Routledge Revivals

A Critical Edition
of Thomas Middleton's
the Witch

A Critical Edition
of Thomas Middleton's
the Witch

Edited by
Edward J. Esche

Routledge
Taylor & Francis Group

First published in 1993 by Garland Publishing, Inc.

This edition first published in 2018 by Routledge
2 Park Square, Milton Park, Abingdon, Oxon, OX14 4RN
and by Routledge
52 Vanderbilt Avenue, New York, NY 10017, USA

Routledge is an imprint of the Taylor & Francis Group, an informa business

Publisher's Note
The publisher has gone to great lengths to ensure the quality of this reprint but points out that some imperfections in the original copies may be apparent.

Disclaimer
The publisher has made every effort to trace copyright holders and welcomes correspondence from those they have been unable to contact.
A Library of Congress record exists under ISBN:

ISBN 13: 978-0-367-18401-8 (hbk)
ISBN 13: 978-0-367-18404-9 (pbk)
ISBN 13: 978-0-429-06136-3 (ebk)

The RENAISSANCE IMAGINATION

Important Literary and Theatrical Texts
from the Late Middle Ages through
the Seventeenth Century

STEPHEN ORGEL, EDITOR

A Garland Series

A Critical Edition
of Thomas Middleton's
The Witch

EDITED BY
EDWARD J. ESCHE

GARLAND PUBLISHING, INC.
New York & London
1993

Library of Congress Cataloging-in-Publication Data

Middleton, Thomas, d. 1627.
    [Witch]
    A critical edition of Thomas Middleton's The witch / edited by
Edward J. Esche.
        p. cm. — (The Renaissance imagination)
    Revision of Edward J. Esche's thesis.
    Includes bibliographical references and index.
    ISBN 0–8153–1090–0 (alk. paper)
    1. Witchcraft—Drama.   I. Esche, Edward J., 1953–
II. Title. III. Series: Renaissance imagination (Unnumbered)
PR2714.W5 1993
822'.3—dc20   92–45122
                                                                              CIP

Printed on acid-free, 250-year-life paper
Manufactured in the United States of America

For

JOHN L HOLMAN
(1908-1976)

and

RONALD MARSH
(1914-1987)

CONTENTS

ACKNOWLEDGEMENTS

Over the time that I have worked on this project, I have had the great fortune to receive help and encouragement from many people within and without the world of academe. My greatest pleasure is now to thank them. Dr. Anne Lancashire, with characteristic generosity, first put me onto *The Witch*, and the University of Toronto first nurtured the seeds of my work. Those who supported thereafter are many, but my special thanks go to Norma Jean Esche, Ouida Thomas, Robert Mountsteven, Dr. E.F.J. Tucker, Dr. Robert Smallwood and Roma Gill. I also wish to thank three of my colleagues at Anglia Polytechnic University for their support: Ian Bonner shared an office and a great deal of worry; Rick Rylance provided a model during the final run to the finish; and Nigel Wheale, who read the thesis, gave the ultimate support as a friend of my heart. Thanks to Dr. Ian Gordon, Head of Arts and Letters, Anglia, for his generous support in the form of financial backing and timetable remission, both of which lightened my load when I needed relief. I sincerely hope that I have repaid his initial trust when he hired me. Thanks to Linda Parkes for help with the photographic reproductions. Thanks too to every member of the Computer Centre at Anglia, including Nicky Morland, Gerry Brown, Andy Geliher, Gill Blackwell, Ian Kitching, Joe McIntyre, Chris Coward and John Blanchfield. I owe a particular thanks to Jonathan Whiteland, who helped me format the text with his own PROFF programme and, more importantly, freely gave his own time. My deepest gratitude goes to Professor Stanley Wells, who took me into the Shakespeare Institute and supervised this thesis, and who remains a model of both academic excellence and human decency within the sometimes troubled world of scholarship. The strengths of this work are his; the weaknesses are, of course, my own. I apologise to my sons, Ben and Nick, who have suffered my absences during the periods of heavy work, and I thank them for their constant interruptions, which always distracted me from this project to things of much greater import. Finally, words of thanks and gratitude are wholly inadequate to express the debt I owe to Rosalind Marsh: she alone keeps me from the abyss.

ILLUSTRATIONS

ABBREVIATIONS

The following abbreviations are used throughout this edition.

(A) TEXTS

(i) *General*

Titles of Shakespeare's plays are abbreviated as in C.T. Onions's *A Shakespeare Glossary*, 3rd ed., revised and enlarged by Robert D. Eagleson (Oxford, 1986), and line references, except where otherwise stated, are to *The Complete Works*, eds. Stanley Wells and Gary Taylor (Oxford, 1986). Play editions appearing in the Revels Plays series are usually cited (except for those listed below) by series and not by editor, unless the matter being quoted is the editor's own.

(ii) *Middleton*

Middleton's works (including some merely attributed to him) are cited, except where otherwise specified, from A.H. Bullen's *The Works of Thomas Middleton* (1885-87). Titles of individual Middleton works, except *The Witch*, are abbreviated as in R.B. Parker's Revels edition (London, 1969) of *A Chaste Maid in Cheapside*:

A.F.Q.L.	*Anything for a Quiet Life.*
B.B.	*The Black Book.*
B.M.C.	*Blurt, Master Constable.*
C.	*The Changeling*, ed. N.W. Bawcutt (London, 1958).

ABBREVIATIONS

C.M. in C.	*A Chaste Maid in Cheapside*, ed. R.B. Parker (London, 1969).
F.Q.	*A Fair Quarrel.*
F. of L.	*The Family of Love.*
F.H.T.	*The Ant and the Nightingale; or Father Hubbard's Tale.*
G. at C.	*A Game at Chess.*
H.K.K.	*Hengist, King of Kent; or the Mayor of Quinborough.*
M.W.M.M.	*A Mad World, My Masters.*
M.T.	*Michaelmas Term.*
M.C.	*Micro-Cynicon.*
M.D.B.W.	*More Dissemblers Besides Women.*
N.W.N.H.	*No Wit, No Help like a Woman's.*
O.L.	*The Old Law.*
P.	*The Phoenix.*
Pur.	*The Puritan; or The Widow of Watling Street*, ed. C.F.T. Brooke, *Shakespeare Apocrypha* (Oxford, 1908).
R.T.	*The Revenger's Tragedy*, ed. R.A. Foakes (London, 1966).
R.G.	*The Roaring Girl*, ed. Paul Mulholland (Manchester, 1987).
S.M.T.	*The Second Maiden's Tragedy*, ed. Anne Lancashire (Manchester, 1978).
S.G.	*The Spanish Gipsy.*
T.C.O.O.	*A Trick to Catch the Old One.*
Wid.	*The Widow.*
W.B.W	*Women Beware Women*, ed. J.R. Mulryne (London, 1975).
Y.F.G.	*Your Five Gallants.*

The Witch is abbreviated *Witch* throughout, and all references are to this edition unless otherwise stated. See Introduction pp. 69-70 for abbreviations used in the collation for the previous editions of *The Witch*.

Works not included in Parker are abbreviated as follows:

1H.W.	*The Honest Whore, Part 1*, ed. Fredson Bowers, in *The Complete Works of Thomas Dekker*, 2 (Cambridge, 1955).
Y.T.	*A Yorkshire Tragedy*, ed. A.C. Cawley and Barry Gaines (Manchester, 1986).

(B) OTHER

Abbott	E.A. Abbott, *A Shakespearean Grammar*, 2nd ed. (London, 1870).
Briggs	Katharine Briggs, *A Dictionary of Fairies: Hobgoblins, Brownies, Bogies and other Supernatural Creatures* (London, 1976).
conj.	conjecture
Dent	R.W. Dent, *Proverbial Language in English Drama Exclusive of Shakespeare, 1495-1616* (London, 1984).
D.N.B.	The Dictionary of National Biography.
Gerarde	John Gerarde, *The Herball or Generall Historie of Plantes* (London, 1597).
Henke	James T. Henke, *Renaissance Dramatic Bawdy (Exclusive of Shakespeare): An Annotated Glossary and Critical Essays* (Salzburg, 1974).
J.W.C.I.	*Journal of the Warburg and Courtauld Institutes.*
Kökeritz	Helge Kökeritz, *Shakespeare's Pronunciation* (London, 1953).
Libr.	*The Library.*

ABBREVIATIONS

Linthicum	M. Channing Linthicum, *Costume in the Drama of Shakespeare and His Contemporaries* (Oxford, 1936).
M.S.R.	Malone Society Reprints.
M.L.N.	*Modern Language Notes.*
M.L.R.	*The Modern Language Review.*
M.P.	*Modern Philology.*
MS	manuscript.
n	note
ns	notes
N.&Q.	*Notes and Queries.*
O.E.D.2	*Oxford English Dictionary*, 2nd ed. (Oxford, 1989).
Opie & Tatem	Opie, Iona and Moira Tatum, *A Dictionary of Superstitions* (Oxford, 1989).
Partridge	Eric Partridge, *Shakespeare's Bawdy* (London, 1968).
P.B.S.A.	*The Papers of the Bibliographical Society of America.*
pres.	presumably
R.E.S.	*The Review of English Studies.*
Robbins	Rossell Hope Robbins, *The Encyclopedia of Witchcraft and Demonology* (1959; rpt. Feltham, Middlesex, 1984).
Rubinstein	Frankie Rubinstein, *A Dictionary of Shakespeare's Sexual Puns and their Significance*, 2nd ed. (London, 1989).
Scot	Reginald Scot, *The Discouerie of Witchcraft* (London, 1584).
S.D.	stage direction.
S.H.	speech heading.
Shakespeare's England	*Shakespeare's England: An Account of the Life and Manners of His Age*, eds. Sidney Lee and C.T. Onions, 2 vols. (Oxford, 1916).

Sh.S.	*Shakespeare Survey.*
S.P.	*Studies in Philology.*
Stow	John Stow, *A Survey of London* (London, 1603), ed. Charles Letherbridge Kingsford, 2 vols. (Oxford, 1971).
subst.	substantially
Sugden	Edward H. Sugden, *A Topographical Dictionary to the Works of Shakespeare and His Fellow Dramatists* (Manchester, 1925).
Tilley	Morris P. Tilley, *A Dictionary of the Proverbs in England in the Sixteenth and Seventeenth Centuries* (Ann Arbor, 1950).
Valiente	Doreen Valiente, *An ABC of Witchcraft Past & Present* (1973; rpt. London, 1984).

Throughout this edition, in quotations and in titles from older works, long 's' is reproduced as a modern 's'.

INTRODUCTION

1. RATIONALE FOR EDITING *THE WITCH*

Although interest in Thomas Middleton's plays has greatly increased in recent years, *Witch* has still not received the distinction of a single-volume edition. It did, however, appear in 1986 in a collection of witchcraft plays edited by Peter Corbin and Douglas Sedge,[1] but that edition is lightly annotated, and the text and apparatus are unreliable.[2] The following is offered as an extended scholarly treatment to fill a significant gap in studies of the author.

2. A SHORT LIFE OF THOMAS MIDDLETON

Sustained biographical interest in Thomas Middleton begins with Alexander Dyce, who was the first to gather together the few facts known in the mid-nineteenth century about the playwright.[3] Since Dyce's investigations, our knowledge has grown as more information has come to light, and a discernible though by no means fully detailed life has emerged.[4]

The precise date of Thomas Middleton's birth is unknown, but he was christened at St. Lawrence in the Old Jewry, London, on 18 April 1580.[5] The entry in the register reads 'Thomas sonn of will: Middleton'. This is most likely the playwright because the pedigree that Middleton furnished to the heralds at the visitation of Surrey in 1623 names his parents as 'Wilimus Midleton' and 'Anna filia Will. Snow',[6] and they were married at St. Lawrence on 17 February 1573/4. Besides Thomas, they had two other children, Avice, christened 3 August 1582, and Bridget, baptized 3 April 1575 and buried 22 May 1576.

Two significant events changed the structure of Middleton's family during his lifetime: William Middleton made his noncupative, or verbal, will 'lyeinge vppon his deathe bedd' on 20 January 1585/6 and subsequently died the same day;[7] and Anne Middleton married again, taking 'Thomas Harvey of St. Dioniss' on 7 November 1586 at St. Lawrence.[8] The marriage was an unfortunate one because Harvey was a reckless adventurer who eventually involved his wife and son in law suits designed to gain total control of family property.[9] Thus before Thomas Middleton was six years old, he had lost his father and gained a difficult stepfather.

The major formative event of Middleton's adolescence was discovered in 1931 but is still often ignored. It had once been assumed that Middleton the playwright was one of three Thomas Middletons who had attended Gray's Inn between 1593 and 1606.[10] But Mark Eccles proved that the playwright was in fact 'matriculated from Queen's College, Oxford, in April 1598, aged eighteen', by identifying Middleton's signature at subscription (that is, to the Thirty-Nine Articles) dated on or soon after 7 April 1598.[11] Despite Eccles's proof, recent bibliographies of the literature of the period still include the erroneous Gray's Inn tradition,[12] possibly because the mistake has been enshrined in *The Dictionary of National Biography*.[13]

Middleton's time at the Queen's College was not that of a typical undergraduate. Mildred G. Christian argues that his stay was continuous from April 1598 to December 1601, when 'he sank all his worldly goods in a determined effort to remain at Oxford', by selling his share in the property that he had inherited from his father for, as he says, money 'paid and disbursed for my advauncement & p[re]ferment in the Vniu[er]sity of Oxford where I am nowe a studient and for my maintenance with meat drinke and apparrell and other necessaries for me meet and convenient'.[14] P.G. Phialas argues that Middleton's residence was probably not continuous, and Eccles points out that Christian is one year out in her dating (it should be 1600 instead of 1601);[15] even so, her interpretation that Middleton wanted to remain at Oxford is still correct, but her conclusion that he 'was headed for the completion of his A.B. degree' is less certain.[16] Middleton's words quoted above point away from serious study: his position as a student is mentioned as a subsidiary point in a dependent clause. The main reason that he is selling his share in the property is, he says, for his 'advauncement & p[re]ferment'. Both words carry the general meaning of 'promotion to a higher position in life', but each also has a more specific meaning. 'Advancement' is a legal term meaning 'the promotion of children in life, especially by the application beforehand of property or money to which they are prospectively entitled under a settlement or will' (*O.E.D.*2, 2). 'Preferment' has a wider meaning of 'that which has been done or given towards the advancement of the children of a family' (*O.E.D.*2, 2). So Middleton is probably being literal here. The secondary reason that he is selling is for his 'maintenance'; this he defines as food, drink, dress and other necessities, which are 'meet and convenient' for him. The passage considered as a whole may indicate that he is trying to keep a level of comfortable living appropriate for making useful contacts and 'getting on' in life, rather than trying to complete his studies.

Middleton did not take a degree. There are two possible explanations: one, he had to return to London to help his mother in a suit brought by Harvey, who was trying to gain control of land that Thomas Middleton had already sold;[17] or, two, he was more interested in pursuing a career as a man of letters than in working towards finishing his degree,[18] and, when he failed to secure patronage with *The Ghost of Lucrece*, a poem he published while he was still at the Queen's College and which was dedicated to William second Baron Compton, he had little alternative but to look for work in London.[19] Whatever the reason, it is likely that Middleton 'gave up residence at Oxford between 28 June 1600 [the date on which he was in London in

3

court to sell his share in his father's property] and 8 February 1600/1, when Antony Snode testified that "he remaynethe heare in London daylie accompaninge the players"'.[20]

Once in London, Middleton served a playwrighting apprenticeship of sorts: he is mentioned in Philip Henslowe's *Diary* several times between May and December 1602,[21] but he probably had been working on plays for some time earlier, perhaps for a year or two.[22] By 1602 or 1603 he was writing for more socially select theatre companies than Henslowe's, notably those of the Children of St. Paul's and the Children of the Chapel. He thus did most of his early writing for the children's companies, but also picked up other work wherever he could: he wrote plays for the Admiral's or Prince Henry's Men and Worcester's Men, collaborated with other dramatists, and contributed to a royal pageant.[23] Middleton seems to have switched to writing plays only for the adult companies between 1606 and 1608, a practice he was to follow for the rest of his life, by giving plays to Prince Henry's Men, Lady Elizabeth's Men and the King's Men.[24] However, if *The Revenger's Tragedy* is his, then he was writing for the King's Men as early as 1605.[25] Similarly, if Middleton wrote *The Second Maiden's Tragedy*, then he was working for the King's Men from 1611.[26] The date at which he began to write extensively for the King's Men is uncertain, but he became one of their principal playwrights from at least the mid-1610s, perhaps around 1615, to well into the 1620s.[27]

Middleton had been thought to have married twice because the name of his widow, 'Magdalen', which is recorded in the Repertories of the Court of Aldermen 7 February 1627/8, does not match the name of his wife given on his 1623 visitation pedigree, 'Maria'. Again, Eccles has looked at the facts and has explained how the two names probably refer to the same woman. The visitation pedigree names Maria as the daughter of Edward Marbeck. Eccles found records of the baptisms of four of Edward Marbeck's children in the register of St. Dunstan in the West, including one 'Maulyn'. He notes

4

that "'Maulyn" is a common form for "Magdalen" and could easily have been confused with "Mary" through the diminuitive "Mall" or "Moll"'.[28] Thus Middleton probably had only one wife, Magdalen Marbeck, whom he had married by 1603 and with whom he had his only son, Edward, in 1604. The family residence from at least 1609 onwards was at Newington Butts in Surrey, where Middleton died and was buried on 4 July 1627.[29]

This is not the place for a full chronological discussion of Middleton's work,[30] but one more important fact of his literary life deserves mention because of the influence it had on his dramatic writing. Quite early in his career he developed a connection with civic pageantry that was to last most of his life. On 15 March 1603/4 he collaborated with Thomas Dekker on an entertainment given to James I by the City of London on the King's official entry into the City; Middleton then went on to write numerous entertainments and pageants for the City, and to become City Chronologer on 6 September 1620. He seems to have carried out his duties adequately until quite near the end of his life; but in 1625 he may have embezzled funds which were meant for an elaborate welcome into the City for Charles I, and in 1626 he had trouble collecting payment for a pageant, *The Triumphs of Health and Prosperity*, written for the Draper's Company, because it was badly organized and poorly performed.[31]

3. THE MANUSCRIPT

The text of Thomas Middleton's play *The Witch* survives in a unique MS held in the Bodleian Library, MS Malone 12, which is bound in late eighteenth-century russia leather.[32] The entire document consists of 55 quarto leaves measuring 19 cm high by 14 cm wide. Of these 55 leaves, 49 are the MS proper, that is, all of the brown ink on seventeenth-century paper; there are three preface fly-leaves and three end fly-leaves. Between the second and third preface fly-leaves 'is a pen-and-ink copy of the "Vera Effigies Tho. Midletoni Gent." published as an engraved frontispiece to Middleton's *Two New Plays* of 1657 and also found in some copies of his *No Wit Like a Woman's* of the same year.'[33] The reason for the odd number of both preface and end fly-leaves is that one piece of paper wraps the document and is pasted to both the front and end paste-downs. A piece of paper has been folded in half to form a gathering of two leaves at the front, and another piece of paper has been folded in half to form a gathering of two leaves at the end. The second and third preface fly-leaves and the effigy copy are paginated only on the recto side in pencil in the upper right-hand corner, as 'iii', 'v', and 'vii'. The writing on these pages is as follows: i verso, in brown ink, 'Malone MSS. 12'; iii recto, in pencil, 'Mal. MSS. 12.' (plus additional material as described below); iii verso, in brown ink and in the same hand as i verso, 'Malone MS. 12.'. The end fly-leaves are paginated only on the recto in the upper right-hand corner in pencil as '97.', '99', and '101'. They are otherwise blank on both recto and verso.

The third preface fly-leaf recto has a great deal of material on it. '7.10.0' is written in the top left-hand corner in pencil, which, as will be seen, is a former sale price of the document (i.e., £7.10s). Below the price and centred is a piece of paper pasted onto the page and printed as follows:

3872 *The Tragi-Comodie, called* The Witch, *long since acted by his Majesty's Servants at Black Friars*, written by Tho. Middleton, MS.

N.B. The above MS. of the Witch, was purchased from the Collection of Benj. Griffin, the Actor.—*See a MS. note of Geo. Steevens, Esq. prefixed to this play.*

This is the actual catalogue listing of the *Witch* MS at the sale of the effects of one of its previous owners, Major Pearson.[34] The MS note referred to is not present. Below the printed material and again centred on the page is the following in the hand of George Steevens:

> The sole tendency of the MS note so formally
> mentioned, was to ascertain that this Play
> passed from the hands of Griffin abovementioned,
> into those of Lockyer Davis Bookseller in
> Holbourn, who sold it to Major Pearson. I bought
> it at The Major's Auction for £2..14..0.
>   N.B. one hundred copies of it had been
> printed off by Mr Reed, as presents to his
> friends. See his Biographia Dramatica, 1782.
> Vol I. p. 314, and his Edition of Shakspeare,
> 1785. Vol. I. p. 335. &c.
> GS.

Frank Sullivan, a previous editor of the play, asserts that 'evidently Steevens was employed by the book seller to give the history of the MS',[35] but there is no evidence to suggest that Davis 'employed' Steevens. Isaac Reed certainly printed the first edition (1778) of *Witch*, but more will be said of that later.[36] Finally, below the Steevens material and again centred on the page is the following in the hand of Edmond Malone:

> Bought at the sale of Mr Steevens's
> books, May 20th 1800, at the enormous
> price of £7. 10. 0
> EM.

W.W. Greg and F.P. Wilson, the Malone Society editors of *Witch*, provide the best commentary on the information that these notes give us about the history of the MS. 'It appears to have been at one time the property of the actor and playwright Benjamin Griffin (1680-1740), to have come into the possession of Lockyer Davis, a bookseller in Holborn from 1753 to 1791, and later into the library of Thomas Pearson. At the sale of Pearson's books on 1 May 1788 Steevens acquired it for £2. 14s., and at the Steevens sale on 20 May 1800 Malone bought it "at the enormous price of £7. 10. 0.". With the bulk of Malone's manuscripts and books it came to the Bodleian in 1821.'[37]

The entire MS proper is in the hand of one scribe, Ralph Crane.[38] The first page is a separate leaf with 'ix' written in pencil in the upper right-hand corner; it is the title page and begins as follows:[39]

> A Tragi- | Coomodie, Called | the | Witch; | ∵ | long since Acted, by his Ma[ties.] Seruants | at the Black-Friers. | ∵ | Written by. Tho. Middleton.

Below this appears the scene and then the dramatis personae, under which and centred at the bottom of the page is 'G. STEEVENS' printed by hand. On the verso of the title page is the dedication, addressed to Thomas Holmes, with the pagination 'x.' written in pencil in the upper left-hand corner.

The rest of the MS text is paginated 1-95 in the same hand as the MS. Crane mistakenly wrote '49' on what would be page 47; thus there are two pages numbered 49. Pages 1-94 are written on twelve quarto sheets, but Crane cancelled the third leaf of the eleventh sheet; the stub of the cancellation can be seen between pages 84 and 85. The last leaf of the MS is separate and contains page 95 of the text and a blank verso.

Crane began his copying task by drawing four rules on the MS page, which created a rectangle 14.5 cm high by 11.5 cm wide on average.[40] He used the outside of the rectangle for nothing except the running title, *'The witch*', and the pagination, which always occurs on the top outer corner of each page. He used the inside of the rectangle for the text of the play. The limitation of writing space for the text appears to have caused Crane some inconveniences. The congestion created by one or more unusually long lines occasionally forced him to copy the stage directions into available white space rather than exactly where the playwright might have intended them to appear; however, he usually indicated the stage direction placement with a dash.[41] He wrote the running title, act divisions, scene divisions, speech prefixes and stage directions in italic hand; he wrote the dialogue in secretary hand with a sprinkling of italic. There are regular catchwords throughout and twenty-five lines per page on average.

Two types of paper are used, one for the preliminaries, and one for the rest of the MS. Greg and Wilson note that 'on the title-leaf of the MS. Malone 12 is the upper half of the same watermark that appears on a blank leaf and the title-leaf of *Demetrius and Enanthe*, two posts with grapes, similar to Heawood's no. 70, for which Heawood cites examples from 1623.'[42]

Except for the title-leaf, the MS bears the same watermark—illustrated below—throughout:[43]

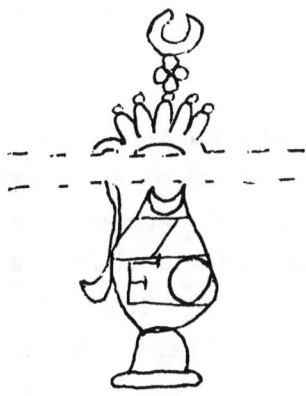

Greg and Wilson think that the above is the same as the watermark of

Bodleian MS Malone 25, *A Game at Chess*, a MS which was also prepared by Crane. They are wrong.[44] The following is an illustration of the MS Malone 25 watermark:

The error is understandable because the pots are almost identical and the lettering could easily be mistaken as the same, especially since the neck portion of the MS Malone 12 watermark can hardly be seen as it falls directly in the binding.[45]

Dating the MS by the watermark is inconclusive because the pot was 'the commonest mark in England in the seventeenth century,'[46] and, as yet, the particular pot of MS Malone 12 has been neither identified nor dated. Heawood illustrates only one mark, no. 3565, dated 1611, with a similar arrangement of symbols—the moon, a vertical line (instead of a diagonal), and the initials 'FO'—but the top portion of the pot is of a different configuration.[47] Heawood no. 3585, is closest in overall shape to the *Witch* MS watermark, and the earliest dates cited for its appearance are 1623-4,[48] but the initials within the pot are 'CC'. Thus a MS dating of 1623-4 to 1627 (the date of Middleton's death) based on watermark evidence seems the most that can be offered given the evidence available.

Ralph Crane was a scrivener who was regularly employed by the King's Men and who did other work for Middleton, including the Folger, Lansdowne, and Malone MSS of *A Game at Chess*. A great deal has been written about him and his scribal practices, particularly in relation to his involvement with the copy for the 1623 Shakespeare First Folio,[49] and some of this information has been of use for this edition of *Witch*. The knowledge of his tendency to over-hyphenate and to use parentheses, for example, is not only helpful in identifying his work but it also allows an editor to remove some accidentals of punctuation with impunity. Another practice of Crane's is his tendency to use heavier punctuation than is grammatically required at the end of a line; this has occasionally provided an explanation for puzzling punctuation problems.[50] Substantive emendations, however, are not usually possible, because even with the full knowledge of Crane's scribal practices, an editor cannot detect exactly where or how Crane may have changed his copy text.[51]

Frank Sullivan tries to establish a compositional date for the *Witch* MS based on Crane's writing habits. First, he cites F.P. Wilson on the MS date, and Wilson's supporting documentation:

... the transcript may have been made at any time between 1620 and the year of Middleton's death. The year 1620 is chosen because in 1621 Crane wrote in the autobiographical preface to his *Works of Mercy*,

> And some imployment hath my vseful *Pen*,
> Had 'mongst those ciuill *well-deseruing Men*,
> That grace the *Stage* with *honour* and *delight*,
> Of whose *true honesties* I much could write
> But will compris't (as in a Caske of Gold)
> Vnder the *Kingly-seruice* they doe hold.[52]

Sullivan then observes that Crane's handwriting changed over the years and that his writing in the *Witch* MS is closer in style to his earlier *An Jnvention* (1622) than to his later *The Faultie Favorite* (1631).[53] These two points, taken together with the fact that 'The only play of the King's Men that we know Crane wrote before 1621 is *Sir John van Olden Barnavelt*, which was submitted to Sir George Buc in the summer of 1619',[54] lead Sullivan to conclude that Crane transcribed the *Witch* MS in about 1620. Sullivan, however, has pushed his argument too far. A specific transcription date simply cannot be assigned to the MS because there is no evidence to suggest that Crane was working on the MS known as Malone 12 on, before, or after he wrote his preface to *The Works of Mercy*; he could have been working on one or more other plays for the King's Men before 1621; and the link in style with *An Jnvention* supplies only an approximate date of composition, say, from 1618-1627. Indeed, Fleay has posited a date of 1627 and has added (without evidence) that the MS was 'probably prepared for publication, but interrupted by his [Middleton's] death'.[55] All that can be said from the handwriting evidence is that Crane might have prepared his transcription of *Witch* sometime between a year or so before 1619 and 1627, a range that begins at a date shortly before we know that Crane was working for the King's Men and ends at the date of Middleton's death, the date after which the playwright clearly could not dedicate a work to anyone.

The copy for the MS is difficult to identify. T.H. Howard-Hill argues that it was an autograph of Middleton's because the text contains fewer parentheses than Crane normally wrote.[56] Greg and Wilson argue that the copy 'was probably a playhouse manuscript' because the 'entrances are usually, though not always, marked a line or two early'.[57] A promptbook, however, was sometimes made of the author's MS itself, and since the stage directions might not have been moved, the Greg and Wilson argument collapses.[58] In other words, the placement of stage directions actually tells us nothing about the nature of the MS copy, but act-end notations may be a different matter. Robert K. Turner has examined a number of documents containing a variety of act-end notations, and has concluded that 'such act-end notations as *finis* and *explicit*, although they may sometimes be carried over into promptbooks, do not—except in extraordinary circumstances, such as revisions affecting the ends of acts—originate there'.[59] His comments on the *Witch* MS are brief, but important: 'if Middleton did give a playhouse manuscript [to Crane] from which to prepare the presentation copy of *The Witch*, it seems most probable that the *finis*'s which appear in the transcription are Crane's versions of Middleton's *finit*', which is found throughout his authorial manuscript of *A Game at Chess*.[60] The implications are clear: the copy for the Crane MS was probably Middleton's authorial manuscript which had been used as a prompt-book.

4. THE REED-STEEVENS EDITORSHIP CONTROVERSY

The catalogue of the British Library cites J. Reed as the editor of the 1778 edition of *Witch*,[61] but *The National Union Catalogue* cites both Reed and George Steevens as possible editors.[62] Sullivan argues that only Reed could have edited the 1778 text, and advances a reason for the catalogue confusion.[63] He points to an entry by Dobell in a 1906 book catalogue which offers for sale a copy of the 1778 edition of *Witch*:

> It is usually supposed that it was edited by Reed; but in Lilly's Catalogue, 1865, a copy was for sale which had on the fly-leaf the following inscription—"Hy. Fuseli, from the Editor, George Steevens."[64]

Furness says in his variorum edition of *Macbeth* that he possesses a copy of the edition under discussion, which was presented to 'Hy. Fuseli from the

Editor George Stevens', but he thinks that the inscription was 'clearly not in the autograph of Steevens' because Steevens would not misspell his own name;[65] however, the inscription may have created doubt as to who was the real editor of the 1778 edition.

Sullivan mistakenly claims that Steevens published his discovery of the source and text of the 'Black spirits and white' and 'Come away, come away, Hecate' songs (both of which are referred to in *Macbeth*, but which survive in their entirety in *Witch*[66]) in the Malone 1790 edition of Shakespeare.[67] He notes that Steevens's name appears on the second (1778) and third (1785) editions of Johnson's Shakespeare,[68] and he asserts that Steevens did not publish his source discovery in either. From this Sullivan concludes that Reed must have edited the 1778 *Witch*, and that Steevens must have made his source discovery after 1787, the date of the sale in which he bought the manuscript of the play.[69]

Sullivan's argument is straightforward, but his facts are incorrect. Steevens's discovery is published in full in both the 1778 and 1785 editions of Shakespeare's plays;[70] therefore, Steevens must have been familiar with the text of *Witch* by 1778 at the latest, which was nine years before he bought the Crane manuscript of the play. Thus Sullivan's argument that Reed was necessarily the editor of the 1778 edition collapses.

The authentic evidence to support the contention that Reed edited the 1778 *Witch* is of some weight. The Crane manuscript contains Steevens's preface note, which says that 'one hundred copies of it had been printed off by Mr Reed as presents to his friends'.[71] Although there is nothing here which clearly indicates that Reed edited the text, the statement does suggest that he was very closely concerned with the project: he financed the printing venture as a gift for his friends. But a copy of the 1778 edition contains an inscription to the Bishop of Dromore.[72] On the title-page of the copy, written in brown ink at the top of the page in Reed's hand, is the following:

No. 53   The Bishop of Dromore
                          with the Editor's
                          Compliments.

This note demonstrates that Reed thought of himself as the editor of the text.

The evidence to suggest that Steevens edited the 1778 *Witch* is, however, overwhelming. A transcription of *Witch* in the hand of George Steevens, held by the Folger Shakespeare Library, has been brought to my attention by Paul Mulholland. It is prefaced by the following inscription:

> This Play is the hand — I writing of Geo: Steevens Esq. I the Editor
> of Shakspeare — I & copied by him from the — I Original Mss. I I.
> Reed. I 1778[73]

The handwriting of the inscription is unmistakably that of Isaac Reed. Mulholland has collated the Crane manuscript of *Witch*, Steevens's transcription and the 1778 printed edition and has discovered that the 1778 edition follows every substantive error that Steevens made in his transcription but one, which strongly suggests that the 1778 edition was printed from the Steevens transcription.[74] Thus Steevens, not Reed, was the editor of the 1778 *Witch*; he published his discovery of the text and source of the 'Black spirits and white' and 'Come away, come away, Hecate' songs in the 1778 edition of Shakespeare's plays because he was working on both projects at roughly the same time. It is even possible that the double accreditation noted on the original Library of Congress card may be rooted in the cataloguer's knowledge of The Folger Shakespeare Library Steevens transcription of the Crane manuscript of *Witch*.

The editorship confusion arises naturally out of a now archaic meaning of the word 'edit'. At the time Reed and Steevens were working, it could mean 'to publish, give to the world (a literary work by an earlier author, previously existing in MS)'[75] as well as 'to prepare an edition of (a literary work or works by an earlier author)'.[76] Thus both men could legitimately claim to be the editor of the 1778 *Witch* even though they carried out separate functions on a joint project: Steevens clearly prepared an edited text for Reed's generously financed publication.

5. DATE

The date of Middleton's *Witch* has never been established with any degree of certainty, yet, as when considering all literature, one's critical perspective needs to be informed either directly or indirectly by the compositional date of the piece under examination. This is particularly so with *Witch* because, as we shall see, some aspects of the characters and events portrayed in the play may be patterned on or intended to represent various aspects of actual, historical personages and events. Such references to contemporary historical events would, in many cases, be a great help in fixing a date, but *Witch* has been particularly resistant to convincing proofs, numerous though the attempts have been.

Scholars have been trying to date *Witch* since the Crane manuscript was first discovered and printed in 1778, and their efforts have varied in thoroughness of scholarly method. In what follows, I will first note the less convincing attempts at dating, and then discuss those which have a serious claim to credibility.

The earliest dating appears to be that of George Steevens, the play's first editor, who noted the dedication to Thomas Holmes and considered it probable 'that the play was written *long* before the dedication, which seems to have been added soon after the year 1603, when the act of K. James against witches passed into a law'[77]. Steevens is wrong about the Holmes dedication: it is the same date as the rest of the MS. He also never specifies the exact duration of '*long* before' or of 'soon after', but even if 'long' is a relatively short period of time, perhaps one year, then Steevens's date of composition for *Witch* is around 1602, which would make it one of Middleton's earliest plays. G. Bengueral also thinks that *Witch* is one of Middleton's earliest creations, but Hugo Jung considers it to be one of his latest.[78] Since Middleton died in 1627, this presents a range of about twenty-five years from 1602 to 1627, and various other scholars have dated the play throughout that range.

A.H. Bullen does not offer a precise year, but he suggests that *Witch* was a composition of the later part of Middleton's career, 'when he was no longer content with composing lively comedies of intrigue, but was turning his attention towards subjects of deeper moment'.[79] Frederick Gard Fleay sees a link between the number of witches in the play and the Edward Fairfax prosecution of six witches in 1621: he accordingly dates the play circa 1621-2.[80] But Fleay bases his conclusions on a faulty premise: the precise number of witches in *Witch* is unclear—the dramatis personae lists three by name and then contains an entry for 'Other Witches and Servants'. He also chooses his historical influences quite arbitrarily: but as we shall see later in this section, there is at least one witchcraft trial in the period which can claim equal attention to that of the Fairfax prosecutions.[81] Felix E. Schelling, following Fleay, guesses a date of the 'early twenties' of the seventeenth century without citing any supporting evidence.[82] Unfortunately, all of the above datings are based at best on faulty information and at worst on vague impressions, techniques which are not, sadly, fully eradicated from more recent dating practice.[83]

Serious but limited work on dating *Witch*, of the kind that we now associate with forming the foundations of solid scholarship, began at a surprisingly early point, with Edmond Malone.[84] He argues against Steevens's pre-1603 dating and places the play in 1613 on the basis of several pieces of internal evidence. Some of these might appear vaguely indeterminate to us now because no precise date can be attached to them: he tries to establish the date at which perfumery became an established trade in London and the date after which 'strokes at Puritans' became 'more frequently introduced' into plays.[85] But other details of evidence carry more argumentative weight precisely because he shifts his approach from trying to identify vague generalities to establishing a clear method of investigation which attempts to identify references to specific places or events at the time the play might have been composed. When Almachildes mentions 'a country house, some mile out of town' (I.i.93), Malone sees a clear reference to a notorious house at Brentford. He claims that 'in the plays written in 1607, and for some years afterwards, there are frequent allusions to the practice of carrying women of the town thither'.[86] He also uses Hecate's reference to 'a five pound picture' (I.ii.142): 'I have reason to believe that this was the ordinary price of a portrait about the year 1612 or 1613'.[87] But the argument here is weakened because he does not supply any hard evidence to support his belief and because he admits that five pounds may also have been the price of a portrait at the beginning of James I's reign. Malone then claims that Antonio's pretence to draw Abberzanes to a meeting with him—an invitation to 'yonder horse race' (IV.iii.107)—is an allusion to specific popular horse races at Croydon in 1612,[88] but why to these particular races and to no others is never explained. He also sees a reference in Francesca's mention of 'an East Indian voyage' (II.i.61) to a specific voyage of 1611 for which the East India Company built a new ship, the Trade's Insurance, with money received from an enlargement of their charter granted by King James I.[89] The venture was popular not only because of its increased English funding but also because James dined on board the Trade's Insurance when she was named; however, the connection between the general and the specific voyage remains unproven. None of the foregoing fixes the date of the play with any certainty, but Malone's *method* of investigation anticipates modern work even if the facts are often too general or even wrong, as is his

1613 date for the King's Men's first possession of Blackfriars.[90] He does, however, succeed in undermining Steevens's dating at a single stroke by pointing out that the words 'long since' occur not only in the dedication of *Witch* but also in the preface to the second edition of Middleton's *A Mad World My Masters* (London, 1640): in the latter play they must mean at least thirteen years, because Middleton died in 1627; in the former play they could (but of course need not) mean the same number of years, which would put the dedication to Holmes at 1627 and the play's performance at 1613 or 1614.[91] Malone's entire argument is faulty because it starts from the supposition that 1613 is the correct date of composition and he is, as it were, arguing backwards to fit his material to that date, but he deserves attention because of his method of investigation.

W.J. Lawrence has probably been the most influential dater of *Witch*.[92] He assumes that some of the King's Men had performed in Jonson's entertainment *The Masque of Queens* on 2 February 1609, and argues that they wished to transfer the witches' dance in it to the public stage. They then commissioned Middleton to write *Witch* as a vehicle for them, and, 'With the renewal of acting in December, 1608 [error for 1609], the King's Men took possession of the Blackfriars, and, in all probability, opened there with *The Witch*'.[93] There is absolutely no evidence associating the King's Men with Jonson's masque, but that has not diminished Lawrence's influence. A large number of subsequent scholars have used his dating, including Frank Sullivan, John Dover Wilson, W.W. Greg and F.P. Wilson, and John Stevens.[94] Lawrence's dating has also influenced the possible earlier dating limit listed by both Gerald Eades Bentley and Samuel Schoenbaum.[95] Frank Sullivan's argument is the only detailed one out of all of these, and therefore merits detailed discussion.

In the introduction to his edition of *Witch*, Sullivan gives a dating range of 1609-1623, and tentatively suggests 1610 for five reasons: one, a large ship (presumably, the Trade's Insurance) was built in 1610 for trade to the

Indies 'and Middleton's reference to the Indies (II.i.61) could easily have sprung out of the excitement attendant upon the building of this vessel'; two, the boy companies, for whom Middleton wrote, were deposed from Blackfriars in 1610, 'leaving Middleton free and probably very willing to accept a commission from a dramatic company like the King's Men'; three, Jonson's *The Masque of Queens* was presented at Court in 1609 and, because 'The citizens were anxious to see some of its dances', the King's Men got Middleton to write a play incorporating one of the dances; four, the King's Men chose Middleton for the job because plague had closed the London theatres for almost all of 1609 and, therefore, their best playwright, Shakespeare, was in Stratford; five, the statute referred to by Francesca at II.i.87-8 most likely refers to the statute of 7 James (1610) against vagabonds and fiddlers.[96] This is Sullivan's argument, and it is obvious that he is basically following Lawrence with a nod to Malone. The argument is suspect and his five points are easily refuted: one, as we shall see, there were ships built for trade to the Indies other than the one to which Sullivan refers;[97] two, that Middleton was available for work in 1610 does not prove that he wrote *Witch* in the same year; three, there is no evidence to suggest that the general populace of London was anxious to see Jonson's witch dances, nor is there any evidence to support the statement that Middleton actually used Jonson's dances in *Witch*; four, Shakespeare's actual whereabouts in 1609 is irrelevant because he may have continued his own output right through the plague years; five, if Francesca is referring to the statute of 7 James (and she may well be), the reference could have been made at any time after 1610.

In direct contrast to the limited work described above, R.C. Bald achieved his results through sound historical research on the play and made the single most important discovery for dating purposes. 'In Sebastian's scheme to prevent Antonio from consummating his marriage with Isabella, and in the charms he seeks from the witches to effect his purpose, there is a clear allusion to the notorious Essex divorce case of 1613, but the play is more likely to date from about 1616, as the parts played by Simon Forman and Mrs Turner in aiding the Countess of Essex were not disclosed until the Overbury murder trials at the end of 1615.'[98] The divorce case referred to here was one in which the marriage between Frances Howard and Robert Devereux, Earl of Essex, was annulled on the grounds of non-consummation which, Frances claimed, resulted from witchcraft.[99] Bald's dating has also been influential and has been followed by Alfred Harbage, Samuel Schoenbaum, David Lake and Margot Heinemann.[100]

David George argues for a date of 1614 based mainly on stylistic grounds, but his logic reads very much like that of his predecessors whom he attacks: he appears to guess 1614 and then fit his facts to accommodate that date. First, he maintains that the source of the Sebastian/Isabella/Antonio plot is not the notorious Essex divorce case but *The Atheist's Tragedy* (printed 1611); second, since there is no firm evidence to associate Middleton with the King's Men before 1614-15, *Witch* must have been the first play that he wrote for them.[101] The argument is suspect on both points: first, if a source of the Sebastian/Isabella/Antonio plot is *The Atheist's Tragedy* (as it probably is[102]), then the only safe statement that one can make is that *Witch* postdates *The Atheist's Tragedy*, which was most likely written in 1611;[103] second, if there is no firm evidence to associate Middleton with the King's Men before 1614-15, then there is no knowing what might have come before that date.

The most detailed arguments for dating *Witch* have all been advanced within the last few years. Anne Lancashire proposes a range from 1610 to 1616 for the play's composition and argues for spring 1613 as the most probable date.[104] She agrees with Bald that the Sebastian/Isabella/Antonio plot refers directly to the Essex divorce case, but argues that he was mistaken in assuming that its details remained unknown until the Overbury murder trials of 1615. The case was in fact 'the talk of the court and country', and was 'almost as sensational in 1613 as the state murder trials were to be in 1615-16'.[105] In addition, there are two major points in the contemporary history not shared with *The Atheist's Tragedy*, but which appear in *Witch*: the Frances Howard claim of Robert, Earl of Essex's impotency through witchcraft parallels the Isabella-Antonio situation, as does the alleged fact of Robert's impotency *only* with his wife. There are three minor points of similarity. Frances's initial separation from Robert was three years and, as the play opens, Sebastian has been separated from Isabella for three years. Frances, like Isabella, claimed that she wished to consummate the marriage in order to have children. Frances's second husband, Robert Carr, for whom she divorced Essex, was Scottish, as is Antonio (see II.i.169ff). The situation in the play is reversed: Isabella's first husband is Scottish, but in the historical liaison Frances's second husband was Scottish. Lancashire thinks that the similarity is close enough to merit mentioning.[106] All of the similarities may be compelling when taken together, and, if Lancashire's date is accepted, then Middleton's dedicatory words referring to the play's 'imprisoned obscurity' may in fact refer to the political suppression of *Witch*, as she argues, rather than to a failure of the play on the popular stage. Thus, when the full details of the involvement of Frances and Robert Carr in the 1613 murder by poisoning of Thomas Overbury became known at the 1615 state trials, the play may have become far too controversial to be allowed to continue being played on the stage.[107]

At the same time that Lancashire wrote her argument, A.A. Bromham was writing his. He, like Lancashire, proves that 'The connection of the Essex Divorce Case with witchcraft ... was clearly made in 1613, without any of the details of the Countess's dealings with Simon Forman and Mrs. Turner being known. Moreover, the situation of Isabella and Antonio in the play relates closely to the plea of *maleficium* since Middleton makes clear that Antonio is only impotent as far as his wife is concerned.'[108] His conclusion is that 'any date for the play after September 1613 (the annulment of the marriage was agreed by the Commission on 25 September 1613) would allow of the possibility of topical allusion in the witch material'.[109]

Paul Yachnin misreads Bromham's article as claiming 1614 as the specific date of *Witch*, but he goes on to supply a considerable amount of detailed historical information to which he sees allusions in the play as evidence for a 1614 dating. He, like Malone, thinks that Francesca's mention of an East Indian voyage at II.i.61 is indeed a direct reference to a specific voyage, but unlike Malone, he thinks the voyage is that of Nicholas Downton, which set sail for the East early in 1614. He gives two reasons for this conjecture: one, 'The preparations for this voyage would no doubt have been of greater public interest than the preparations for any of the previous expeditions' because 'the subscribed capital for the 1614 voyage was five times as great as that for the previous most subscribed voyage, the one of 1609'; and, two, 'Middleton himself had created the single most important advertisement for the East Indian venture, a pageant of five lush Indian islands which formed part of his 1613 Lord Mayor's Show, *The Triumphs of Truth.*'[110] Yachnin's facts appear to be sound, but they are far from putting 'the whole issue of dating beyond question.'[111] First, the entire argument rests on the four words 'an East Indian voyage' being a reference to a *specific* voyage, but Yachnin simply has not proved that it refers to Downton's of 1614. Second, and much more importantly, if Middleton himself created an advertisement for the 1614 voyage in 1613 with the entertainment *The Triumphs of Truth*, then he could well have written a single general allusion to it any time after that year. In short, Yachnin's argument has proved nothing, although, like many scholars before him, he may well be correct in his guess.

There is, however, another tenuous piece of internal evidence which may point to a later date. At I.ii.34, Hecate claims to be able to recognize the Mayor of Whelpley's son 'by his black cloak lined with yellow'. Yellow as

23

applied to clothing is a rare colour in the Middleton canon. It is, however, mentioned here and in three other plays: *A Fair Quarrel* (IV.iv.189: 'Thy ruff starched with rotten eggs!'), *More Dissemblers Besides Women* (V.i.104-5: 'Ay, and his jealous laundress / That for the love she bears him starches yellow'), and *The Widow* (V.i.51-3: 'it [a suit] will disgrace / My master's fashion for ever, and make it as hateful / As yellow bands'). Yellow in all three plays is an allusion to the hanging of Mrs. Anne Turner on 14 November 1615, for her part in the murder of Sir Thomas Overbury: 'Mistress *Turner*, the first inventress of *yellow starch*, was executed in a Cobweb Lawn Ruff of that colour at *Tyburn*'.[112] The colour evidently caught on as a fashion for dyeing bands or ruffs.[113] The reference in *Witch* is to the lining of a cloak, but like the 'suit' of *More Dissemblers Besides Women*, it is the right colour for the fashion. If the allusion is to the fashion begun by Mrs. Turner, then *Witch* must date from after her November 1615 execution, and most likely from 1616, as do *More Dissemblers Besides Women* (*c.* 1615 (?)), *The Widow* (*c.* 1615-1617), and IV.iv. of *A Fair Quarrel*, (an addition to the original play, probably added in 1617).[114]

One final argument demands attention. Nicholas Brooke has put forward an interesting case for dating *Witch* in 1615 based on the surviving manuscripts of two of the songs, 'Come away, come away, Hecate' and 'In a maiden time professed'.[115] His argument is that since the writer of the first, Robert Johnson, composed for the King's Men from *c.* 1609 to *c.* 1615, and since the writer of the second, John Wilson, probably worked for the King's Men from about 1615, then the date of overlap would be the logical date for the composition of the play. The argument is very interesting, but does not fully allow for the re-use of song materials after the original date of composition.

The conclusions to be drawn from all of this information are by no means clear, but summations can be made. The evidence which seems incontrovertible and which has a direct bearing on the possible dating of

Witch comes down to two facts, both of which involve sources: one, some details of the plot of *The Atheist's Tragedy* are similar enough to some details of the plot of *Witch* to suggest that it is probably a source for the latter play, and since *The Atheist's Tragedy* is dated 1611, Middleton could have borrowed his material at any time after 1611; two, the similarities between the Essex divorce case and the Isabella-Antonio material in *Witch* are close enough to make the contemporary historical scandal a likely source for the play, and since the details of the case were common knowledge from 1613 onwards, they could have been used at any point after that date. But whether they could have been used in 1613 or shortly after, say 1614, is highly doubtful.

If the contemporary political parallel is to hold, then Middleton is identifying the morally corrupt fictional Scottish Antonio with the real-life Scottish Robert Carr. But in 1613-14 Carr was a court favourite close to James I, and if such an identification was made in 1613-14, then Middleton risked offending the King's favourite and making an extremely powerful enemy in Carr. Moreover, he would have been writing a public anti-Carr play at the same time as he was writing *The Masque of Cupid*, a private entertainment commissioned to celebrate the occasion of Carr's marriage to Frances.[116] Such a series of events does not seem consistent. It is much more likely that he was writing later, specifically in early 1616, when the existence of an anti-Carr play would be popular because of the Overbury trial, and safer from Middleton's point of view because Carr had been exposed and convicted as a murderer. The play would then form part of the considerable body of anti-Carr literary work.[117]

Witch might still have been suppressed for political reasons because the Overbury trial was the greatest scandal of James's reign and he would not wish to have it in the public eye on the popular stage, but the play might also have found disfavour in the highest circles for another reason. There was a witchcraft trial at Leicester in August of 1616 involving six alleged witches.

The number may or may not be significant, but one of the events surrounding that trial is James I himself exposed the witches in this particular case to be fraudulent.[118] Several historians have taken his actions as proof of his desire to distance himself from associations with witchcraft.[119] If true, then Middleton's play might have annoyed the patron of the King's Men not only because of its political content but also because of its witchcraft content. Since this would have been against precedent (*Macbeth* found favour with the King), Middleton could justifiably claim, as he does in his dedication, that *Witch* was '*ignorantly* ill-favoured' (my italics).

6. SOURCES

The Witch has three separate plots: the successful attempt of Sebastian to reclaim his legally betrothed partner, Isabella, from her marriage with Antonio; the revenge of the Duchess against her husband, the Duke, for his 'barbarous act' of forcing her to drink from the skull of her dead father; and the illicit love affair between Abberzanes and Francesca. The three witchcraft scenes of the play contribute to the two main plots, but also stand on their own to some extent as a separate body of material.

Sebastian/Isabella/Antonio

Frank Sullivan cites an argument made by Karl Christ that a novella by Cinthio is a very close analogue and possible source for this plot.[120] Sullivan summarizes the novella as follows:

> Cinthio's story is of a servant who was in love with the wife of his master. He zealously served both master and mistress so that he was taken into the confidence of both and when the lady, jealous

without cause, asked him if her husband was being unfaithful to her, he, seeing a chance to have his will with the lady, replied that such was truly the case and that her husband's paramour was the lady's very good friend.

The lady wished to confront her husband with this guilt immediately, but the servant dissuaded her by pointing out that such a revelation would bring about a duel between her lord and the husband of the other woman, and that he, the servant—being the only one who could possibly have informed on his master—would certainly be killed. He suggests a better plan would be for the lady to take the place of her husband's mistress and after her husband has lain with her (supposing her to be another woman) she may accuse him of his guilt.

The servant manages to procure the use of the house of his cousin without informing her of his purpose, and, after escorting his lady there, he disguises himself and sleeps with her that night. In the morning the lady, having risen, sees her husband riding back from the farm in the country he had told her he intended to visit. She realizes that she has been tricked into adultery; so, returning to the servant, she pretends to want more love play and stabs him.

A hue and cry is raised which attracts the lady's husband, but before he can reach her, she stabs herself, also, and dies protesting to her lord that she has remained faithful to him in mind if not in body.[121]

Cinthio's novella is in parts an analogue to the Sebastian/ Isabella/Antonio plot in *Witch*, but there are several important differences between the two. First, the servant in the novella has not suffered, as has Sebastian, the dreadful misfortune (later revealed to be an injustice) of losing his betrothed wife to another man, and thus the crucial element of character motivation is elevated in *Witch* from the simple lust of the novella to a legitimate search for redress. Second, Cinthio's lady, unlike Isabella, suspects her husband without cause. Third, the lady in the novella consents to a bed-trick, but Isabella is unknowingly lured towards an attempted rape as she tries to catch Antonio in the act of adultery. Fourth, Cinthio's servant succeeds in raping his lady using the bed-trick, but Sebastian aborts his attempted rape and repents his bad intentions. Fifth, Cinthio's story ends in death for the lady and her servant, but Middleton's plot has a fortunate and happy ending.

Sullivan is correct to question Karl Christ's identification of Cinthio's novella as a possible source for *Witch*,[122] because, although there are similarities of action between the two, there are enough significant differences of motivation, action and resolution to indicate that Middleton was using a version of the story other than Cinthio's for his inspiration. Mary Scott suggests that Middleton came to know the Cinthio novella through Painter's novel number 57, but her identification of that translation has been discredited.[123] Several scholars have more recently suggested other sources for the plots of *Witch*.

David George argues that *The Atheist's Tragedy* contains material in the Charlemont/Castabella/D'Amville action which served as a source for Middleton's Sebastian/Isabella/Antonio plot.[124] He identifies multiple similarities between the loving couples' situations, including a betrothal, the male partner's absence and supposed death in war, the female partner's subsequent marriage, the male's return from battle and his frustration over the marriage, the non-consummation of the marriage because of a husband's impotence, the establishment of a situation for forced sexual intercourse but a rape not attempted, the fortunate death of the husband, the final defence of the male partner's actions throughout the play, and the happy reunion of the loving couple in marriage. But there are also several differences between the two stories. First, D'Amville, the character who corresponds to the Lord

Governor, is an arch-villain who engineers Castabella's marriage to his son, Rousard, through various plots and intrigues. In *Witch* the Lord Governor is clearly not a vilainous character, but rather a pillar of moral righteousness.[125] Second, the causes of the husbands' impotence are different: Rousard is ill; Antonio has been bewitched. Third, the deaths of the husbands differ: Rousard simply succumbs to his illness, but Antonio dies as he enters Fernando's house furious with rage and falls sixty fathoms to his death through a trapdoor. Finally, the lovers' reunions are also different. Towards the end of *The Atheist's Tragedy*, Charlemont and Castabella courageously face a possible double execution, but Sebastian and Isabella benefit from the common dramatic technique of the final discovery and accept what seems likely to be a happily-ever-after married life. The similarities are striking and the differences fairly slight, so David George is probably correct in assuming that *The Atheist's Tragedy* is a direct source for *Witch*.

Anne Lancashire persuasively argues that several of the plot differences between *Witch* and *The Atheist's Tragedy* are the result of Middleton deliberately paralleling the contemporary political scandal known as the Essex divorce case. This case and its specific influences on *Witch* are discussed fully in the 'Date' section of this introduction.[126]

Duchess/Duke/Almachildes

Middleton's main source for this plot is the Rosamund/Alboine story found in Machiavelli, Bandello, and Belleforest.[127] George Steevens first identifies the story as the source of the plot;[128] and then Alexander Dyce attempts to identify the specific source version, but he wrongly thinks that Middleton is following Belleforest's story,[129] when in fact the playwright is using Machiavelli. Both Belleforest and Bandello have major differences from *Witch* not shared by Machiavelli. In Belleforest two men (instead of *Witch*'s one) kill Alboine (the figure corresponding to the Duke); Rosamund (the character who corresponds to the Duchess) has been having an affair with

Helmige (the figure corresponding to Almachildes) long before she tricks him into killing her husband. Bandello's version does not contain the complication of the illicit love intrigue, but it does have two men, one of whom may be Almachildes, kill Alboine.[130] The main situation of the Duchess's plot to kill the Duke in *Witch* is most closely paralleled in the original of Machiavelli:[131] Rosamund is privy to one of her maids' consent to lie with Almachildes. Rosamund then takes her maid's place, sleeps with Almachildes in a room without light, reveals herself to him, and coerces him into killing Alboine with the threat that if he does not, she will claim that Almachildes has abused her and Alboine will kill him. Clearly Middleton is following Machiavelli.

Karl Christ argues that Middleton is following the original Italian of Machiavelli and not an existing English translation of *The Florentine History* because of a single detail of Queen Rosamund's plot to kill her husband: in both the original Italian of Machiavelli and *Witch*, the Queen/Duchess contrives with her maid to kill Alboine/Duke, but in the Bedingfield translation the Queen appears to act on her own initiative without the maid's knowledge.[132] Christ bases his argument on a comparison of the following two passages:

> sapiendo ... Elmichilde ... amava una sua ancilla, tratte con quella che celatamente desse opera che Elmachilde, in suo scambio dormisse con lei essendo Elmichilde secundo l'ordine di quella venuto a trovarla in loco obscuro credendosi essere con l'ancilla, iace con Rosimunda.[133]

> Then knowing that Almachilde ... loued a maiden of hers, of whome hee obtained to lie with her, and the Queene being priuy to that consent, did herself tarry in the place of their meeting, which being without a light, Almachilde came thither, and supposing to

INTRODUCTION

have been with the mayden, enjoyed the Queen....[134]

Christ quotes from a 1929 edition (it is, in fact, the same as the original), but
his translation of the passage is wrong. Here is a modern translation of the
entire passage, including Christ's extract:

> Deciding on revenge and knowing that Almachild, a noble and fiery
> Longobard youth, loved her handmaid, she planned with her a
> secret arrangement for Almachild to sleep with the queen instead of
> the maid. Almachild, coming into a dark place according to her
> plan and believing he was with the maid, lay with Rosamunda.[135]

Thus, all three versions—the original Italian of Machiavelli, the Bedingfield
translation and *Witch*—contain the crucial point of Rosamunda/Duchess's
collusion with her maid. It therefore seems likely that since a translation of
Machiavelli's *The Florentine History* existed, Middleton probably used it.

Francesca/Abberzanes
Margot Heinemann was the first to identify a source for this material. She
notes the similarity between the names and the characters of Middleton's
Francesca and Frances Carr, Countess of Somerset: 'In her irresponsibility,
her terror of exposure, and the utter ruthlessness she shows in trying to avoid
it, she may well have been suggested to the dramatist's imagination by
Frances Countess of Somerset herself.'[136]

Witchcraft Scenes
The main source for most of Middleton's witchcraft material is Reginald
Scot's *The Discouerie of Witchcraft* (London, 1584). Sullivan argues that all
of it comes from Scot,[137] but as we shall see, other sources have recently
come to light. Witchcraft was also a subject that existed in the popular

imagination of the time;[138] thus, when Middleton makes use of its better-known practices, such as witches dancing when they meet together (V.ii.86.1), he need not have been borrowing from a specific source. Scot himself often rehearsed what appeared to be common knowledge, and many of these beliefs appear in *Witch*. Here, for example, is just one extract.

And first *Ouid* affirmeth, that they can raise and suppresse lightening and thunder, raine and haile, clouds and winds, tempests and earthquakes. Others doo write, that they can pull downe the moone and the starres. Some write that with wishing they can send needles into the liuers of their enimies. Some that they can transferre corne in the blade from one place to another. Some, that they can cure diseases supernaturallie, flie in the aire, and danse with diuels. Some write, that they can plaie the part of *Succubus*, and contract themselues to *Incubus*; and so yoong prophets are vpon them begotten, &c. Som saie they can transubstantiate themselues and others, and take the forms and shapes of asses, woolues, ferrets, cowes, apes, horsses, dogs, &c. Some say they can keepe diuels and spirits in the likenesse of todes and cats.

They can raise spirits (as others affirme) drie vp springs, turne the course of running waters, inhibit the sunne, and staie both day and night, changing the one into the other. They can go in and out at awger holes, & saile in an egge shell, a cockle or muscle shell, through and vnder the tempestuous seas. They can go invisible, and depriue men of their priuities, and otherwise of the act and vse of venerie. They can bring soules out of the graues. They can teare snakes in peeces with words, and with looks kill lambes.[139]

And there are other general quotations that could be cited from Scot as proof that many of the isolated instances of witchcraft in *Witch* could come from common knowledge;[140] thus for any witchcraft material to be a specific source for the play, the respective passages must be very close. The present edition quotes source passages only when Middleton is clearly borrowing or when there is a particularly striking similarity which helps to illuminate a section of the play.

Alexander Dyce claims that Middleton is following a source other than Scot for some of the Latin in *Witch*.[141] He argues that Middleton took the Ovid Latin quotation at V.ii.18-25 from Jean Bodin[142] because, unlike Scot, both Bodin and Middleton omit one line of text (in *Witch* it would have appeared between ll. 22 and 23). Dyce actually cites a reprint of the Lotarium Philoponum translation of Bodin's French original.[143] Dyce went to a Latin text probably because Scot's marginal note cites a Latin edition of Ovid's *Metamorphoses*; however, if Dyce had looked at a reprint of the French original, he would have noted that the same line is omitted.[144] Thus Middleton could have been following either a Latin translation or the French original of Bodin's work. The playwright had plentiful references to Bodin's work because Scot lists his sources in the margins of his text. In any event, he was researching his material fairly thoroughly. Scot's reference beside the Ovid passage just mentioned above is, in fact, not to Bodin, but to the *Metamorphoses*.[145] The Ovid passage must have been relatively well-known; otherwise, Middleton would not have been able to cross-refer so easily.

David George suggests that there must be a specific source for the Latin at II.ii.11-14. He identifies these lines as being taken from Virgil's *Eclogue*, VII, and also argues that Middleton's mistaken '*nodo*' for '*modo*' in the line '*Nete tribus nodis ternos Amoretta colores*' must be an indication of the existence of a Latin original containing the same mistake.[146] He is absolutely correct, and Gareth Roberts identifies the original Latin mistake, not in a copy of Virgil, as George had predicted, but in another source for some of the witchcraft material, Le Loyer, *A Treatise of Spectres*.[147] Robarts also argues that the St. Oses witchcraft trial record is a source for *Witch*,[148] but at least some of the identifications, such as the record of mother-son incest, seem part of the general witchcraft lore of the period rather than a direct influence. Again, this edition only prints material in the explanatory notes when the parallel is compelling.

Such are the specific literary sources for *Witch*, but the general popular witchcraft beliefs of the time are also sources, and they too must be considered.

7. WITCHCRAFT IN THE RENAISSANCE POPULAR IMAGINATION

The Witch is difficult to appreciate without first understanding the supernatural phenomenon of witchcraft belief at the beginning of the seventeenth century in England. Middleton's witchcraft material is a mixture of literary tradition, derived from the *Mallevs Malificarvm*[149] by way of Reginald Scot's *The Discouerie of Witchcraft*, and popular English belief. The witches' actions and behaviour in the play conform in most respects to what a recent historian has called 'the cumulative concept of witchcraft', a concept that was firmly established by the end of the sixteenth century across Europe.[150] In general the English experience shared the broad outlines of the cumulative concept, but, as we shall see, differed in some details.

Two separate but related ideas formed the basis of popular witchcraft belief at the time Middleton wrote. The first idea was that of *maleficium*, an idea which derives from ancient folk beliefs about sorcery and is defined by two elements: first, that witches possessed some sort of extraordinary or mysterious power, magic, to perform their deeds;[151] second, that all deeds so performed were 'by definition harmful, not beneficial. They are intended to bring about bodily injury, disease, death, poverty or some other misfortune', usually concerning the loss or damaging of property.[152] Their method of enactment varied widely and included a range of actions from simple looks

34

to charms, chantings and image magic.[153] *Witch* contains numerous examples of this belief. There are, for example, lists of general *maleficium* at I.ii.57-67 and I.ii.135-50, mention of charms, such as a remora (I.ii.211) and knots (I.ii.160), chantings at I.ii.1-7, I.ii.107-10, and V.ii.18-25, and mention of image magic dealing with a heart (I.ii.46-7), a needle (I.ii.169), a gristle (I.ii.171) and pictures (I.ii.48-9, V.ii.4-6).

The second major idea of witchcraft was the belief that witches made pacts with the Devil, whereby they exchanged their souls for cooperation from him when performing *maleficium*.[154] This idea is obviously Christian in origin and dates back to the writings of St. Augustine, although it was not widely disseminated until the ninth century, and not fully officially codified until 1484 in the Papal Bull, *Summis desiderantes affectibus*.[155] The notion of the diabolical pact clearly incorporated *maleficium*: all evil derives from the Devil and he lends his power as magic to the witch. It also classed witchcraft as an heretical practice, and therefore firmly antithetical to Christianity. The pact with the Devil enjoys a long literary tradition, but its origin in popular imagination is difficult to locate. Its first mention in English trial records occurs in 1612,[156] and Middleton only barely alludes to it at I.ii.131-2 where Hecate mentions that she, like all other witches is 'sworn / To sweat for such a spirit' as Sebastian, and at I.ii.186 where Hecate professes to be motivated by 'mischief', which 'we're sworn to, the first oath we take'.

There were five other widespread beliefs concerning witches: the sabbath, flight, metamorphosis, the bodily mark and familiars. First, the sabbath was 'the belief that those witches who made pacts with the Devil also worshipped him collectively and engaged in a number of blasphemous, amoral and obscene rites'.[157] The worship took various forms, but often included actions such as sexual intercourse with the Devil and/or his attendants, general promiscuous heterosexual and homosexual activity, kissing the Devil's buttocks or anus, trampling on the cross, cannibalistic infanticide, and dancing, sometimes naked.[158] The first trial record of a possible sabbath in England is again 1612.[159] *Witch* contains a scene of a sabbath in V.ii. complete with a 'Witches' Dance', and III.iii. may well be the preparations for a flight to attend one. Second, flight was the belief that witches could transport themselves great distances through the air, usually to sabbaths or on child-killing missions. They were thought to ride beasts, sticks, brooms or gusts of wind, or to fly simply under their own power after having anointed themselves with unguents.[160] Middleton obviously capitalized upon the theatrical sensationalism of such an activity: III.iii. is entirely devoted to preparations for and the enactment of flying. Third, metamorphosis was the belief that witches could transform themselves (or others) into another shape, usually that of an animal,[161] but also into the shape of another person, which was called either *succubus* if male or *incubus* if female.[162] Although no witches change shape in *Witch*, Hecate twice refers to the practice of becoming an incubus, once at I.ii.30-1 and again at I.ii.202 when she notices Almachildes, 'I have had him thrice in incubus already'. Fourth, the bodily mark was a way of identifying a witch by a distinctive feature on her body, usually a spot or excrescence.[163] There is no reference to this in *Witch*, possibly because the decorum of playacting would not allow the disclosure of such an intimate detail. Fifth, familiars were imps or devils which witches kept; they usually took the shape of an animal or insect.[164] Middleton makes ample use of this belief with references to such animals as owls (III.iii.5, III.iii.10, V.ii.40), a bat (III.iii.7) and a raven (V.ii.40), and the actual presentation of the cat at I.ii.235.1-238 and at III.iii.52.1-78.

These ideas were disseminated in various treatises and trial reports; however, they were also directly challenged by exactly the same documents that scholars have used to substantiate widespread belief in them. The English writings on witchcraft from the time of the St. Osyth trial in 1582 to the Leicester witch trials of 1616 do not present a consistent attitude to popular notions of witchcraft; some even express doubts about the very existence of witches. The author of the St. Osyth trial record and other writers, such as Perkins and Potts, were obvious believers in witchcraft, but presented differing concepts of it,[165] whilst writers such as Scot and Gifford were severe sceptics.[166]

Scholars today also disagree widely in their interpretations of the three Acts of Parliament (1542, 1563, 1604) passed against witchcraft; some interpret the last as more severe in character than both its predecessors and therefore as evidence of a growing climate of persecution in Jacobean England,[167] but others argue more closely and perceptively that there is little difference between the implementation of the Act of 1563 and the implementation of that of 1604.[168] And even the King's position on witchcraft at the time *Witch* was written is unclear. In Scotland, a notoriously rich area for witch-hunting, James VI, when supposedly personally attacked by witches, participated in witch persecution and wrote about it.[169] But in England, a comparatively less virulent country for witch-hunting, James I apparently lost interest in witch persecutions by his courts, and there is strong evidence that his personal intervention in the famous Leicester trial of 1616 and exposure of it as a sham may have led to effective suppression of some subsequent prosecutions in England as a whole.[170] Middleton's literary use of his sources is fairly easy to gauge, but how that material functioned against such a fluid and uncertain background at the time *Witch* was written is less clear.

Such ambiguity of response has repercussions upon discussion of the play. The most obvious consequence is that if James I was *not* the fanatical witch-hunter that many historians have claimed he was throughout his life, if he in fact was keen to minimize his witch-hunting past at or around the time *Witch* was written, then Middleton's play was an ill-judged piece with which to court royal favour.[171]

The final point to be made here is that Middleton is using his witches as credible potent forces of evil, and thus he is not writing in the sceptical English tradition of witchcraft. The witches control human actions and have complete success with their charms: the Isabella-Antonio marriage is not consummated because of Hecate's knotted snake-skins; and for the time that Almachildes's love charm is actually on Amoretta's person, it is fully effective. The Duchess is caught before she can act to kill Almachildes, but if she had not been caught, there is little doubt that Hecate's methods would have worked.

8. THE PLAY

Critical History. The scant critical history of *Witch* is one of extreme variation. The first document that can be cited as evidence of a critical response is the Dedication to Thomas Holmes:

> I have merely upon a taste of your desire recovered into my hands
> (though not without much difficulty) this ignorantly ill-fated labour
> of mine. Witches are *ipso facto* by the law condemned and that
> only, I think, hath made her lie so long in an imprisoned obscurity.
>
> (ll. 3-7)

These lines point to an admission by Middleton that he had trouble recovering his work, probably because plays were the property of acting companies, not individual authors,[172] which may explain why the play lay 'so long in an imprisoned obscurity', but he also says that his labour was 'ignorantly ill-fated'. Every critic except one who has addressed this phrase has interpreted it to be an admission that 'the play failed upon the stage'.[173] But Anne Lancashire argues that the words need not be interpreted as an admission of failure: the play might have been a political mistake, and therefore suppressed because it reflected current court scandal of the Essex divorce case too closely.[174] Lancashire has clearly opened debate, but in the absence of conclusive evidence, one cannot make a final judgement about the play's early reception.

The next critical responses to *Witch* occur when it is rediscovered by George Steevens. The play then becomes interesting mainly because it is the earliest source of two songs referred to in *Macbeth* only by their first two lines.[175] Most of the subsequent writing on *Witch* centres on its relationship to Shakespeare's play, with the unfortunate result that *Witch* is generally judged as an inferior creation when compared to its illustrious predecessor. This introduction will be returning to the issue of the relationship of *Witch* to *Macbeth* from time to time, but it is also worth some extended consideration here.

The earliest questions raised concern the relative dating of the two plays, or to put it simply, which came first and who was borrowing from whom. Then by the middle of the eighteenth century it became clear that the original composition of *Macbeth* was the earlier play, and that *Witch* followed. But there was a further complication. The text of *Macbeth* preserved in the First Folio of Shakespeare's plays was held to be a revision, so the question then became, was the revised *Macbeth* earlier or later than *Witch*. Today, that question remains unanswered, even though Middleton is by consensus the most likely candidate for the reviser of *Macbeth*.[176]

There are other areas of interest in the relationship between the two plays, and the one often discussed is the different effects of the use of witches and witchcraft. Shakespeare's witches have again received much better reviews; Charles Lamb's opinion is a good example:

His [Shakespeare's] witches are distinguished from the witches of Middleton by essential differences. These [Middleton's] are

39

creatures to whom man or woman plotting some dire mischief might resort for occasional consultation. Those [Shakespeare's] originate the deeds of blood, and begin bad impulses to men. From the moment that their eyes first meet with Macbeth's, he is spell-bound. That meeting sways his destiny. He can never break the fascination. These witches can hurt the body: those have power over the soul.... Their names, and some of the properties, which Middleton has given to his hags, excite smiles. The Weird Sisters are serious things. Their presence cannot co-exist with mirth. But in a lesser degree, the Witches of Middleton are fine creations. Their power too is, in some measure, over the mind. They raise jars, jealousies, strifes, like a thick scurf o'er life.[177]

This is a typically Romantic view of Shakespeare, which emphasizes the cerebral rather than the theatrical, but even at that level, the argument is curious. Lamb begins by asserting what he sees as essential differences between the Shakespeare and Middleton witches, but by the end of his short paragraph he appears to be reversing his opening position and arguing that Middleton's witches are similar to Shakespeare's in that they too can affect the mind. Furthermore, and this is the curious part, the rhetorical effect seems to be cumulative for Middleton's creations: they affect *both* the mind and the body; Shakespeare's can be said to affect the mind only, but, of course, to a greater extent. Lamb did not fully understand theatre, which is why Middleton's stage properties only excite mirth in him; but, as we shall see later, an understanding of those stage properties is central to the meaning of the play's action.[178]

A line of critical response to *Witch* on its own as a play exists beside, and sometimes in the shadow of the *Macbeth* discussion, and it covers the full range of aesthetic judgement. Lamb's type of qualified praise continues throughout the nineteenth century and into the twentieth: '*The Witch* is a good but not a distinguished play.'[179] And although high praise for *Witch* is rare, it actually begins surprisingly early, in 1832, with the claim that 'it is a very good play' from John Genest, a critic who obviously read the text closely because he provides a detailed synopsis of it.[180] But damning critical responses are also prevalent throughout the nineteenth and well into the twentieth century: 'it rises little above mediocrity';[181] 'The construction or composition of the play, the arrangement and evolution of event, the distinction or development of character, would do less than little credit to a boy of twelve ...';[182] 'The plot is a tissue, not worth unravelling, of intrigues ...'.[183]

Much more recent criticism has tried to address *Witch* mainly in terms of its professed tragicomic form, and in relation to other tragicomedies in the middle period of Middleton's career. The play is sometimes still seen as a flawed achievement, or, at best, a rehearsal for later tragic masterpieces. Thus *Witch* is 'the least interesting play in the group' of tragicomedies circa 1613-18;[184] 'the play has less intellectual complexity and coherence than *More Dissemblers* ... [and] the consequent loss of intellectual focus in the play creates structural problems ...';[185] 'one senses for the first time the gathering darkness of Middleton's later drama'.[186]

But *Witch* is also sometimes seen in a more positive light as a successful achievement in its own right. Carolyn Asp thinks that the play is 'deliberately constructed to parody, burlesque, or critically examine the stage conventions of both the public and the private playhouses ... [and] it also examines the social mores that accept these conventions'.[187] Margot Heinemann observes that even though it 'is not as a whole a satisfactory play ... it does, in a strange way, suggest an atmosphere of court corruption, of sexual intrigue and fashionable witchcraft, that is both more realistic and more disturbing than has commonly been allowed'.[188] And Inga-Stina Ewbank argues for a 'particularly Middletonian version of scepticism: scepticism, that is, applied to the substance of human affairs as well as to theatrical forms and conventions'.[189] In *Witch* in particular she sees that scepticism directed 'at the sheer fragility of the enacted "if" which underpins the tragicomic form Middleton is using, and at the belief in human perfectability which alone could underpin a truly moral tragicomedy'.[190]

Anne Lancashire picks up the point of Middleton as a moral writer from Asp and others and sees the playwright combining entertainment and morality in a new way: 'although Middleton is doubtless in part influenced by Fletcher, another tradition, given the play's reflection of the Jacobean court, and its use of song, dance, and spectacle, would seem to stand as strongly, or more só, behind *The Witch*'s plot endings: that of the court masque'. And near the end of her article, she notes several instances of 'allegorical motifs'.[191] Lancashire also calls for a re-examination of *Witch* to 'endeavour to discover the play's own terms'.[192] The following discussion attempts to do just that by examining how Middleton generates meaning through plotting, action, staging and language.

Plotting. Middleton plots *Witch* from two literary sources (Tourneur's *The Atheist's Tragedy* and Machiavelli's *The Florentine History*) and one historical source (the exposure of the Somersets' role in the Essex divorce case and the Thomas Overbury murder). He adapts his materials in such a way as to present his characters with forced choices within various dilemmas, usually associated with love relationships, and most often with marriage. The action is also governed by the tragicomic form in which it occurs. The form thus accounts for Middleton's reworking of the tragic death ending of Machiavelli's tale of Albovine and Rosamund into a story of redemptive reconciliation between the Duke and Duchess. But the selection and use of *The Atheist's Tragedy* material is considerably more involved. Middleton's main change is to cut everything preceding the central love dilemma of that play, the point at which the two main romantic characters, Charlemont and Castabella, find that Castabella has been forced into marrying Rousard after having been incorrectly informed of Charlemont's death. This cut has two effects. First, Middleton immediately focuses attention upon the predicament of the returning wronged fiancé/husband, Sebastian, as he faces the *fait accompli* marriage of his fiancée/wife, Isabella, to another man, Antonio. Second, Middleton's cut also suppresses the reasons for the marriage; thus, the audience is ill-informed about why Isabella married Antonio, which leaves the action open to active audience speculation.

Middleton reshapes the historical events by distributing characteristics of the Somerset couple between various characters. Thus Robert and Frances, are actually not Antonio and Isabella, but rather Antonio and Francesca, and some of the specific events attaching to Frances in particular are attributed to characters other than Francesca. Hence the allusion to Frances's divorce from Essex on the grounds of non-consummation through bewitched impotency of her husband finds expression in *Witch* in the Antonio/Isabella marriage, not the Francesca/Abberzanes relationship. The confusion is not unusual in drama of the period, and a contemporary audience would have had little trouble in catching the allusions,[193] but direct satire is probably not Middleton's main concern in adapting his sources. His aim in reworking his materials is a didactic one: he wishes to make absolutely clear what is and what is not correct moral behaviour in love between the sexes. He achieves his aim mainly through the technique of parallel action, language and staging.

Action. There are three plots in *Witch*. The main plot includes the Sebastian/Isabella/Antonio material. Sebastian has been away from his fiancée/wife at war for three years, and has been reported killed in action by Gaspero and Antonio, but before he left, he and Isabella agreed a legally binding verbal marriage known as *sponsalia per verba de praesenti*.[194] Sebastian returns to Ravenna on the day Isabella and Antonio wed. The 'question' of the main plot can thus be loosely phrased as 'How can Sebastian save his marriage now that his betrothed has formally wed Antonio?'

The two sub-plots also pose direct questions. The Duchess/Duke material is the most straightforward of the two. The Duke has been playing, and continues to play, a 'horrid game' (I.i.111-32, II.ii.58-62), which he presumably thinks proves the Duchess's love for him: he publicly and privately forces her to pledge a drink to him from a cup made out of the skull of her father, whom he has killed in battle. She plots a revenge for the Duke's behaviour, so the question of this plot becomes 'How will she kill her husband and get away with the murder?' The second sub-plot is a bit more complex because it slightly overlaps the main plot. It involves the Francesca/Abberzanes material, but because Francesca is Antonio's sister and because she lives in his household, it also involves Antonio and Isabella. Francesca is heavily pregnant when she first appears, but has managed to conceal the fact from everyone except her lover, Abberzanes. As the play opens, the birth of the child is seven weeks away (I.i.134-7), but there is a sense of imminence nevertheless (II.i.40-2, 161-2), so the question of this plot is 'How will Francesca manage to have the child and keep the birth secret?' All three plots are introduced in the first three scenes of the play and develop from that point.

The main character of each plot needs an agent to help him or her because each is powerless on his or her own. Sebastian's first problem is how to stop the wedding-night consummation of the Antonio/Isabella marriage. He finds a solution by resorting to a group of witches led by Hecate for a charm to make Antonio impotent with Isabella. We have, of course, seen the witches before Sebastian meets with them: Almachildes, a court rake, has sought them out to get a love charm to seduce Amoretta, the Duchess's maidservant. The two scenes, both of which occur in I.ii., are an excellent example of Middleton's use of parallel plotting, not so much because they present the same dramatic situation (two consultations with dealers in the supernatural for a charm of some kind), but because the parallel action forces consideration beyond that action.

Sebastian wants to save his legally sound marriage, but Almachildes wants to seduce Amoretta, an objective with no legal justification. And there are further moral implications which arise: Sebastian uses his consultation and charm to prevent bigamy and save Isabella's honour/virginity for love within the state of marriage; Almachildes uses his consultation and charm to attempt fornication, which would destroy Amoretta's honour/virginity in an act of lust. The parallel actions thus appear to be opposites, but Middleton's technique raises more complex questions. Compare each character's words when they decide to search out the witches. Almachildes is simplistically straightforward:

> I will to the witches.
> They say they have charms and tricks to make
> A wench fall backwards, and lead a man herself
> To a country house some mile out of the town
> Like a firedrake. (I.i.90-4)

Sebastian is obscurely guarded, even to his closest friend, Fernando:

> Sir, I've a world of business. Question nothing;
> You will but lose your labour. 'Tis not fit
> For any, hardly mine own secrecy,
> To know what I intend. I take my leave, sir.
> I find such strange employments in myself
> That unless death pity me and lay me down,
> I shall not sleep these seven years; that's the least, sir. (I.i.17-23)

Almachildes exhibits no sign of uneasiness or apprehension, and he makes his choice willingly, but Sebastian is clearly distressed at the action he thinks he is forced to take: far from making his choice willingly, he can hardly consider it even in the secrecy of his own mind. Almachildes does not comment on his emotional state, but Sebastian notes the 'strange employments within myself', or the odd purposes to which he is now devoted contained within his very being, and this so disturbs him that he sees his future as one of endless sleeplessness, or, if he is lucky, he will die and so end his torment. Almachildes goes to the witches in gleeful anticipation of a charm which will give him sexual satisfaction, but Sebastian resorts to them in a distraction that fractures his usual sense of self. The two characters' words upon entering the witches' domain reinforce the point more clearly:

> *Almachildes.* Call you these witches?
>> They be tumblers, methinks, very flat tumblers. (I.ii. 198-9)

> *Sebastian.* Heaven knows with what unwillingness and hate
>> I enter this damned place; but such extremes
>> Of wrongs in love fight 'gainst religious knowledge,
>> That were I led by this disease to deaths
>> As numberless as creatures that must die
>> I could not shun the way.   (I.ii.111-16)

Almachildes makes bawdy jokes and is very much at home in this environment, whereas Sebastian sees the area as a 'damned place' to which he is unwillingly driven by 'extremes / Of wrongs in love'; and his distress must be extreme because it overrides the absolute law of religious knowledge, of which his conscience reminds him. The difference of response is again brought out in the ending of each character's scene—Almachildes stays and dines with Hecate, but Sebastian leaves indicating his relief to be gone:

> I depart happy
> In what I have then, being constrained to this.
> [*Aside*] And grant you, greater powers, that dispose men,
> That I may never need this hag again.   (I.ii.180-3)

The point of the parallel action of the two characters is not merely that Sebastian knows the moral implications of his behaviour and that Almachildes does not, and so Sebastian's resorting to the witches demonstrates the depth of his desperation whereas Almachildes's visit simply re-emphasizes his corruption, but rather that Sebastian's awareness clouds the justification of his actions right from the opening lines of the play. In other words, enlisting the agents of darkness, even when no other solution presents itself and even when the result of their involvement could be described as 'good', is morally dubious—and the point is that Sebastian knows this at the precise moment he finds himself forced to act. The fact that the charm works—Antonio is unable to consummate his marriage to Isabella—further complicates matters, because the 'right' result, the preservation of Isabella's virginity for her first marriage to Sebastian, derives from 'wrong' behaviour, choosing to rely on the evil of witchcraft for help. Similar choices of agents have to be made in the sub-plots, but the moral questions thereby raised are less complex.

In the first sub-plot, the initial choice for an agent is altogether different. The Duchess intends to have her husband, the Duke, killed in revenge for his 'horrid game' (II.ii.56-64). The Duchess thus needs someone to kill the Duke for her, and she chooses Almachildes, 'a fantastical gentleman' (Dramatis Personae) for the task. (Again, Middleton has quite clearly outlined Almachildes's moral character, as discussed above). Like

47

Sebastian's understanding of the witches, the Duchess has no illusions about Almachildes's character: in fact, she chooses to use him precisely because the public knowledge of his immorality opens him to blackmail, but unlike Sebastian, she shows no signs of hesitation or conscience in her choice, which indicates that she is perfectly contented to use the morally dubious for her own (at least equally morally dubious) ends. Her plan of entrapment combines Almachildes's attraction to Amoretta, the loose moral behaviour prevalent at court, and the theatrical convention of the bed-trick (she pretends to sleep with Almachildes, and then threatens to call the coupling rape). The plan succeeds in extracting the promise from Almachildes to kill the Duke, which it seems he does, but Almachildes does not carry out the assassination—a fact which is importantly withheld from the audience until the final scene. This opens a whole new area of consideration, but one which is again based upon volition. When the Duchess offers Almachildes a choice, after revealing herself and threatening to accuse him of rape ('take thy choice', 'either die or kill the Duke', III.i.38, III.i.16), we, like Almachildes, might conclude that this is not a real choice at all, because either may lead to death (III.i.38-9). But we would be wrong, as is proven in the final scene when the Duke appears alive. Thus, the highly morally corrupt character, Almachildes, is still capable of correct moral choice, but whether he does it for his own self-interest or not is another matter. The point of the suppression of Almachildes's real behaviour is that we as an audience are 'caught out' as it were the first time through, and the ending forces us to rethink the 'certainties' of our first viewing. Middleton uses the same technique of suppression with Isabella, but to greater effect. Because we do not know initially why she married Antonio, we are likely to be swayed by either Ferdinand's explanation—the Lord Governor 'clapped it up'—or Sebastian's diatribes against women's 'faithless vows' into judging Isabella harshly. But the real reason for her marriage to Antonio is that he and Gaspero swore to her Sebastian's death in battle. In other words, the later revelation effectively clears her of any accusation of making a faithless vow to Sebastian, but also forces us into rethinking an earlier judgement that we might have made, and once rethought, we might see that we were wrong, and this, in turn might force us into reviewing the criteria of our judgements.

The second choice the Duchess makes for an agent is straightforward in meaning. She promises to marry Almachildes if he kills the Duke, and after the supposed assassination, she wants to kill Almachildes so that she can marry the Lord Governor. Marriage is thus used in both cases as a means to an end which is despicable. The Duchess consults the witches for a means to carry out the deed, and, as she does, she places herself in exactly the same position as Almachildes and Sebastian earlier, but, like Almachildes rather than Sebastian, she shows no hesitation or pangs of conscience over her behaviour. Middleton's technique of parallelling is again very revealing. Almachildes and the Duchess follow actions that lead them into life-threatening situations (IV.i.44ff, V.iii.91ff), as does Francesca in the other sub-plot.

But Francesca's dilemma is considerably different from either those of Sebastian or the Duchess: whereas both of the other characters have been the victims of other characters' wills, Francesca has become pregnant through voluntary and repeated sexual intercourse with Abberzanes (II.i.34-56), 'a gent[leman] neither honest, wise, nor valiant' (Dramatis Personae). He, of course, must be her choice of agent because her dilemma precludes choice of anyone else, but the point here is that Francesca has effectively made her choice before the play begins, and self-motivated moral corruption has informed it. This becomes absolutely clear when her three soliloquies (II.i.34-61, III.ii.113-40, IV.iii.1-21) are compared to Sebastian's soliloquies.

Middleton very carefully charts Sebastian's personal mental states as he progresses towards reunifying his marriage through a series of soliloquies (or in one case an aside which functions as a soliloquy). There are four of these: I.ii.111-22, II.i.206-24, III.ii.14-28, IV.ii.95-111. They map a different and, most importantly, a changing attitude of character to action, and, beyond that, action to interpretation within the moral context of the play. Francesca's soliloquies, on the other hand, demonstrate exactly the opposite: hers reassert a complete absence of any moral awareness and a total obsession with self-preservation.

The first of the speeches is an aside which functions as a soliloquy:

Heaven knows with what unwillingness and hate
I enter this damned place; but such extremes
Of wrongs in love fight 'gainst religious knowledge,
That were I led by this disease to deaths
As numberless as creatures that must die
I could not shun the way. I know what 'tis
To pity madmen now; they're wretched things
That ever were created, if they be
Of woman's making and her faithless vows.
I fear they're now a-kissing. What's o'clock?
'Tis now but supper-time; but night will come,
And all new-married couples make short suppers.   (I.ii.111-22)

The speech divides into three parts. The first section, ll. 111-16, is a disclaimer showing an awareness of conscience, knowledge of 'this damned place' and desperation. The second section, ll. 116-19, is an imaginative leap to a consideration of the plight of others, specifically madmen—a unique example of such thought in *Witch*, and rare in other plays of the period. The third section, ll. 120-22, is another imaginative leap, but this time to the possible simultaneous actions of his betrothed, Isabella, and her 'new' husband—their kissing and imminent consummation of their marriage. This is the problem he faces and his obsession with it has driven Sebastian to the witches.

Francesca's first soliloquy (II.i.34-61) by contrast is an extended whine about the misfortune of her situation:

> I have had the hardest fortune, I think, of a hundred
> gentlewomen.
> Some can make merry with a friend seven year
> And nothing seen; as perfect a maid still,
> To the world's knowledge, as she came from rocking.
> But 'twas my luck, at the first hour, forsooth,
> To prove too fruitful.
>   ...
>
> These bastards come upon poor venturing gentlewomen ten to one
> faster than your legitimate children. If I had been married, I'll be
> hanged if I had been with child so soon now.   (II.i.34-40, 43-5)

And she then goes on to praise the 'pains a friend will do' over those of a husband (ll. 46-50), to blame various aphrodisiacal foods for her sexual behaviour (ll. 50-51), to admit that sex was a regular occurrence from which even her brother benefitted (ll. 52-6), to hope that her friend will 'provide safely' for her (ll. 56-8), and to note that her brother would kill her if he knew about the situation (ll. 56-8). The soliloquy is twenty-seven lines long and, unlike Sebastian's aside, does not contain any hint of the presence of a conscience beyond a parenthetical and clichéd 'Honesty forgive me'. In fact the whole soliloquy points directly away from any notion of personal responsibility: she has had the most misfortune; she has had bad luck; the food made her do it, etcetera. There is no imaginative leap to anything beyond herself here either; it is one great 'poor me' speech, of extreme self-interest, complete with no fewer than twenty-one uses of first-person pronouns. There are, however, pointed ironies: her criterion of judgement (moral or otherwise) for her behaviour rests in that nothing is 'seen'; and her

51

claim that this would not have happened to her had she been married conveniently ovelooks the logical point that if she had been, she would not have the problem she now faces. Everything points to the obvious 'fact' that by the official Christian codes of Jacobean morality, her behaviour is morally unsound. And Francesca never shifts from her position of self-centred self-preservation. Sebastian, too, becomes utterly self- absorbed to the point of forgetting or redefining moral correctness.

His second speech (II.i.206-24), this time soliloquy, expresses a confusion of emotion that the impotency charm has worked. He begins by complimenting Isabella on her ability to bear sexual abstinence in marriage and commends the concept of women's 'honesty', but the speech also contains a telling point of self-realization: 'Yet I'm not throughly happy' (l. 211), because 'Still she's not mine ...' (l. 221). And the soliloquy ends with a cry of frustration, which re-emphasizes the legal and religious 'fact' of his marriage to Isabella: 'Holy vows, witness that our souls were married' (l. 224). This speech does not point towards action; it merely states what has become a position of deadlock in the plot: Isabella's virginity is preserved but she is still Antonio's wife, which places Sebastian in a living hell:

> What makes the greatest torment 'mongst lost souls?
> 'Tis not so much the horror of their pains,
> Though they be infinite, as the loss of joys.   (II.i.215-17)

The third speech (III.ii.14-28), again in soliloquy, directs Sebastian towards a piece of information, that Antonio is still keeping and having sex with Florida, his whore, after his marriage to Isabella. As an audience, we, of course, already knew that this was his intention *before* he was charmed impotent, which indicates the extreme depth of his moral weakness.[195] Sebastian will now use this information, together with the fortuitous absence of Antonio, to further his own ends. He tells Isabella of her husband's adultery with Florida (ll. 187-94); Isabella does not initially believe the allegation (ll. 195-8), but after some argument she seems to think that it may be true (ll. 216-7); and Sebastian undertakes to prove his allegations if she will follow him out of her house that night (ll. 221-9). Sebastian's intentions are dishonourable. His double plan becomes clear later in IV.ii.: he intends to confirm his allegations by using Ferdinand's house to establish the appearance of a regular meeting place where Antonio commits adultery with Florida, but Sebastian also intends to rape Isabella. He tries to justify his actions:

> I will think
> This night my wedding-night; and with a joy
> As reverend as religion can make man's,
> I will embrace this blessing. Honest actions
> Are laws unto themselves, and that good fear
> Which is on others forced grows kindly there.   (IV.ii.60-5)

But the logic is nothing more than a rather unsophisticated 'the ends justifies the means' argument to satisfy himself; he is now at a point of development similar to the self-centredness of Francesca.

Her second soliloquy (III.ii.113-40) occurs just after Isabella has told her that she knows about the clandestine birth. After many lines bemoaning this embarrassing discovery, Francesca forms a plan to disgrace Isabella, even though Isabella had promised her that she would not relate the information to Antonio if Francesca reformed her behaviour:

> I must be quit with her in the same fashion,
> Or else 'tis nothing. There's no way like it
> To bring her honesty into question cunningly.
> My brother will believe small likelihoods,

> Coming from me too. I lying now i'th' house
> May work things to my will, beyond conceit too.
> Disgrace her first, her tale will ne'er be heard;
> I learned that counsel first of a sound guard. (III.ii.130-7)

Like Sebastian, Francesca is now, as throughout the play, only thinking of herself, arguing that she must destroy Isabella's honesty before her own immorality is exposed. There is a classic case of transference embedded within this soliloquy, which provides Francesca with a spurious motive for her actions. She comments upon Isabella's promise of confidentiality:

> She can keep it secret?
> That's very likely, and a woman too!
> I'm sure I could not do't; and I am made
> As well as she can be for any purpose. (III.ii.120-3)

The joke is not just gratuitous misogyny. The important point is that Francesca is judging others by referring to her own behaviour: she transfers her world view onto Isabella, and finds Isabella wanting. The irony is that the system of values for which Francesca condemns Isabella is, in fact, Francesca's. Similarly, Sebastian's plan to rape Isabella is a severely limited view of religious doctrine interpreted according to his self-centred desires—obviously sexual as well as spuriously religious—to reclaim Isabella as his wife. The final and ultimate difference between the two highlights this point of moral knowledge: Sebastian comes to understand, and more importantly, comes to avoid the terrible deed of rape through a deeply realized repentance; or, to put it simply, he chooses to learn, whereas Francesca chooses not to. His final soliloquy reveals a repentance for his misguided intentions:

> I cannot so deceive her, 'twere too sinful;
> There's more religion in my love than so.
> ...
> No, he that would soul's sacred comfort win
> Must burn in pure love like a seraphin.　　　(IV.ii.95-6, 110-11)

This is the moral centre of the play because it marks the point where personal will guided by Christian ideology triumphs over personal will guided by selfish reason and logic. Far from being either haphazard or simplistically convenient, the repentance is perfectly plotted to demonstrate the possibility of correct moral behaviour even in the face of both the desire and the opportunity to act otherwise.

Francesca, on the other hand, is still plotting mayhem in her final soliloquy (IV.iii.1-21):

> I must bestir my wits now
> To catch this sister of mine and bring her name
> To some disgrace first, to preserve mine own.
> There's profit in that cunning.　　　(IV.iii.4-7)

Here are the values by which she lives: others' disgrace, self-preservation ('mine own'), profit and cunning. There is no sense of compassion for others, and certainly no appeal to any system of moral order. Even after she is forced to admit what she has done (IV.iii.81-96), there is not the slightest hint of repentance, and she ends the play in utter silence still committed to herself. Quite simply, Francesca is the immoral touchstone of the play. But *Witch* is refreshing in its sense of positive didacticism, that is, in its presentation of the positive power of moral correction. Consider, for instance, how the idea of revenge functions.

Standard revenge plotting necessitates the annihilation of the revenger's opponents through his revenge and, most often, a resolution steeped in blood through multiple murder. This is Antonio's intention: he wishes to kill at least Isabella, Gaspero, Francesca and Abberzanes (Florida could also die in the malaise). But he kills no one. Antonio's revenges are completely ineffectual: Florida and Gaspero survive his direct attack; Francesca simply will not descend from 'above' to her slaughter; and Hermio refuses to follow his master's orders to poison the wine. Again, Middleton's parallelisms point the meaning: Antonio's impotency in revenge parallels his impotency in his marriage. Like the marriage, which is founded upon the lie of Sebastian's death in battle, the revenge is founded upon a lie, that of Isabella's unfaithfulness. One of the possible moral 'truths' of *Witch* is that action based upon lies cannot succeed. Thus, as Antonio's second revenge is also founded upon a lie—Isabella's supposed infidelity with Celio/Sebastian—it is likewise doomed to failure, but the implications are more complicated, because the revenge attacks a relationship legitimized through legal marriage. So, instead of revenge destroying all around it in a great conflagration as is so often the pattern, the parody of form internalizes the process: Antonio progresses towards his own destruction, because he, like Spenser's Ire, can attack only himself with his rage.

The Duchess/Duke subplot follows similar lines of development. As the Duchess moves into her revenge, she moves deeper and deeper into the complications that ensue, but the resolution of this subplot is far simpler, although just as didactic, as that of the other subplot. There is a similarity in that the action breaks down: Almachildes does not kill the Duke; the Duchess with the witches' aid does not kill Almachildes. Instead, the Duchess is exposed by the Lord Governor as an intentional killer, but redeemed by a benevolent Duke who dramatically rises from a faked death and forgives the Duchess her actions. The crucial factor here is again located in a first cause, and that cause is a mitigating circumstance: the Duke's atrocious behaviour of forcing the Duchess to drink to him out of her father's skull. The Duchess was wrong for her attempted murder, but forgiven because she was driven to it—again, a judicial moral result.

Staging. Middleton achieves particularly noteworthy effects, which contribute to various meanings of the play, by the full use of stage properties, costume, off-stage sounds, and blocking and movement. In fact, Middeleton's work is so sophisticated that it has led several critics to attack his staging as flawed or unintelligible,[196] but such is not the case.

    Witch contains a variety of stage properties which are actually named or implied in the dialogue. Sometimes, as at the opening of I.ii., they are named as simply 'properties' without detailed explanations, but we know from other productions of the period which use witches, most notably Jonson's *The Masque of Queens*, that the properties are likely to have been spectacular; we also know from the same source that the costuming was likey to have been theatrically flamboyant.[197]

    Generalities are notoriously vague; exact meanings are harder to establish, but they are most often recoverable when Middleton is at pains to name or directly to imply specific stage properties. When Hecate enters at the opening of I.ii., she must be carrying at least two snakes: this is obvious from what she says later in the scene ('Send Stadlin to me with a brazen dish / That I may fall to work upon these serpents': I.ii.14-15). The audience 'reads' the property as a sign on various levels. At the most immediate it is simply one kind of reptile known as snake (the particular kind is of no importance), but there is also a wider range of associated meanings which are generated by the larger shared cultural world of Jacobean England, a world that included the virtually universal belief in Christianity and a popular belief in witchcraft. In this larger cultural world a snake would have meanings associated with the biblical myth of the temptation of Eve: it would be seen as a creature of the Devil and thus an appropriate accoutrement to the demonic practices of witches. The actual language of description of the stage property reinforces these meanings by using the biblically charged word 'serpents'. The Jacobean 'facts' of a Christian devil who had inhabited a snake to tempt mankind into the Fall and the popular notion of the widespread practice of witchcraft fuse in the stage property to create resonances of meaning which must have been clear, and possibly horrific for those in an audience drawn from that cultural world. As that audience watched the property (snake-skins now, after Hecate's 'squeezing') move from the environment of the witches into the environment of the court characters of the play, the evil associated with the snakes spreads beyond its first location: in other words, it loses its character specificity, which, of course, is exactly the extended meaning of the Fall. Middleton thus connects the underworld of demonstrable evil with the world of court, using the literal device of a stage property.

He creates a similar effect with the most shocking stage property in the play, the baby. We see it twice. It first appears as a dead child, another one of the properties with which Hecate enters at the beginning of I.ii., and then as Francesca's newborn infant in II.iii. When the property is among the witches it generates meanings of horror associated with child abuse. These meanings range from at worst infanticide—a particularly obnoxious form of murder because it combines the brutality of killing with the innocence of its victim—and at best a disrespect for the dead and hideous treatment of the body. When the property is later among the court characters Francesca and Abberzanes in II.iii., the meanings that we have already seen with the witches carry over into the court realm. Although they are not actually murdering the child, they are handing it on to an old woman for disposal, exactly the same stage image created in I.ii. when Hecate gives the dead child to Stadlin. Each action of handing over the child leads to abuse: in the case of the witches, the abuse is that of mistreating the corpse; in the case of the court characters, the abuse is that of abandonment. This particular

58

parallel drawn through the stage property of the child also points to Francesca being the court counterpart to Hecate, and thus specifically the human witch of the title.[198] The parallel also provokes an interesting question: which character's actions with the child is more 'evil'? The answer is most probably Francisca's, because in every major moral decision involving right and wrong the factor of choice is emphasized, whereas the witches are defined as morally wrong from the beginning of the play—we never see Stadlin, for instance, reflecting upon whether or not she should remain in the diabolical sisterhood.

Paradoxically, one of the most significant symbols of the play is a piece of furniture which, though it appears as a stage property in other plays of the period, is evoked rather than represented in *Witch*—the bed referred to at IV.ii.88-9. This is the scene in which Sebastian plans to consummate his marriage contract with Isabella through a 'legal' rape. The bed functions as a heavily charged icon of marriage; the sexual union in it is the final act of proper marriage bonding in Jacobean society. But like so many ideals, marriage is open to corruption. Middleton had used a bed as a stage property to underscore just such corruption in *A Chaste Maid in Cheapside*, where Mrs. Allwit is 'thrust out' onto the stage still in her bed after giving birth to her seventh child by Sir Walter Whorehound (III.ii.0.1). There the bed functioned as an inverted or corrupt icon of marriage because it became the territory upon which marriage's opposite, adultery, was not only practised but celebrated. Here in *Witch* the stage use is much more refined: the bed functions as a potential icon; it contains several possibilities of moral conduct within it. It represents correct marriage behaviour in proper consummation of the relationship of man and wife, but it also contains its opposite in adultery (Isabella's inevitable position in relation to Antonio after the proposed rape) or rape (again, Isabella's inevitable position as victim in relation to Sebastian because she has not consented). But the bed is an even more complex icon than that: because of the specific situation of the play and the complicated points of view (sexual intercourse upon it represents various things depending upon the character's perspective), the bed is a completely open sign gathering to it a range of possible interpretations. Middleton's genius in this play is that he keeps it open, even after the scene is over: it is a positive 'proof' for Isabella of Antonio's adultery; it is negative 'proof' of Sebastian's 'pure love' for Isabella. It is finally nothing less than the central icon of the play.

Middleton achieved far more spectacular theatrical effects in III.iii. with the flight of Hecate and her cat. Again, like the stage property of the snakes, flying had certain Jacobean cultural resonances, all associated with the supernatural, both good and evil. Witches are defined as evil, so, again, the dramatic effect supports and elaborates definition: the audience is witness to titillatingly horrific actions. Glynne Wickham argues that the scene is notably successful from a theatrical point of view;[199] his argument is particularly interesting because it places *Witch* III.iii. firmly in a progression of stage witchcraft spectacles, most notably between the original *Macbeth* and the revival *Macbeth*. This in turn at least raises the possibility of the kind of intertextuality that Inga-Stina Ewbank identifies as existing within the King's Men acting company: 'as Middleton must have known—the effect on the audience of the tragicomedy of *The Witch* would be conditioned by the fact that, in the same playhouse and with the same cast, they had seen the tragedy of *Macbeth*'.[200] Ewbank's admirably subtle argument is aimed at the overall effect or meaning of *Witch*, but effects and meanings can also be traced from Shakespeare's play to Middleton's through stage properties and stage sounds. I should like to examine one stage sound, knocking, one further stage property, the cauldron, and one stage body, Hecate.

The staging in IV.iii. is complex, but absolutely perfect for the effect that is to be created. Francesca wishes to discredit Isabella's reputation because Isabella is the only character in the play who knows that Francesca

60

has had an illegitimate child by Abberzanes. Francesca has therefore contrived a situation whereby Antonio, whom she has sent away from his home for a period of time, is to return unexpectedly and find his wife, Isabella, in a compromising position with Gaspero, his servant. The major difficulty that Francesca faces is getting Isabella and Gaspero into the same room in the dead of night, but this she accomplishes by telling Gaspero that the knocking waks him from his sleep comes from Isabella's room. It is, in fact, made by Antonio, and that knocking is extremely interesting because it is another example of intertextuality: here we have a direct aural quotation from *Macbeth*. Although there are no original stage directions for it in the MS, it is clearly marked in the text. At l. 27 Francesca says, 'My sister hath both knocked and called this hour', so we must have heard the knocking shortly before that point. It could have occurred at l. 19 just before Francesca notes Antonio's return: 'My brother's come'. There is no other way for her to note his arrival except through some sound, and since knocking is mentioned just six lines later, knocking is the likeliest sound. Then at l. 29 Francesca exclaims, 'Hark, hark again!' This must be a recognition of at least the second knocking in the scene. Finally, at l. 31, Francesca repeats the exclamation, 'Hark, hark again!' for the same reason. During this scene, Francesca has been frantically trying to manoeuvre a dazed and sleepy Gaspero into the correct room: he has been making bawdy jokes as the knocking continues, and just before the knocking started, Francesca told us that she had drugged the rest of the servants of the house, who are curiously all female: 'I spiced them lately with a drowsy posset' (l. 18). The knocking, the bawdy joking servant, and the woman who drugs servants are all paralleled in *Macbeth*, and Middleton may well be playing upon an audience's knowledge of that King's Men's play. But to what effect? The parallel is not direct, mainly because the overall situation of *Witch* is not precisely that of *Macbeth*: no king lies dead during the knocking and no tyrant is to rule afterwards. The scene actually descends into ineffectual ranting by Antonio, and even his moral boast, 'I'll make base lust a terrible example', (1.39) is ridiculous in our ears since we know that he has kept his whore long after his marriage to Isabella—and *not* only because of his bewitched impotency with his wife. We do not know it at the time, but his off-stage attempted murder of the couple in Isabella's room is also ineffectual: he has only wounded them, and he has actually attacked Florida who, unbeknown to Francesca, earlier entered Isabella's room as part of Sebastian's plot to discredit Antonio. But the *Macbeth* parallel is clear, and works to align Francesca with Lady Macbeth as an evil female force in the play even though that evil is held in the check of relative ineffectuality because the form of the play is tragicomedy rather than tragedy.

There are other parallels with *Macbeth* and earlier Renaissance drama. G.K. Hunter has noted that Marlowe uses standard medieval hell imagery in *The Jew of Malta* to emphasize the damnation of Barabbas at the end of that play when he falls through a trap door into a cauldron and boils to death. The imagery derives directly from the description of Leviathan in *Job* 41:20 and 31: 'Out of his nostrils goeth smoke, as out of a sething pot or caldron ... He maketh the deep to boil like a pot ...'.[201] Shakespeare similarly depends upon this iconic tradition in *Macbeth* when he puts a cauldron on stage as an accompanying property for his witches, and Shakespeare also uses the wider and subtler iconography of Hell Castle to tie the witches' iconography directly to the Macbeths and thereby link them to practices of demonic evil. [202] Middleton is using the same iconic tradition with his cauldron; the stage property is probably a direct iconic quotation from *Macbeth*. The cauldron is associated with hell, and thus the Duchess's visit to the witches in V.ii. directly encodes her actions as evil in exactly the same way that Macbeth's visit to the witches in IV.i. encodes his behaviour. Similarly, Antonio's death is described in terms that recall the morality play tradition and both *Macbeth* and *The Jew of Malta*:

Blinded with wrath and jealousy, which scorn guides,
From a false trap-door [Antonio] fell into a depth
Exceeds a temple's height, which takes into it
Part of the dungeon that falls threescore fathom
Under the castle.   (V.iii.29-33)

Here we have a classic description of one of the deadly sins, wrath, running completely out of control and killing its victim. Far from being selective retribution,[203] it is absolutely determined: Antonio, unlike most of the other characters, has become irrational through anger. This fact, coupled with his underhanded lies to steal Isabella from Sebastian (V.i.59-66), condemns him ultimately to damnation. The castle too may be another iconic quotation from *Macbeth*. The descent through the trap-door draws attention to itself not as parody or as plot convenience,[204] but as a direct moral feature which helps us interpret the meaning of the play: only lost souls inhabit the kingdom of hell. Of course, there are other morally unrepentant characters who do not die (most notably Almachildes, Francesca and Abberzanes), but their sins are not as great as Antonio's and they are punished in kind.

Hecate is another parallel with *Macbeth*. If the Oxford editors and Nicholas Brooke are correct, then the Hecate of both *Witch* and *Macbeth* was written by the same man, Thomas Middleton; the Hecate scenes in *Macbeth* could have been added in the revision of the play. In *Witch* Hecate's behaviour with the dead child is directly paralleled to Francesca's actions with her live child, thereby linking the two. The roles of Hecate and Francesca could also have been doubled because they never appear on stage at the same time. Isabella is the only other major female character that could have been doubled with Hecate, but the general thematic connections are not so persuasive as to link those two characters. If one extends the idea of intertextuality and marries it with Lancashire's 'heresy' about the revision of *Macbeth*, then one gets an amazing line of associations which read from the contemporary historical situation through *Witch* and the *Macbeth* revision. Frances Howard/Essex/Somerset = Francesca/Hecate (*Witch*) = Hecate (*Macbeth*).[205] My own feeling is that the equation depends far too heavily upon a number of suppositions, any one of which may be wrong, but the connections would not be so far-fetched if the same actor played all the roles, as he could well have done in the King's Men.

Finally, both *Witch* and *Macbeth* contain groups of witches. Shakespeare's combine the effects of classical fates and physical manifestations of Macbeth's psychology. They can predict the future, but not the precise way the future will manifest itself: Macbeth is to become king, but the way that he will become king is not specified. Thus the witches' prophecy acts as a trigger to the play's action, but that action is determined by the evil that is latent in Macbeth's being. The witches do not, as Lamb says above, have power over Macbeth's soul: in fact, the idea of freewill and choice is emphasized throughout the play, especially by the protagonist himself. Middleton's witches *are* different; they have almost nothing of the classical fates about them, except in the name of Hecate. They do not predict the future, and they are not confined to the manifestations of any single person's thought. They are *more* than that: they are representations of one aspect of several, perhaps of all of the character psychologies in *Witch*, and they are infinitely more dangerous than anything except Macbeth himself in Shakespeare's play. They grant several characters' wish fulfilments, and thus are a much more tempting force at large in a society, which is why they function as a resource to be sought out and used. They are successful on the level of specific detail—no tempting prophecies here. Finally, as forces within the play, they can be activated by consultation, but they can also be nullified or defeated as well. Thus, they remain at the heart of the meaning of *Witch*, which focuses on the clear power of moral choice in all of the plots of the play.

Language. Most of *Witch* is written in Middleton's characteristic loose iambic pentameter, which is used by characters of rank in both the social and supernatural contexts. Prose is reserved for figures of inferior rank or dubious status: most notably Firestone, Hecate's loutish son, who speaks almost entirely in prose befitting his low status, and for some of the less attractive characters such as Almachildes and Francesca, whose long speeches sometimes move in and out of verse and prose (see, II.ii.1-35, IV.i.1-21 and II.i.34-61, respectively). The occasional chants and songs are written in doggerel. The diction and syntax that Middleton employs throughout *Witch* are fairly straightforward and present few problems of interpretation or understanding; he seems to be taking considerable pains to be as clear as possible.

The tone of *Witch* is overwhelmingly moral, at times approaching biblical. Within this there is also a characteristically Middletonian bawdy lexis, which is most oftenly used to point immorality (as in the case of the witch scenes, the Francesca and Abberzanes material, or the language surrounding Florida), but which also appears in a less virulent form to mark, perhaps, acceptable sexual jesting within marriage (the wedding night/morning jokes of the Lord Governor and Isabella). The imagery ranges from the wicked grotesquery of the witches to the, again, biblical allusion of Sebastian's long repentance soliloquy. Since that speech is actually the moral centre of the play, it provides an excellent example of Middleton's use of language.

> I cannot so deceive her, 'twere too sinful;
> There's more religion in my love than so.
> It is not treacherous lust that gives content
> T'an honest mind; and this could prove no better.
> Were it in me a part of manly justice,
> That have sought strange hard means to keep her chaste

To her first vow, and I t'abuse her first?
Better I never knew what comfort were
In woman's love than wickedly to know it.
What could the falsehood of one night avail him
That must enjoy for ever or he's lost?
'Tis the way rather to draw hate upon me;
For, known, 'tis as impossible she should love me
As youth in health to dote upon a grief,
Or one that's robbed and bound t'affect the thief.
No, he that would soul's sacred comfort win
Must burn in pure love like a seraphin.   (IV.ii.95-111)

The religious coding of the opening sets the register for the rest of the speech: Sebastian's planned rape is a deceitful sin of 'treacherous lust'; his 'honest mind' informed by the tenets of Christian 'religion' forces him to recognize his error. The remainder of the speech drives the point home. If Sebastian carried through his plan, he would 'abuse' Isabella by 'wickedly' knowing her love through a 'falsehood', which would bring nothing but 'hate' from her. The sacrament of marriage is actually realized in terms of an eternal context, suggesting the enormity or the absoluteness of the action he has been contemplating and the enormity of the destruction that he would have inflicted but has now fortunately avoided: one night's pleasure is balanced against an eternity of enjoyment (ll. 104-5), and nothing short of the 'soul's sacred comfort' is at issue here. Finally the purity of the love that is compared to the angelic is ultimately an abdication of the pursuit of personal justice and a statement of faith and hope in providential aid, given proper moral behaviour.[206] Far from being deeply ironic, Sebastian's language is straight recognition of morally reprehensible behaviour coupled with its probable outcome, ending with a resolution to emulate angelic love.

INTRODUCTION

The paralleling of diction that codes as either morally good or morally bad is a technique that Middleton uses throughout the text, and, although this is not the place for an involved linguistic analysis of the language of *Witch*, a simple short list of the basic binary oppositions can easily illustrate Middleton's didactic technique.

love	lust
virtue	sin, mischief
wife, husband	strumpet, friend
honesty	folly
honour	shame
truth	falseness, wrongs
innocence	guilt
justice	revenge, cruelty
joy	grief
noble	baseness

This is just one possible list of key words, but the point is obvious: Middleton is using heavily-laden moral diction which is absolutely straightforward, and there are surprisingly few instances of ambiguously ironic usages of any of the words listed above which are not clearly signalled as ironic. For example, when Sebastian describes his planned rape of Isabella as an 'honest action', the irony, if not clear at his point of utterance, becomes unavoidable when he comments in his repentance soliloquy. At other times, after the coding of the language is fully understood from such a list as the one above, then the irony, such as it is, is again straightforward. So, if Francesca, for instance, launches into a disquisition on how much more caring a 'friend' is than a husband, her language is coded as morally corrupt, no matter how true her observations might be.

The Duke's final speech, then, is not, I think, ironic at the level of, for lack of a better phrase, moral correctness: it is a straight summation of the positive values of the play:

> Nay, since in honour thou canst justly rise,
> Vanish all wrongs, thy former practice dies.
> I thank thee, Almachildes, for my life,
> This lord for truth, and heaven for such a wife,
> Who, though her intent sinned, yet she makes amends
> With grief and honour, virtue's noblest ends.
> What grieved you then shall nevermore offend you:
> Your father's skull with honour we'll inter
> And give the peace due to the sepulchre.
> And in all times may this day ever prove
> A day of triumph, joy and honest love.   (IV.ii.128-38)

'Honour' is 'justly' restored after the Duchess's repentance through 'grief' (and the maintenance of her 'honour') for her 'sin' of attempting to kill the Duke. 'Truth' has been a guiding principle, and 'heaven' has been, very importantly, a providential influence leading to this happy conclusion. Finally, the speech and the play end on the phrase 'honest love', which takes us back to Sebastian's repentance and conversion to 'pure love', again, the central moral issue of the play.

Witch is a play that is fully successful in it own terms, and its clarity of meaning is its major strength. It applies its moral view even-handedly among the characters. Its ultimate punishment, death, is meted out to only one character, Antonio, and he is irredeemable because of his irrational violence. Its other irredeemable characters, Francesca, Abberzanes and the witches, are in fact not severely but rather appropriately punished, and, finally, tolerated as examples of moral misbehaviour. Its ultimate reward, happiness in marriage, is shared equally between characters, men and women alike, who have repented their 'sins'. In this final concentration upon positive didacticism, that is, upon the rewards of correct moral choice, *Witch* refreshingly presents a world that can improve through human learned behaviour, which is, finally, what we mean by civilization.

9. PRINCIPLES OF THIS EDITION

The text of this edition is a modernization of the unique MS of the play written in the hand of Ralph Crane. The conventions used in editing are mainly those of The Revels Plays Series.[209] The MS text has been collated with three diplomatic editions of the play (which are all essentially reproductions, in type, of the MS text) and with six other previous modern editions. Texts are cited in the collation as follows:

MS	Bodleian Library MS Malone 12 (original scribal MS).
Steevens	George Steevens, ed., *A Tragi-coomodie, Called The Witch* (London, 1778).
Scott	Sir Walter Scott, supposed ed., in *Ancient British Drama*, III (London, 1810).
Dyce	Alexander Dyce, ed., in *The Works of Thomas Middleton*, III (London, 1840).
Bullen	A.H. Bullen, ed., in *The Works of Thomas Middleton*, V (London, 1885).
Ellis	Havelock Ellis, ed., in *Thomas Middleton*, II (London, 1890).

Sullivan	Frank Sullivan, ed., 'Thomas Middleton's *The Witch*' (Ph.D. thesis, Yale University, 1939).
Drees & de Vocht	L. Drees and Henry de Vocht, eds., in *Materials for the Study of Old English Drama*, XVIII (Louvain, 1945).
Greg & Wilson	W.W. Greg and F.P. Wilson, eds., *The Witch* (M.S.R., 1950 for 1948).
Corbin & Sedge	Peter Corbin and Douglas Sedge, eds., in *Three Jacobean Witchcraft Plays* (Manchester, 1986).

All substantive departures of this edition from the MS text are recorded in the collation as are all defensible readings of previous editors, even though unadopted. Where the reading of the MS is in question because of unclear scribal handwriting, every plausible reading introduced by modern editors is collated. Incorrect and implausible readings of previous editors are not noted. Only the earliest source of a reading in previous editions is cited, and citations do not necessarily conform in spelling or punctuation to the original, except where spelling or punctuation is the matter being collated. Peculiarities of italics, capitalization and word division are silently normalized according to modern usage. Speech prefixes are also silently regularized throughout.

Spelling. Spelling is silently modernized along the lines suggested by Stanley Wells.[208] Verbal forms ending in '-ed' are printed as '-èd' when syllabic and '-ed' when non-syllabic. The '-est' termination is printed 'est' when syllabic and ''st' or 'st' (depending upon modern usage) when non-syllabic. The long s is always transcribed as the modern short s.

The scribe, Ralph Crane, has peppered the MS with elisions indicated by apostrophes; this edition handles them as follows. The apostrophe indicating such an elision is retained but not noted in the collation where Crane has joined two words written out in full with an apostrophe and an elision or slur is possible in modern usage (e.g. 'we'are' as 'we're' at I.i.124 or 'it'had' as 'it'd' at IV.iii.54). If the elision of two words indicated with an apostrophe offers no modern solution (e.g. at'hart, II.i.199), then the apostrophe is omitted, but recorded in the collation immediately after the siglum (e.g. II.i.199 *at heart*] at'hart *MS*). If the elision seems wrong even by seventeenth-century usage, the siglum is followed by citation of the first modern editor to remove it, then the elision (e.g. II.i.229, I ha'] *Steevens* I'ha' *MS*). ''Please' and ''pray' are silently regularized throughout to 'please' and 'pray'. But the apostrophe is retained in this edition where it is essential to meaning (e.g. ''Give', II.iii.21), or where it provides a useful hint of meaning to the reader (e.g. ''Morrow', II.i.63 or 'This'', III.i.1). Contractions are silently regularized throughout according to modern usage (e.g. 'ne'er' for 'neu'r', and 'I'm' for 'I'me').

MS readings are unclear in several places. In cases involving a choice between one of two possible readings, the unchosen alternative is recorded in the collation (e.g. II.i.46 once] *MS; poss.* oure).

Punctuation. Ralph Crane's punctuation has its own peculiarities, which include an excessive use of hyphens, parentheses and apostrophes, but it is systematic and fairly consistent throughout the MS. With the exception of apostrophes as outlined immediately above, this edition silently modernizes all punctuation throughout, unless a choice of meaning is involved, in which case the choices are recorded. Crane uses a question mark, an inverted semicolon and combinations of these with a comma to indicate both exclamations and questions; this edition notes the MS punctuation always as a question mark in the collation. Often the choice for modernization is of equal weight between the modern exclamation point or question mark; this edition does not collate the choice between the two or that of previous editors unless genuinely different meanings are involved. All plausible punctuation of previous editions is collated when it is different from the punctuation of this edition and when it changes meaning. In every case, only the earliest text with the specific meaning is cited either as the source for this edition or as an example of a different interpretation.

Stage Directions. Most of the stage directions in the MS were added by Crane probably after he wrote out the text.[209] He seems to have been concerned about their placement because he began most of them, particularly entrance stage directions, with a dash which appears to indicate specific positions for placement.[210] The general practice of this edition is to print the MS stage direction immediately after a line of text when the dash is either directed at the last word of that line or to the white space immediately above it. All exceptions to this practice are noted in the collation.

Adopted or unadopted asides which originated with previous editors are collated at the lines where they would stand according to Revels practice, rather than at the actual lines of text where in their own editions they occur. 'Pres.' (i.e., presumably) is used in the collation wherever the existence of an aside is in question (a dash, for instance, is sometimes particularly ambiguous) or wherever the amount of material marked as an aside is in question.

All substantive editorial additions to MS stage directions are enclosed within square brackets; such additions are recorded in the collation only when they have originated with a previous editor. All other plausible editorial additions except scene locations of previous editors unadopted by this edition are recorded in the collation.

Abbreviations. All MS abbreviations have been silently expanded, including those in Latin act endings and in stage directions. The unique instance of E^{xt} meaning *'Exit'* rather than its usual *'Exeunt'* has been collated. Abbreviations in the collation have the following meanings: 'conj.' indicates the conjecture, rather than emendation, of a modern editor; 'pres.' indicates a presumed but unclear reading of a modern editor; 'subst.' indicates a reading substantially though not exactly that of a previous editor; 'poss.' indicates a possible but unclear reading of the MS.

Lineation. In the MS a new line is begun at every change of speaker, even though a second speaker may be completing the line of blank-verse begun by the first. This edition silently indents lines by new speakers which are part of verse lines begun in preceding lines. This edition also relines irregular MS blank-verse lines to create one or two regular lines and one short or long line. All relineations of the MS are noted in Appendix A, and all relineations of previous editors, whether adopted or unadopted by this edition, are also collated. 'So' indicates an arrangement of text by a previous editor which has been adopted by this edition.

Endnotes

1   Peter Corbin and Douglas Sedge, eds., *Three Jacobean Witchcraft Plays* (Manchester, 1986).
2   See Edward J. Esche, review of Peter Corbin and Douglas Sedge, eds., *Three Jacobean Witchcraft Plays* (Manchester, 1986), in *Ideas and Production*, 8 (1988), 108-10.
3   Alexander Dyce, ed., *The Works of Thomas Middleton*, I (London, 1840), pp. ix-xiii.
4   The best and fullest discussions of Middleton's life are to be found in Mark Eccles, '"Thomas Middleton a Poett"', *S.P.*, 54 (1957), 516-36;

Richard Hindry Barker, *Thomas Middleton* (New York and London, 1958); and N.W. Bawcutt, ed., Thomas Middleton, *The Changeling* (London, 1958), pp. xvii-xxi.

5   Mark Eccles, 'Middleton's Birth and Education', *R.E.S.*, 7 (1931), 431.

6   See the visitation pedigree reproduced in Dyce, I, p. xii.

7   Mildred G. Christian, 'A Sidelight on the Family History of Thomas Middleton', *S.P.*, 44 (1947), 490; Eccles, '"Middleton a Poett"', 516; P.G. Phialas, 'Middleton's Early Contact with the Law', *S.P.*, 52 (1955), 187.

8   Eccles, 'Middleton's Birth', 431.

9   Christian, 'A Sidelight', 490-6.

10 Dyce, I, p. xiii.

11 Eccles, 'Middleton's Birth', 434-7: see also Mildred G. Christian, 'An Autobiographical Note by Thomas Middleton', *N.&Q.*, 175 (1938), 259-60.

12 See, for instance, Roma Gill, 'Middleton', in *Renaissance Drama*, ed. James Vinson (London, 1980), pp. 87-91.

13 C. H. Herford, 'Middleton (Thomas)', in *D.N.B.*, 13, eds. Leslie Stephen and Sidney Lee (1885-90; rpt. Oxford, 1921-2), p. 357.

14 Mildred G. Christian, 'Middleton's Residence at Oxford', *M.L.N.*, 61 (1946), 90-1.

15 Eccles, '"Middleton a Poett"', 525; Phialas, 193.

16 Christian, 'Middleton's Residence', 91.

17 Phialas, 193.

18 Middleton had published *Micro-cynicon. Six Snarling Satyres* in 1599 while at Oxford, and *The Wisdom of Solomon Paraphrased* in 1597 before he went up.

19 David George, 'Thomas Middleton at Oxford', *M.L.R.*, 65 (1970), 734-6; see also Joseph Quincy Adams, ed., *The Ghost of Lucrece*

(New York, 1937), pp. xxiii-xxxi.

20   Eccles, '"Middleton a Poett"', 525.

21   Philip Henslowe, *Henslowe's Diary*, eds. R.A. Foakes and R.T. Rickert (Cambridge, 1961), pp. 201-7.

22   See Phialas, 194 and Barker, pp. 9-10.

23   Barker, p. 11.

24   Barker, p. 13.

25   See R.A. Foakes, ed., Cyril Tourneur, *The Revenger's Tragedy* (London, 1966), pp. xlviii-liv and lxvi-lxix for a full discussion of Middleton's authorship of the play.

26   See Anne Lancashire, ed., *The Second Maiden's Tragedy* (London, 1978), pp. 15-22 for a full discussion of Middleton's authorship of this anonymous play.

27   Margot Heinemann, *Puritanism and Theatre: Middleton and Opposition Drama under the Early Stuarts* (Cambridge, 1980), p. 107.

28   Eccles, '"Middleton a Poett"', 535-6.

29   Eccles, '"Middleton a Poett"', 536.

30   See instead R.C. Bald, 'The Chronology of Thomas Middleton's Plays', *M.L.R.*, 32 (1937), 33-43 and David J. Lake, *The Canon of Thomas Middleton's Plays* (Cambridge, 1975).

31   R.C. Bald, 'Middleton's Civic Employments', *M.P.*, 31 (1933), 65-78.

32   This section of the introduction is based upon a close examination of the MS, which verified most of the excellent work recorded in the introduction to Thomas Middleton, *The Witch*, eds. W.W. Greg and F.P. Wilson (M.S.R., Oxford, 1950 for 1948), pp. v-xv.

33   Greg and Wilson, p. v.

34   Frank Sullivan, 'Thomas Middleton's *The Witch*', Ph.D. dissertation, Yale University 1939, p. 230.

35   Sullivan, p. 230.

36   See pp. 13-16 below.

37   Greg and Wilson, p. v.

38   F.P. Wilson, 'Ralph Crane, Scrivener to the King's Players', *Libr.*, 4th series, 7 (1926-7), 194-215.

39   See photocopy on p. 88 for the full page reproduction.

40   See photocopy on p. 89 as an example of a typical MS page.

41   Again, see photocopy on p. 90 as an example. Crane obviously added the stage directions after he wrote the dialogue: see also T.H. Howard-Hill, *Ralph Crane and Some Shakespeare First Folio Comedies* (Charlottesville, 1972), pp. 25-6.

42   Greg and Wilson, p. viii.

43   My illustration is hand drawn from viewing the watermarks of Bodleian Library, MS Malone 12, pp. 19, 32, 46, 62, and 87.

44   It is possible that Greg and Wilson were relying upon the work of R.W. Hunt and P. Long: see Greg and Wilson, p. viii.

45   See pp. 19 and 46 of Bodleian Library, MS Malone 12.

46   Edward Heawood, 'Papers Used in England after 1600: I. The Seventeenth Century to c. 1680', *Libr.*, 4th series, 11 (1930-1), 288.

47   Edward Heawood, *Watermarks: Mainly of the 17th and 18th Centuries* (Hilversum, Holland, 1950), pl. 481 and p. 143.

48   Heawood, *Watermarks*, pl. 482 and p. 143, and Heawood, 'Papers Used in England', no. 78, 299.

49   See Howard-Hill, *Ralph Crane* for a full discussion, with bibliography, of Ralph Crane's work; see also T.H. Howard-Hill, 'Shakespeare's Earliest Editor, Ralph Crane', *Sh.S. 45* (1992), 113-29.

50   Howard-Hill, *Ralph Crane*, pp. 38-9.

51   Howard-Hill, *Ralph Crane*, pp. 59-60.

52   This quotation is taken from Ralph Crane, *The Pilgrimes New-yeares-Gift; or, Fourteen Steps to the Throne of Glory* (London, 1621), Bodleian Library, Vet. A2 f. 257, p. 6, ll. 7-12, because

Sullivan makes twelve errors in his transcription and gives an inaccurate reference: see Sullivan, p. 210.

53   Sullivan, pp. 211-14.

54   Sullivan, p. 210.

55   G.F. Fleay, *A Biographical Chronicle of the English Drama 1559-1642*, II (London, 1891), p. 104.

56   T.H. Howard-Hill, 'Ralph Crane's Parentheses', *N.&Q.*, 210 (1965), 334-40; Howard-Hill, *Ralph Crane*, pp. 24, 58.

57   Greg and Wilson, p. xii; see also John Fletcher, *Demetrius and Enanthe*, eds. Margaret McLaren Cook and F.P. Wilson (M.S.R., Oxford, 1951 for 1950), p. viii, where the placing of stage directions one or two lines early is again noted but suggested to be Crane's scribal habit.

58   See G.R. Proudfoot, 'Dramatic Manuscripts and the Editor', in *Editing Renaissance Dramatic Texts English, Italian, and Spanish: Papers Given at the Eleventh Annual Conference on Editorial Problems, University of Toronto, 31 October - 1 November 1975*, ed. Anne Lancashire (New York and London, 1976), pp. 9-39, especially p. 10.

59   Robert K. Turner Jr., 'Act-End Notations in Some Elizabethan Plays', *M.P.*, 72 (1975), 246.

60   Turner, 'Act-End Notations', 245.

61   *The British Library General Catalogue of Printed Books to 1975*, 221 (London, 1962), p. 56.

62   *The National Catalogue Pre 1956 Imprints*, 382 (London, 1975), p. 623.

63   The argument which follows is taken from Sullivan, pp. 221-3.

64   Bertram Dobell, *Catalogue of Books Printed for Private Circulation* (London, 1906), p. 122.

65   Horace Howard Furness, ed., *Macbeth*, by William Shakespeare, revised by Horace Howard Furness, Jr. (London, 1873 and 1903), p.

368.

66 See *Witch*, V.ii.60-78 and III.iii.39-79, and *Macbeth*, IV.i.44-60 and III.v.34-73, respectively.

67 William Shakspeare, *The Plays and Poems of William Shakspeare*, ed. Edmond Malone, I (London, 1790), pp. 359-364.

68 See title page of William Shakespeare, *The Plays of William Shakspeare*, notes by Samuel Johnson and George Steevens, 2nd ed. (London, 1778) and William Shakespeare, *The Plays of William Shakspeare*, notes by Samuel Johnson and George Steevens, 3rd ed., revised by Isaac Reed, 10 vols. (London, 1785).

69 Falconer Madan, *A Summary Catalogue of Western Manuscripts in the Bodleian Library at Oxford*, IV (Oxford, 1897), p. 427. See the transcription of Steevens's preface note, p. 7 above.

70 Shakespeare, *Plays*, I (1778), pp. 324-30 and Shakespeare, *Plays*, I (1785), pp. 336-41.

71 See the transcription of Steevens's preface note, p. 7 above.

72 Bodleian Library, Percy 30.

73 Folger Shakespeare Library, D.A. 47.

74 Paul Mulholland, 'Notes on Several Derivatives of Crane's Manuscript of Middleton's *The Witch*', *P.B.S.A.*, 78 (1984), 75-81.

75 *O.E.D.2*, vb., 1, which cites 1791 as the earliest date for this usage.

76 *O.E.D.2*, vb., 2a, which cites 1793 as the earliest date for this usage.

77 Shakespeare, *Plays*, I (1778), p. 329.

78 G. Benguerel, *Thomas Middleton: Part 1* (Nordhausen, Kirchner, 1870), p. 23, as noted by Sullivan, p. 98; Hugo Jung, *Das Vërhaltnis Thomas Middleton's zu Shakspere*, Müchener Beiträge zur Romanischen und Englischen Philologie, 29 (Leipzig, 1904), p. 65, as noted by Sullivan, p. 98.

79 A.H. Bullen, ed., *The Works of Thomas Middleton*, I (London, 1885), p. liii.

80 Fleay, II, p. 104.

81 See pp. 25-6 below.

82 Felix E. Schelling, *Elizabethan Drama 1558-1642: A History of the Drama in England from the Accession of Queen Elizabeth to the Closing of the Theatres, to which is Prefixed a Résumé of the Earlier Drama from Its Beginnings*, II (London, 1908), p. 245.

83 See, for instance, David L. Frost, *The School of Shakespeare: The Influence of Shakespeare on Elizabethan Drama 1600-42* (Cambridge, 1968), pp. 52 and 262-7.

84 Edmond Malone, ed., *The Plays and Poems of William Shakspeare*, II (London, 1821), pp. 420-38.

85 Malone, II, pp. 427-8.

86 Malone, II, p. 428.

87 Malone, II, p. 429.

88 Malone, II, pp. 430-1.

89 Malone, II, pp. 431-3.

90 Malone, II, p. 434. The date should be 1608-9: see J. Leeds Barroll, *et al.*, *The Revels History of Drama in English, Volume III, 1576-1613* (London, 1975), p. 33.

91 Malone, II, pp. 433-6.

92 W.J. Lawrence, 'The Mystery of *Macbeth*: A Solution', in *Shakespeare's Workshop* (Oxford, 1928), pp. 24-38. Lawrence claims that this is a reprint of an article of the same title which appeared in *The Fortnightly Review*, 108 (1920), 777-83, but it is in fact a revision of the original.

93 Lawrence, p. 33.

94 Sullivan, p. 129; John Dover Wilson, ed., William Shakespeare, *Macbeth* (Cambridge, 1947), p. xxvii; Greg and Wilson, pp. vi-vii; John Stevens, 'Shakespeare and the Music of the Elizabethan Stage: An Introductory Essay', in *Shakespeare in Music*, ed. Phyllis Hartnoll

(London, 1964), p. 40.

95 Gerald Eades Bentley, *The Jacobean and Caroline Stage*, IV (Oxford, 1941), p. 903; Samuel Schoenbaum, revisor of Alfred Harbage, *Annals of English Drama 975-1700: An Analytical Record of All Plays, Extant or Lost, Chronologically Arranged and Indexed by Authors, Titles, Dramatic Companies, etc.* (London, 1964), p. 104.

96 Sullivan, p. 126-9.

97 See p. 23 below.

98 Bald, 'Chronology', 41.

99 See T.B. Howell, *A Complete Collection of State Trials, Volume II: 1603-1627* (London, 1816), pp. 785-862.

100 Alfred Harbage, *Annals of English Drama 975-1700: An Analytical Record of All Plays, Extant or Lost, Chronologically Arranged and Indexed by Authors, Titles, Dramatic Companies, etc.* (London, 1940), p. 86; Schoenbaum, *Annals*, p. 104; Lake, p. 26; Heinemann, pp. 107-8.

101 David George, 'The Problem of Middleton's *The Witch* and Its Sources', *N.&Q.*, 212 (1967), 209-11.

102 See pp. 28-9 below.

103 See Irving Ribner, ed., Cyril Tourneur, *The Atheist's Tragedy, or, The Honest Man's Revenge* (London, 1964), pp. xxiii-xxv.

104 Anne Lancashire, '*The Witch*: Stage Flop or Political Mistake?', in *'Accompaninge the players'; Essays Celebrating Thomas Middleton, 1580-1980* ed. Kenneth Friedenreich (New York, 1983), pp. 163-88.

105 Lancashire, 'Stage Flop', pp. 165 and 166.

106 Lancashire, 'Stage Flop', p. 169 and p. 179, n. 45.

107 Lancashire, 'Stage Flop', p. 174. Lancashire also entertains the possibility that Middleton might have written the play before early 1613 and, if so, he must then 'have been astonished when life began to imitate his fictional drama', but the supposition is unconvincing.

108 A.A. Bromham, 'The Date of *The Witch* and the Essex Divorce Case', *N.&Q.*, 225 (1980), 151.

109 Bromham, 'Date', 150.

110 Paul Yachnin, '"This Great Game": The Opportunism of Thomas Middleton,' Ph.D. thesis, University of Toronto, 1983, p. 105

111 Yachnin, p. 104.

112 James Howell, *Familiar Letters*, ed. J. Jacobs (London, 1892), p. 20, as quoted by R.V. Holdsworth, ed., Thomas Middleton and William Rowley, *A Fair Quarrel*, IV.iv.164n (London, 1974).

113 See Dyce, III, p. 422, and I.ii.34n below.

114 Schoenbaum, *Annals*, p. 104; and see Holdsworth, ed., *Fair Quarrel*. pp. xiv-xv.

115 Nicholas Brooke, ed., William Shakespeare, *The Tragedy of Macbeth* (Oxford, 1990), pp. 65-6 and 225.

116 See Barker, *Middleton*, p. 19, and Heinemann, p. 108-9.

117 Heinemann, p. 111-14.

118 George Lyman Kittredge, *Witchcraft in Old and New England* (Cambridge, Mass., 1929), pp. 322-3.

119 Kittredge, 'Witchcraft and James', pp. 57-63; see also Keith Thomas, *Religion and the Decline of Magic*, p. 546.

120 Sullivan, p. 193.; Karl Christ, *Quellenstudien zu den Dramen Thomas Middleton* (Borna-Leipzig, 1905), p. 26 (all Christ citations are taken from Sullivan); Giovanni Battista Giraldi-Cinthio, *Hecatommithi* (Venezia,1574), Deca Quarta, Novella IIII, pp. 184-7.

121 Sullivan, p. 192.

122 Sullivan, p. 193.

123 Mary Augusta Scott, *Elizabethan Translations from the Italian* (Boston and New York, 1916), pp. 14 and 41; Willian Painter, *The Firste Tome of the Palace of Pleasure* (London, 1575), The LVII Nouell, pp. 252v-254v; René Pruvost, *Matteo Bandello and*

Elizabethan Fiction (Paris, 1937), note 1, pp. 32-3; note 1, pp. 33-4; note 2, p. 77.

124 George, 'The Problem', 209-10. See also David George, 'Thomas Middleton's Sources: A Survey', *N.&Q.*, 216 (1971), 17-24.

125 George, 'The Problem', 210 mistakenly thinks that the 'devil in a sheep-skin' is the Lord Governor, rather than Antonio.

126 See pp. 20-3 above.

127 Niccolo Machiavelli, *Istorie Fiorentine*, I; Matteo Bandello, *Novelle*, III; Francois Belleforest, *Histoire Tragiques*, IV, iv.

128 Shakespeare, *Plays*, I (1778), p. 330.

129 Dyce, III, pp. 247-8.

130 Sulllivan, pp. 197-8.

131 See Appendix C for the story printed in full.

132 Christ, *Quellenstudien*, pp. 27-31.

133 Niccolo Machiavelli, *Tutti le Opera*, I (Firenze, 1929), p. 386.

134 Niccolo Machiavelli, *The Florentine History*, trans. T[homas]. B[eddingfield]. (London, 1595), pp. 6-7.

135 Machiavelli, *The Chief Works and Others*, III, trans. Allan Gilbert (Durham, North Carolina, 1965), p. 1044.

136 Heinemann, p. 111.

137 Sullivan, p. 186.

138 See pp. 34-8 below.

139 Scot, *Discouerie*, p. 10.

140 See, for instance, Scot, *Discouerie*, pp. 9-10 and 33.

141 Dyce, III, note k, p. 326.

142 Jean Bodin, *De Magorvm Daemonomania* (Francofvrti, 1590), p. 230 [misprinted 130] is the text that Dyce cites.

143 Jean Bodin, *De Magorvm Daemonomanie*, trans. Lotarivm Philoponvm (Basileae, 1581), p. 116.

144 Jean Bodin, *La Demonomanie Des Sorciers*, ed. derniere (Paris, 1598), p. 178.

145 Scot, *Discouerie*, p. 225.

146 George, 'The Problem', 209 and 211.

147 Gareth Roberts, 'A Re-examination of the Sources of the Magical Material in Middleton's *The Witch*', *N.&Q.*, 221 (1976), 216-19. Pierre Le Loyer, *A Treatise of Specters*, trans. Zachery Jones (London, 1605).

148 Roberts, p 217; W.W., *A True and Iust Recorde, of the Information, Examination and Confession of All the Witches, Taken at S. Oses in the Countie of Essex* (London, 1582).

149 Jacob Sprenger and Heinrich Kramer, *Mallevs Malificarvm* (1486).

150 See Brian P. Levack, *The Witch-Hunt in Early Modern Europe* (London and New York, 1987), pp. 27-45. For other clear presentations of witchcraft material see George Lyman Kittredge, *Witchcraft in Old and New England* (Cambridge, Mass., 1929), and Keith Thomas, *Religion and the Decline of Magic* (London, 1971).

151 Levack, p. 4.

152 Levack, p. 6; see also Kittredge, *Witchcraft*, pp. 4-10, 24-6, and Thomas, p. 519.

153 Thomas, pp. 519-20, and see also Kittredge, *Witchcraft*, pp. 73-103, 141-51 for detailed examples.

154 Levack, p. 32, Thomas, p. 521, and see Kittredge, *Witchcraft*, pp. 239-75 for extended explanation with detailed examples.

155 Levack, p. 32, Thomas, p. 521.

156 Thomas Potts, *The Wonderfvll Discoverie of Witches in the Covntie of Lancaster* (London, 1613); see also Thomas, pp. 528-9

157 Levack, p. 35; see Kittredge, *Witchcraft*, pp. 239-75, particularly pp. 243-50, and Thomas, p. 521.

158 Levack, pp. 35-40, Kittredge, *Witchcraft*, pp. 239-75.

159 Kittredge, *Witchcraft*, pp. 247-51, Thomas, p. 529.

160 Levack, pp. 40-5; see also Kittredge, *Witchcraft*, pp. 243-5 and Thomas, p. 529.

161 Kittredge, *Witchcraft*, pp. 174-84 and Levack, p. 45.

162 Kittredge, *Witchcraft*, pp. 115-23.

163 Thomas, p. 530; see also Kittredge, *Witchcraft*, pp. 236 for passing reference.

164 Kittredge, *Witchcraft*, pp. 174-83, Thomas, p. 530.

165 See W.W., *A True and Iust Recorde*; William Perkins, *A Discovrse of the Damned Art of Witchcraft* (Cambridge, 1608); and Potts, *The Wonderfvll Discoverie*.

166 Scot, *Discouerie*; George Gifford, *A Discourse of the Subtill Practises of Deuilles by Witches and Sorcerers* (London, 1587) and *A Dialogue Concerning Witches and Witchcrafts* (London, 1593).

167 Wallace Notestein, *A History of Witchcraft in England from 1558-1718* (New York, 1911), pp. 101-4; H.R. Trevor-Roper, *The European Witch-Craze of the 16th and 17th Centuries* (1967; revised, Harmondsworth, 1969), pp. 69-70; Anthony Harris, *Night's Black Agents: Witchcraft and Magic in Seventeenth-Century English Drama* (Manchester, 1980), p. 9.

168 George Lyman Kittredge, 'English Witchcraft and James the First', in *Studies in the History of Religions Presented to Crawford Howell Toy by Pupils, Colleagues and Friends* (New York, 1912), pp. 1-65, particularly pp. 1-13; Stuart Clark, 'King James *Daemonologie*: Witchcraft and Kingship', in Sydney Anglo, *The Damned Art: Essays in the Literature of Witchcraft* (London, 1977), pp. 156-81; Christina Larner, 'James VI and I and Witchcraft', in Alan G.R. Smith, ed., *The Reign of James VI and I* (London, 1973), pp. 74-90.

INTRODUCTION

169 James I, *Newes from Scotland* (Edinburgh, 1591).

170 Kittredge, 'Witchcraft and James', pp. 57-63; see also Thomas, *Religion*, p. 546.

171 See pp. 25-6 above for discussion of the influence of the historical context upon *Witch*.

172 See Gerald Eades Bentley, *The Profession of Dramatist in Shakespeare's Time, 1560-1642* (London, 1971), pp. 62-87.

173 Greg and Wilson, p. vii. See also Bentley, p. 904; Samuel Schoenbaum, 'Middleton's Tragicomedies', *M.P.*, 54 (1956), 8.

174 Anne Lancashire, 'Stage Flop'.

175 See Steevens's note in Shakespeare, *Plays*, I (1778), pp. 324-30.

176 For full discussions of the textual relationships of the two plays, see H.H. Furness, ed., Shakespeare, *Macbeth*, New Variorum Shakespeare (London, 1915), pp. 361-79; J. Dover Wilson, ed., Shakespeare, *Macbeth*, (London, 1947), pp. xxii-xxviii; Kenneth Muir, ed., Shakespeare, *Macbeth*, 9th ed. (London, 1962), pp. xxxiii;-xxxvi; J.M. Nosworthy, *Shakespeare's Occasional Plays* (London, 1965), pp. 32-5; Stanley Wells, *et al.*, *William Shakespeare A Textual Companion*, (Oxford, 1987), pp. 129 and 543; and Nicholas Brooke, ed., Shakespeare, *The Tragedy of Macbeth* (Oxford, 1990), pp. 57-9 and 64-6.

177 Charles Lamb, *Specimens of English Dramatic Poets Who Lived about the Time of Shakespeare* (London, 1808), p. 152.

178 See pp. 57-60 below.

179 Montague Summers, *The History of Witchcraft and Demonology* (London, 1926), p. 290.

180 John Genest, *Some Account of the English Stage, from the Restoration in 1660 to 1830*, VI (Bath, 1832), pp. 72-3.

181 Dyce, I, p. liv.

85

182 Swinburne in Havelock Ellis, ed., *Thomas Middleton*, I (London, 1887), p. xxvi.

183 Adolphus William Ward, *A History of English Dramatic Literature to the Death of Queen Anne*, II (London, 1875), p. 75.

184 Barker, p. 92.

185 John F. McElroy, *Parody and Burlesque in the Tragicomedies of Thomas Middleton* (Salzburg, 1972), pp. 155-6.

186 Schoenbaum, 'Middleton's Tragicomedies', 10.

187 Carolyn Asp, *A Study of Thomas Middleton's Tragicomedies* (Salzburg, 1974), p. 224.

188 Heinemann, p. 111.

189 Inga-Stina Ewbank, 'The Middle of Middleton', in *Arts of Performance in Elizabethan and Early Stuart Drama: Essays for G.K. Hunter*, eds., Murray Biggs, *et al.* (Edinburgh, 1991), p. 156.

190 Ewbank, p. 160.

191 Lancashire, 'Stage Flop', pp. 170-1 and 172-3.

192 Lancashire, 'Stage Flop', p. 174

193 See Lancashire, 'Political Mistake', p. 169 and A.A. Bromham and Zara Bruzzi, *The Changeling and the Years of Crisis, 1619-1624*, (London, 1990), pp. 26-7.

194 See I.i.3-4n.

195 See I.i.52-9, I.i.54n and III.ii.191-2n.

196 See, for example, Swinburne's Introduction in Ellis, I, p. xxvi; Sullivan, p. 127; and Corbin and Sedge, pp. 17-18; but Lancashire, 'Stage Flop', p. 174 defends Middleton's craftsmanship.

197 See, for example, Ben Jonson, *The Masque of Queens*, in *Ben Jonson*, eds. C.H. Herford and Percy and Evelyn Simpson, VII (Oxford, 1941), pp. 282-3.

198 But see Lancashire, who has argued that 'The witch is not only Hecate but also the various characters in all plots who sexually enchant one

another by fair means or foul' ('Stage Flop', p. 173).

199 See Glynne Wickham, 'To Fly or Not to Fly? The Problem of Hecate in Shakespeare's 'Macbeth'', in *Essays on Drama and Theatre: Liber Amicorum Benjamin Hunningher* (Amsterdam, 1973), pp. 171-182 for a full discussion of the scene and its position in a series of witchcraft spectacles from Jonson's *The Masque of Queens* to the *Macbeth* revival.

200 Ewbank, p. 157.

201 G.K. Hunter, 'The Theology of Marlowe's The Jew of Malta', *J.W.C.I.*, 27 (1964), 234.

202 See John Doebler, *Shakespeare's Speaking Pictures: Studies in Iconic Imagery* (Albuquerque, New Mexico, 1974), pp. 132-7.

203 Ewbank, p. 160.

204 McElready, p. 163-4; Ewbank, p. 160.

205 Lancashire, 'Stage Flop', p. 174.

206 The necessity to trust in providential assistance, even in the face of seemingly insoluble human dilemma, is precisely the advice given to Charlemont in *The Atheist's Tragedy*.

207 See 'The Revels Plays: Notes for the Use of Editors' and 'Some Informal Notes', unpublished editing guidelines, available from the general editors of The Revels Plays Series.

208 See Stanley Wells, 'Modernizing Shakespeare's Spelling', in Stanley Wells and Gary Taylor, *Modernizing Shakespeare's Spelling, with Three Studies in the Text of 'Henry V'* (Oxford, 1979), pp. 3-36.

209 See T.H. Howard-Hill, *Ralph Crane*, pp. 25-6.

210 See photocopy on p. 89 for a typical example of his practice.

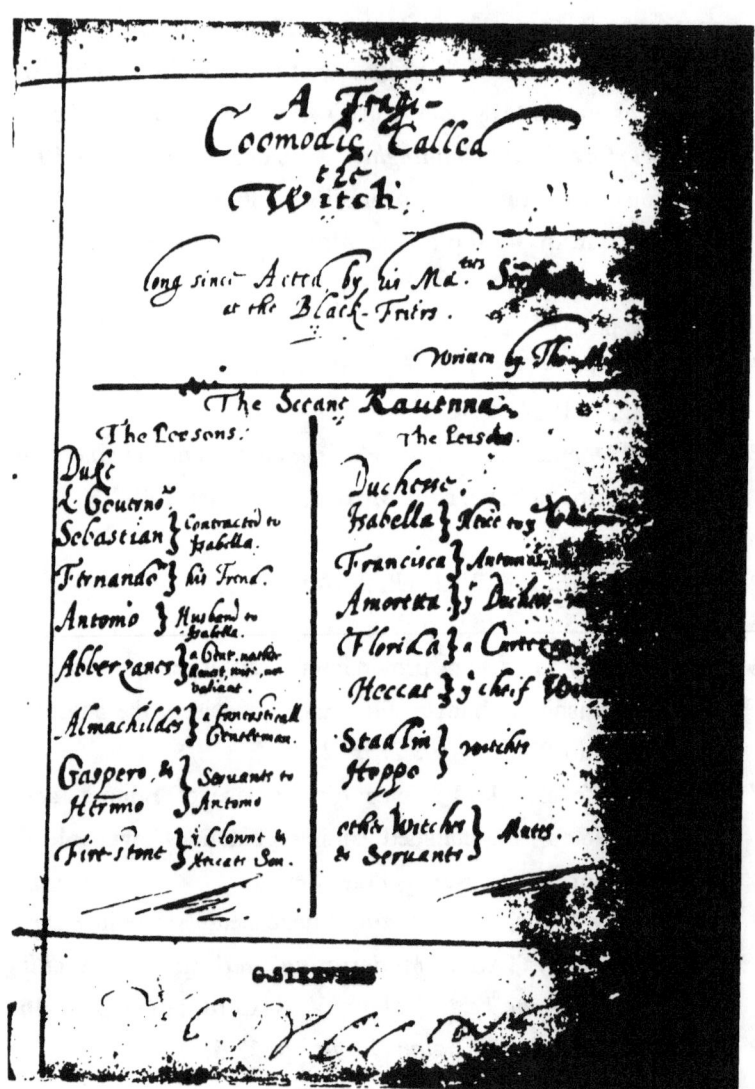

to the poore Mariner, Man; it is not possible
A voung wife can wash a husband cleane,
(he found stranges but stocket storvie to this (Brother)
An. to this, and all thou will grant.
Fra. then this followes, Sir.   — Enter
                                                                              Isabella.
An. A praise thou durrst not for put in whe straytest
    See white: thy comes herselfe kind, honest Lady,
    I must now borrow a triflle for the night Cradle of the
Isa. how Sir? a forthnight?
An. It may be but ten daies; I know not yet
    hed husband for thy State and't must be done
Isa. I wish good sped to't then.
An.   why that was well spoake,
    I'le take but a fhott — boy: I need no more,
    the reste I'le leave at home to doe the studies.
Isa. just your owne pleasure, Sir.
An. till my Returne
    you'le be good Company: my sister, and you
Isa. we shall make shift Sir.
An. I am glad, now that's done,
    And so the rest of my Love to bothe. — Exit   — Enter
Isa. and our good praiers with you Sir.   Sebastian
                                                                              New

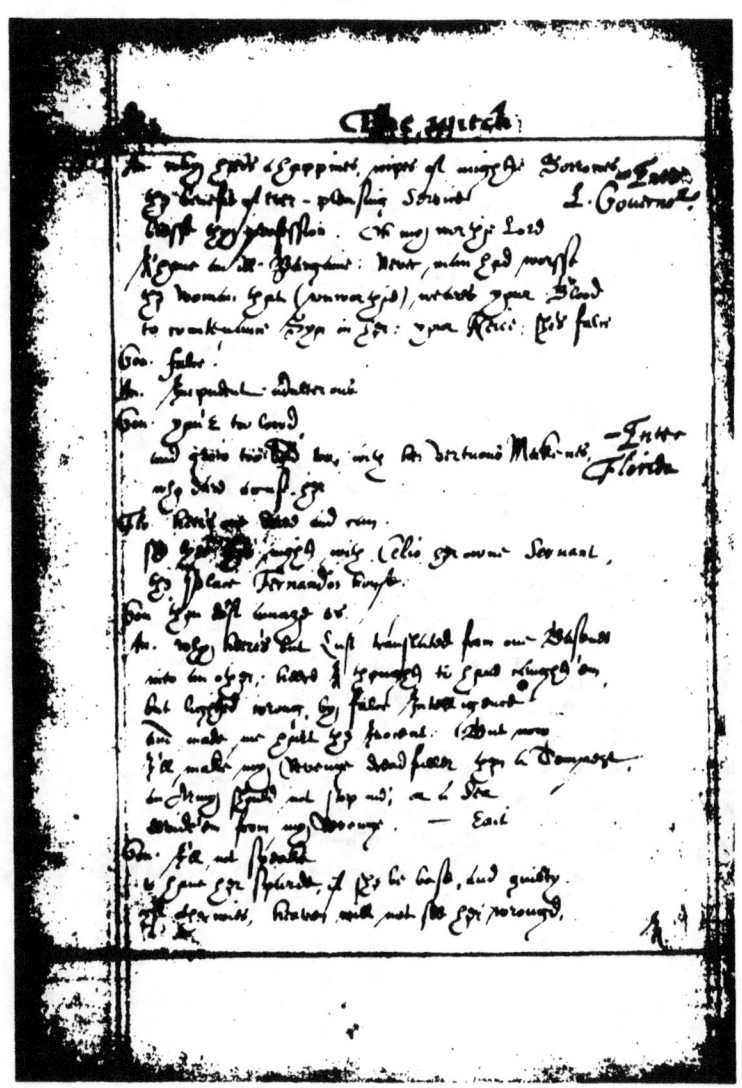

A Tragicomedy Called The Witch

Long Since Acted by His Majesty's Servants at the Blackfriars

Written by Thomas Middleton

[DRAMATIS PERSONAE]

The Scene: Ravenna

The Persons

DUKE
LORD GOVERNOR
SEBASTIAN, *contracted to Isabella*   5
FERNANDO, *his friend*
ANTONIO, *husband to Isabella*
ABBERZANES, *a gentleman, neither honest, wise nor valiant*
ALMACHILDES, *a fantastical gentleman*
GASPERO and HERMIO, *servants to Antonio*   10
FIRESTONE, *the clown and Hecate's son*
[Boy]
[Attendants]

The Persons

DUCHESS   15
ISABELLA, *niece to the Governour*
FRANCESCA, *Antonio's sister*
AMORETTA, *the Duchess's woman*
FLORIDA, *a courtesan*
HECATE, *the chief witch*   20
STADLIN, HOPPO, *witches*
Other Witches and Servants, *mutes*
[Old Woman]

92

[Dedication]

To the truly worthy and generously affected Thomas Holmes, Esquire

Noble Sir

As a true testimony of my ready inclination to your service, I have
merely upon a taste of your desire recovered into my hands (though
not without much difficulty) this ignorantly ill-fated labour of mine.   5
Witches are *ipso facto* by the law condemned and that only, I think,
hath made her lie so long in an imprisoned obscurity. For your sake
alone she hath thus far conjured herself abroad, and bears no other
charms about her but what may tend to your recreation, nor no other
spell but to possess you with a belief that as she, so he that first taught   10
her to enchant, will always be

your devoted
Tho[mas] Middleton

ACT I

Scene i

Enter SEBASTIAN *and* FERNANDO.

Sebastian. My three years spent in war has now undone
     My peace for ever.
Fernando.   Good, be patient, sir.
Sebastian. She is my wife by contract before heaven
     And all the angels, sir.
Fernando.   I do believe you,
     But where's the remedy now? You see she's gone;   5
     Another has possession.
Sebastian.   There's the torment.
Fernando. This day, being the first of your return,
     Unluckily proves the first too of her fast'ning.
     Her uncle, sir, the Governor of Ravenna,
     Holding a good opinion of the bridegroom,   10
     As he's fair-spoken, sir, and wondrous mild—
Sebastian. There goes the devil in a sheepskin!
Fernando.   —with all speed
     Clapped it up suddenly. I cannot think, sure,
     That the maid over-loves him; though being márried,
     Perhaps, for her own credit, now she intends   15
     Performance of an honest duteous wife.
Sebastian. Sir, I've a world of business. Question nothing;
     You will but lose your labour. 'Tis not fit

For any, hardly mine own secrecy,
To know what I intend. I take my leave, sir.   20
I find such strange employments in myself
That unless death pity me and lay me down,
I shall not sleep these seven years; that's the least, sir.   *Exit.*
Fernando. That sorrow's dangerous can abide no counsel;
   'Tis like a wound past cure. Wrongs done to love   25
Strike the heart deeply. None can truly judge on't
But the poor sensible sufferer whom it racks
With unbelievèd pains, which men in health
That enjoy love not possibly can act,
Nay, not so much as think. In truth I pity him;   30
His sighs drink life-blood in this time of feasting.
A banquet towards too! Not yet hath riot
Played out her last scene? At such entertainments still
Forgetfulness obeys and surfeit governs.
Here's marriage sweetly honoured in gorged stomachs   35
And overflowing cups.

         Enter GASPERO *and* Servant.

Gaspero.   Where is she, sirrah?
Servant. Not far off.
Gaspero.   Prithee where? Go fetch her hither;
   I'll rid him away straight.   [*Exit* Servant.]
           The Duke's now risen, sir.
Fernando. I am a joyful man to hear it, sir.
   It seems he's drunk the less, though I think he   40
   That has the least, he's certainly enough.   *Exit.*
Gaspero. I have observed this fellow: all the feast-time
   He hath not pledged one cup, but looked most wickedly

Upon good Malaga, flies to the black-jack still
And sticks to small drink like a water-rat.   45

Enter FLORIDA.

[*Aside*] O, here she comes! Alas, the poor whore weeps!
'Tis not for grace now, all the world must judge;
It is for spleen, and madness 'gainst this marriage.
I do but think how she could beat the vicar now,
Scratch the man horribly that gave the woman,   50
The woman worst of all, if she durst do it.
[*Aloud*] Why, how now, mistress? This weeping needs not,
      for though
My master marry for his reputation,
He means to keep you too.

Florida.   How, sir?

Gaspero.   He doth indeed;
He swore't to me last night. Are you so simple   55
(And have been five years traded) as to think
One woman would serve him? Fie, not an empress!
Why, he'll be sick o'th' wife within ten nights,
Or never trust my judgement.

Florida.   Will he, think'st thou?

Gaspero. Will he!

Florida.   I find thee still so comfortable,   60
Beshrew my heart if I knew how to miss thee.
They talk of gentlemen, perfumers and such things;
Give me the kindness of the master's man
In my distress, say I.

Gaspero.   'Tis your great love, forsooth.
Please you, withdraw yourself to yon private parlour.   65

I'll send you venison, custard, parsnip pie;

For banqueting stuff, as suckets, jellies, syrups,

I will bring in myself.

Florida.   I'll take 'em kindly, sir.   *Exit.*

Gaspero. She's your grand strumpet's complement to a tittle.

'Tis a fair building. It had need; it has   70

Just at this time some one-and-twenty inmates.

But half of 'em are young merchants; they'll depart shortly.

They take but rooms for summer, and away they

When't grows foul weather. Marry, then come the termers,

And commonly they're well-booted for all seasons.   75

Enter ALMACHILDES *and* AMORETTA [*severally*].

But peace, no more; the guests are coming in.   [*Retires.*]

Almachildes. The fates have blessed me. Have I met you privately?

Amoretta. Why, sir! Why, Almachildes!

Almachildes.   Not a kiss?

Amoretta. I'll call aloud, i'faith.

Almachildes.   I'll stop your mouth.   [*Kisses her.*]

Amoretta. Upon my love to reputation,   80

I'll tell the Duchess once more.

Almachildes.   'Tis the way

To make her laugh a little.

Amoretta.   She'll not think

That you dare use a maid of honour thus.

Almachildes. Amsterdam swallow thee for a Puritan

And Geneva cast thee up again, like she that sunk   85

At Charing Cross and rose again at Queenhithe!

Amoretta. Ay, these are the holy fruits of the sweet vine, sir.

[*Retires.*]

Almachildes. Sweet venery be with thee, and I at the tail
    Of my wish! I am a little headstrong, and so
    Are most of the company. I will to the witches.   90
    They say they have charms and tricks to make
    A wench fall backwards and lead a man herself
    To a country house some mile out of the town
    Like a firedrake. There be such whoreson kind
    Girls and such bawdy witches, and I'll try   95
    Conclusions.

      Enter DUKE, DUCHESS, LORD GOVERNOR, ANTONIO,
          and ISABELLA, FRANCESCA.

Duke. A banquet yet? Why surely, my Lord Governor,
    Bacchus could never boast of a day till now
    To spread his power and make his glory known.
Duchess. Sir, you've done nobly. Though in modesty   100
    You keep it from us, know we understand so much:
    All this day's cost, 'tis your great love bestows
    In honour of the bride, your virtuous niece.
Lord Governor. In love to goodness and your presence, madam,
    So understood, 'tis rightly.
Duke.   Now will I   105
    Have a strange health after all these.
Lord Governor.   What's that, my lord?
Duke. A health in a strange cup, and't shall go round.
Lord Governor. Your grace need not doubt that, sir, having seen
    So many pledged already. This fair company
    Cannot shrink now for one, so it end there.   110
Duke. It shall, for all ends here.   [*Produces a cup made from a skull.*]
          Here's a full period.

Lord Governor. A skull, my lord?

Duke.   Call it a soldier's cup, man.
    Fie, how you fright the women! I have sworn
    It shall go round, excepting only you, sir,
    For your late sickness, and the bride herself,   115
    Whose health it is.

Isabella.   Marry, I thank heaven for that.

Duke. Our Duchess, I know, will pledge us, though the cup
    Was once her father's head, which as a trophy
    We'll keep till death in memory of that conquest.
    He was the greatest foe our steel e'er struck at,   120
    And he was bravely slain. Then took we thee
    Into our bosom's love. Thou mad'st the peace
    For all thy country; thou; that beauty did.
    We're dearer than a father, are we not?

Duchess. Yes, sir, by much.

Duke.   And we shall find that straight. [*Drinks.*]   125

Antonio. [*Aside*] That's an ill bride-cup for a marriage-day;
    I do not like the fate on't.

Lord Governor.   Good my lord,
    The Duchess looks pale. Let her not pledge you there.

Duke. Pale?

Duchess.   Sir, not I.

Duke.   See how your lordship fails now:
    The rose' not fresher, nor the sun at rising   130
    More comfortably pleasing.

Duchess.   Sir, to you,
    The lord of this day's honour.   [*Drinks.*]

Antonio.   All first moving
    From your grace, madam, and the Duke's great favour.
                         [*Drinks.*]

[*To Francesca*] Sister, it must.

Francesca. [*Aside*]   This' the worst fright that could come

 To a concealed great belly. I'm with child   135

 And this will bring it out, or make me come

 Some seven weeks sooner than we maidens reckon. [*Drinks*.]

Duchess. [*Aside*] Did ever cruel barbarous act match this?

 Twice hath his surfeits brought my father's memory

 Thus spitefully and scornfully to mine eyes,   140

 And I'll endure't no more; 'tis in my heart since.

 I'll be revenged as far as death can lead me.

Almachildes. Am I the last man then? I may deserve

 To be first one day.   [*Drinks*.]

Lord Governor.   Sir, it's gone round now.

Duke.The round? An excellent way to train up soldiers. 145

 Where's bride and bridegroom?

Antonio.   At your happy service.

Duke. A boy tonight at least! I charge you look to't,

 Or I'll renounce you for industrious subjects.

Antonio. Your grace speaks like a worthy and tried soldier.

        Exeunt [*all but* GASPERO].

Gaspero. And you'll do well for one that ne'er tossed pike, sir. *Exit*. 150

Scene ii

Enter HECATE *and other witches, with properties*
and habits fitting.

Hecate. Titty and Tiffin,

 Suckin and Pigeon,

 Liard and Robin.

White spirits, black spirits,
Grey spirits, red spirits.   5
Devil-toad, devil-ram,
Devil-cat and devil-dam.   [*Exeunt all but* HECATE.]
Why, Hoppo and Stadlin, Hellwain and Puckle!
Stadlin. [*Within.*] Here, sweating at the vessel.
Hecate.   Boil it well.
Hoppo. [*Within.*] It gallops now.
Hecate.   Are the flames blue enough,   10
Or shall I use a little seeton more?
Stadlin. [*Within.*] The nips of fairies upon maids' white hips
Are not more perfect azure.
Hecate.   Tend it carefully.
Send Stadlin to me with a brazen dish
That I may fall to work upon these serpents   15
And squeeze 'em ready for the second hour.
Why, when?

[*Enter* STADLIN.]

Stadlin.   Here's Stadlin and the dish.
Hecate. There, take this unbaptisèd brat;
Boil it well; preserve the fat.
You know 'tis precious to transfer   20
Our 'nointed flesh into the air,
In moonlight nights o'er steeple-tops,
Mountains and pine-trees, that like pricks or stops
Seem to our height; high towers and roofs of princes
Like wrinkles in the earth. Whole provinces   25
Appear to our sight then ev'n leek
A russet mole upon some lady's cheek.

When hundred leagues in air, we feast and sing,
Dance, kiss and coll, use everything.
What young man can we wish to pleasure us   30
But we enjoy him in an incubus?
Thou know'st it, Stadlin?
Stadlin.   Usually that's done.
Hecate. Last night thou got'st the Mayor of Whelpley's son;
I knew him by his black cloak lined with yellow.
I think thou'st spoiled the youth, he's but seventeen.   35
I'll have him the next mounting. Away, in;
Go feed the vessel for the second hour.
Stadlin. Where be the magical herbs?
Hecate.   They're down his throat,
His mouth crammed full, his ears and nostrils stuffed.
I thrust in *eleoselinum* lately,   40
Aconitum, frondes populeas, and soot—
You may see that, he looks so black i'th' mouth—
Then *sium, acarum vulgaro* too,
Pentaphyllon, the blood of a flitter-mouse,
Solanum somniferum et oleum.   45
Stadlin. Then there's all, Hecate?
Hecate.   Is the heart of wax
Stuck full of magic needles?
Stadlin.   'Tis done, Hecate.
Hecate. And is the farmer's picture and his wife's
Laid down to th' fire yet?
Stadlin.   They're a-roasting both, too.
Hecate. Good;   [*Exit* STADLIN.]   50
Then their marrows are a-melting subtly,
And three months' sickness sucks up life in 'em.

They denied me often flour, barm and milk,
Goose-grease and tar, when I ne'er hurt their charmings,
Their brew-locks, nor their batches, nor forespoke   55
Any of their breedings. Now I'll be meet with 'em.
Seven of their young pigs I've bewitched already,
Of the last litter.
Nine ducklings, thirteen goslings, and a hog
Fell lame last Sunday after evensong too.   60
And mark how their sheep prosper, or what soap
Each milch-kine gives to th' pail; I'll send those snakes
Shall milk 'em all beforehand.
The dewed-skirted dairy-wenches
Shall stroke dry dugs for this and go home cursing.   65
I'll mar their syllabubs and frothy feastings
Under cows' bellies with the parish youths.
Where's Firestone? Our son, Firestone?

Enter FIRESTONE.

Firestone.   Here am I, mother.
Hecate. Take in this brazen dish full of dear ware.
Thou shalt have all when I die, and that will be   70
Ev'n just at twelve o'clock at night come three year.
Firestone. And may you not have one o'clock into th' dozen,
     mother?
Hecate. No.
Firestone. Your spirits are then more unconscionable than bakers.   75
     You'll have lived then, mother, sixscore year to the hundred;
     and, methinks, after sixscore years, the Devil might give you
     a cast, for he's a fruiterer too, and has been from the
     beginning. The first apple that e'er was eaten came through

103

his fingers. The costermonger's, then, I hold to be the   80
ancientest trade, though some would have the tailor pricked
down before him.

Hecate. Go, and take heed you shed not by the way;
 The hour must have her portion. 'Tis dear syrup:
 Each charmèd drop is able to confound   85
 A family consisting of nineteen,
 Or one-and-twenty feeders.

Firestone. [*Aside*]   Marry, here's stuff indeed!
 Dear syrup call you it? A little thing
 Would make me give you a dram on't in a posset,
 And cut you three years shorter.

Hecate.   Thou'rt now   90
 About some villainy.

Firestone.   Not I, forsooth.
 [*Aside*] Truly the Devil's in her, I think. How one villain
smells out another straight! There's no knavery but is nosed
like a dog, and can smell out a dog's meaning. [*Aloud*]
Mother, I pray, give me leave to ramble abroad tonight with   95
the Nightmare, for I have a great mind to overlay a fat
parson's daughter.

Hecate. And who shall lie with me then?

Firestone.   The great cat
 For one night, mother; 'tis but a night.
 Make shift with him for once.

Hecate.   You're a kind son!   100
 But 'tis the nature of you all, I see that.
 You had rather hunt after strange women still
 Than lie with your own mothers. Get thee gone!
 Sweat thy six ounces out about the vessel

And thou shalt play at midnight. The Nightmare   105
Shall call thee when it walks.

Firestone.   Thanks, most sweet mother.

                                                     Exit.

Enter SEBASTIAN.

Hecate. [*Sits*.] Urchins, Elves, Hags, Satyrs, Pans, Fauns, Silens, Kit
    with the candlestick, Tritons, Centaurs, Dwarfs, Imps, the
    Spoorn, the Mare, the Man i'th' oak, the Hellwain, the
    Firedrake, the Puckle. *A ab hur hus*.   110
Sebastian. [*Aside*] Heaven knows with what unwillingness and hate
    I enter this damned place; but such extremes
    Of wrongs in love fight 'gainst religious knowledge,
    That were I led by this disease to deaths
    As numberless as creatures that must die   115
    I could not shun the way. I know what 'tis
    To pity madmen now; they're wretched things
    That ever were created, if they be
    Of woman's making and her faithless vows.
    I fear they're now a-kissing. What's o'clock?   120
    'Tis now but supper-time, but night will come,
    And all new-married couples make short suppers.
    [*Aloud*] Whate'er thou art, I have no spare time to fear thee;
    My horrors are so strong and great already
    That thou seem'st nothing. Up and laze not.   125
    Hadst thou my business, thou couldst ne'er sit so;
    'Twould firk thee into air a thousand mile
    Beyond thy ointments. I would I were read
    So much in thy black power as mine own griefs.
    I'm in great need of help; wilt give me any?   130

Hecate. Thy boldness takes me bravely. We're all sworn

    To sweat for such a spirit. See, I regard thee:

    I rise and bid thee welcome. What's thy wish now?

Sebastian. O, my heart swells with't! I must take breath first.

Hecate. Is't to confound some enemy on the seas? 135

    It may be done tonight. Stadlin's within.

    She raises all your sudden ruinous storms

    That shipwreck barks and tears up growing oaks,

    Flies over houses and takes *Anno Domini*

    Out of a rich man's chimney—a sweet place for't! 140

    He would be hanged ere he would set his own years there.

    They must be chambered in a five-pound picture,

    A green silk curtain drawn before the eyes on't—

    His rotten diseased years! Or dost thou envy

    The fat prosperity of any neighbour? 145

    I'll call forth Hoppo, and her incantation

    Can straight destroy the young of all his cattle,

    Blast vineyards, orchards, meadows, or in one night

    Transport his dung, hay, corn, by ricks, whole stacks,

    Into thine own ground.

Sebastian.   This would come most richly now 150

    To many a country grazier; but my envy

    Lies not so low as cattle, corn or vines.

    'Twill trouble your best powers to give me ease.

Hecate. Is it to starve up generation?

    To strike a barrenness in man or woman? 155

Sebastian. Ha!

Hecate. Ha? Did you feel me there? I knew your grief.

Sebastian. Can there be such things done?

Hecate.   Are these the skins

Of serpents? These of snakes?

Sebastian.   I see they are.

Hecate. So sure into what house these are conveyed,   160

                      [*Gives snake-skins to Sebastian.*]

Knit with these charmèd and retentive knots,

Neither the man begets nor woman breeds,

No, nor performs the least desires of wedlock,

Being then a mutual duty. I could give thee

Chiroconita, adincantida,   165

Archimadon, marmaritin, calicia,

Which I could sort to villainous barren ends,

But this leads the same way. More I could instance:

As the same needles thrust into their pillows

That sews and socks up dead men in their sheets;   170

A privy gristle of a man that hangs

After sunset. Good, excellent; yet all's there, sir.

Sebastian. You could not do a man that special kindness

To part 'em utterly now? Could you do that?

Hecate. No, time must do't. We cannot disjoin wedlock;   175

'Tis of heaven's fast'ning. Well may we raise jars,

Jealousies, strifes and heart-burning disagreements,

Like a thick scurf o'er life, as did our master

Upon that patient miracle, but the work itself

Our power cannot disjoint.

Sebastian.   I depart happy   180

In what I have then, being constrained to this.

[*Aside*] And grant you, greater powers, that dispose men,

That I may never need this hag again.   *Exit.*

Hecate. I know he loves me not, nor there's no hope on't.

'Tis for the love of mischief I do this,   185

And that we're sworn to, the first oath we take.

[*Enter* FIRESTONE.]

Firestone. O mother, mother!

Hecate.   What's the news with thee now?

Firestone. There's the bravest young gentleman within, and the
    fineliest drunk. I thought he would have fallen into the vessel.
    He stumbled at a pipkin of child's grease, reeled against   190
    Stadlin, overthrew her, and in the tumbling-cast struck up old
    Puckle's heels with her clothes over her ears.

Hecate. Hoyday!

Firestone. I was fain to throw the cat upon her to save her
    honesty, and all little enough. I cried out still, 'I pray be   195
    covered!'

Enter ALMACHILDES.

See where he comes now, mother.

Almachildes. Call you these witches?
    They be tumblers, methinks, very flat tumblers.

Hecate. [*Aside*] 'Tis Almachildes—fresh blood stirs in me—   200
    The man that I have lusted to enjoy.
    I have had him thrice in incubus already.

Almachildes. Is your name Goody Hag?

Hecate.   'Tis anything.
    Call me the horrid'st and unhallowed'st things
    That life and nature trembles at, for thee   205
    I'll be the same. Thou com'st for a love-charm now?

Almachildes. Why, thou'rt a witch I think.

Hecate. Thou shalt have choice of twenty, wet or dry.

Almachildes. Nay, let's have dry ones.

108

Hecate. If thou wilt use't by way of cup and potion,   210
    I'll give thee a remora shall bewitch her straight.

Almachildes. A remora? What's that?

Hecate.   A little suck-stone;
    Some call it a sea-lamprey, a small fish.

Almachildes. And must' be buttered?

Hecate. The bones of a green frog too, wondrous precious,   215
    The flesh consumed by pismires.

Almachildes. Pismires? Give me a chamber-pot!

Firestone. [*Aside*] You shall see him go nigh to be so unmannerly
    he'll make water before my mother anon.

Almachildes. And now you talk of frogs, I have somewhat here.   220
    I come not empty-pocketed from a banquet;
    I learned that of my haberdasher's wife.
    Look, Goody Witch, there's a toad in marchpane for you.

Hecate. O, sir, you've fitted me.

Almachildes.   And here's a spawn or two
    Of the same paddock-brood, too, for your son.   225

Firestone. I thank your worship, sir. How comes your handkercher
    So sweetly thus berayed? Sure, 'tis wet sucket, sir.

Almachildes. 'Tis nothing but the syrup the toad spit.
    Take all I prithee.

Hecate.   This was kindly done, sir;
    And you shall sup with me tonight for this.   230

Almachildes. How? Sup with thee? Dost think I'll eat fried rats
    And pickled spiders?

Hecate.   No. I can command, sir,
    The best meat i'th' whole province for my friends,
    And reverently served in too.

Almachildes.   How?

Hecate.   In good fashion.

Almachildes. Let me but see that and I'll sup with you.   235

                       She conjures, and enter a cat, playing
                            on a fiddle, and spirits with meat.

    The Cat and Fiddle? An excellent ordinary.

    You had a devil once in a fox-skin?

Hecate. O, I have him still. Come walk with me, sir.

                    Exeunt [all but FIRESTONE.]

Firestone. How apt and ready is a drunkard now to reel to the Devil!

    Well, I'll even in and see how he eats; and I'll be hanged if I   240

    be not the fatter of the twain with laughing at him.   *Exit.*

              Finis Actus Primi.

ACT II

Scene i

Enter ANTONIO *and* GASPERO.

Gaspero. Good sir, whence springs this sadness? Trust me, sir.
    You look not like a man was married yesterday.
    There could come no ill tidings since last night
    To cause that discontent. I was wont to know all
    Before you had a wife, sir; you ne'er found me   5
    Without those parts of manhood, trust and secrecy.
Antonio. I will not tell thee this.
Gaspero.   Not your true servant, sir?
Antonio. True? You'll all flout according to your talent,
    The best a man can keep of you; and a hell 'tis
    For masters to pay wages to be laughed at.   10
    Give order that two cocks be boiled to jelly.
Gaspero. How? Two cocks boiled to jelly?
Antonio. Fetch half an ounce of pearl.   *Exit.*
Gaspero.   This is a cullis
    For a consumption; and I hope one night
    Has not brought you to need the cook already,   15
    And some part of the goldsmith. What, two trades
    In four-and-twenty hours and less time?
    Pray heaven the surgeon and the pothecary
    Keep out, and then 'tis well. You'd better fortune,
    As far as I see, with your strumpet sojourner,   20

Your little four-nobles-a-week. I ne'er knew you

Eat one panada all the time you've kept her;

And is't in one night now come up to two-cock-broth?

I wonder at the alteration strangely.

Enter FRANCESCA.

Francesca. Good morrow, Gasper.

Gaspero. Your hearty wishes, mistress, 25

And your sweet dreams come upon you.

Francesca. What's that, sir?

Gaspero. In a good husband, that's my real meaning.

Francesca. Saw you my brother lately?

Gaspero. Yes.

Francesca. I met him now,

As sad, methought, as grief could make a man.

Know you the cause?

Gaspero. Not I. I know nothing 30

But half an ounce of pearl and kitchen-business,

Which I will see performed with all fidelity;

I'll break my trust in nothing, not in porridge, I. *Exit.*

Francesca. I have the hardest fortune, I think, of a hundred

gentlewomen. 35

Some can make merry with a friend seven year

And nothing seen; as perfect a maid still,

To the world's knowledge, as she came from rocking.

But 'twas my luck, at the first hour, forsooth,

To prove too fruitful. Sure I'm near my time. 40

I'm yet but a young scholar, I may fail

In my account; but certainly I do not.

These bastards come upon poor venturing gentlewomen ten to

one faster than your legitimate children. If I had been
married, I'll be hanged if I had been with child so soon now.   45
When they are once husbands, they'll be whipped ere they
take such pains as a friend will do: to come by water to the
back door at midnight, there stay perhaps an hour in all
weathers with a pair of reeking watermen laden with bottles
of wine, chewets and curran custards. I may curse those   50
egg-pies: they are meat that help forward too fast.

This hath been usual with me night by night
(Honesty forgive me) when my brother has been
Dreaming of no such junkets; yet he hath fared
The better for my sake, though he little think   55
For what, nor must he ever. My friend promised me
To provide safely for me, and devise
A means to save my credit here i'th' house.
My brother sure would kill me if he knew't,
And powder up my friend and all his kindred   60
For an East Indian voyage.

Enter ISABELLA.

Isabella.   Alone, sister?
Francesca. [*Aside*] No, there's another with me, though you see't
          not.
          [*Aloud*] 'Morrow, sweet sister; how have you slept tonight?
Isabella. [*Aside*] More than I thought I should. [*Aloud*] I've had good
          rest.
Francesca. I'm glad to hear't.   65
Isabella. Sister, methinks you are too long alone,
          And lose much good time, sociable and honest.
          I'm for the married life; I must praise that now.

113

Francesca. I cannot blame you, sister, to commend it;

    You have happened well, no doubt, on a kind husband,   70

    And that's not every woman's fortune, sister.

    You know if he were any but my brother

    My praises should not leave him yet so soon.

Isabella. I must acknowledge, sister, that my life

    Is happily blessed with him. He is no gamester,   75

    That ever I could find or hear of yet,

    Nor midnight surfeiter. He does intend

    To leave tobacco too.

Francesca.   Why, here's a husband!

Isabella. He saw it did offend me and swore freely

    He'd ne'er take pleasure in a toy again   80

    That should displease me. Some knights' wives in town

    Will have great hope, upon his reformation,

    To bring their husbands' breaths into th' old fashion,

    And make 'em kiss like Christians, not like Pagans.

Francesca. I promise you, sister, 'twill be a worthy work   85

    To put down all these pipers. 'Tis great pity

    There should not be a statute against them

    As against fiddlers.

Isabella.   These good offices,

    If you'd a husband, you might exercise

    To th' good o'th' commonwealth, and do much profit.   90

    Beside, it is a comfort to a woman

    T'have children, sister, a great blessing certainly.

Francesca. They will come fast enough.

Isabella.   Not so fast neither

    As they're still welcome to an honest woman.

Francesca. [*Aside*] How near she comes to me! I protest she grates   95

My very skin.

Isabella.   Were I conceived with child,

Beshrew my heart, I should be so proud on't.

Francesca. [*Aside*] That's natural; pride is a kind of swelling.

And yet I've small cause to be proud of mine.

Isabella. You are no good companion for a wife.   100

Get you a husband; prithee, sister, do,

That I may ask your counsel now and then.

'Twill mend your discourse much; you maids know nothing.

Francesca. [*Aside*] No, we are fools; but commonly we prove

Quicker mothers than you that have husbands.   105

I'm sure I shall else; I may speak for one.

Enter ANTONIO.

Antonio. [*Aside*] I will not look upon her; I'll pass by

And make as though I see her not.

Isabella.   Why, sir—

Pray, your opinion—by the way—with leave, sir,

I'm counselling your sister here to marry.   110

Antonio. To marry? Soft; the priest is not at leisure yet;

Some five year hence. Would you fain marry, sister?

Francesca. I have no such hunger to't, sir, [*Aside*] for I think

I've a good bit that well may stay my stomach,

As well as any that broke fast a sinner.   115

Antonio. Though she seem tall of growth, she's short in years

Of some that seem much lower. How old, sister?

Not seventeen, for a yard of lawn!

Francesca.   Not yet, sir.

Antonio. I told you so.

Francesca. [*Aside*] I would he'd laid a wager of old shirts rather;   120

115

I shall have more need of them shortly; and yet

A yard of lawn will serve for a christ'ning-cloth.

I have use for everything as my case stands.

Isabella. I care not if I try my voice this morning,

But I have got a cold, sir, by your means.   125

Antonio. I'll strive to mend that fault.

Isabella.   I thank you, sir.   [*Sings.*]

Song.

In a maiden-time professed,

Then we say that life is best;

Tasting once the married life,

Then we only praise the wife.   130

There's but one state more to try,

Which makes women laugh or cry:

Widow, widow. Of these three,

The middle's best and that give me.

Antonio. [*Kisses her.*] There's thy reward.

Isabella.   I will not grumble, sir,   135

Like some musician; if more come, 'tis welcome.

Francesca. [*Aside*] Such tricks has made me do all that I've done.

Your kissing married folks spoils all the maids

That ever live i'th' house with 'em.

Enter ABBERZANES [*and* Servants].

O, here

He comes with his bags and bottles! He was born   140

To lead poor watermen and I.

Abberzanes. Go, fellows, into th' larder. Let the bakemeats

Be sorted by themselves.

Antonio.   Why, sir?

Abberzanes. Look the canary-bottles be well stopped;

The three of claret shall be drunk at dinner. [*Exeunt* Servants.]   145

Antonio. My good sir, you're too plenteous of these courtesies,

Indeed you are. Forbear 'em, I beseech ye.

I know no merit in me, but poor love

And a true friend's well-wishing, that can cause

This kindness in excess. [*Aside*] I'th' state that I am,   150

I shall go near to kick this fellow shortly,

And send him downstairs with his bag and baggage.

Why comes he now I'm married? There's the point.

[*Aloud*] I pray, forbear these things.

Abberzanes.   Alas, you know, sir,

These idle toys, which you call courtesies,   155

They cost me nothing but my servants' travail.

One office must be kind, sir, to another;

You know the fashion. What, the gentlewoman

Your sister's sad methinks.

Antonio.   I know no cause she has.

Francesca. [*Aside*] Nor shall you, by my good will. [*To Abberzanes*]

What do you mean, sir?   160

Shall I stay here to shame myself and you?

The time may be tonight for aught you know.

Abberzanes. [*To Francesca*] Peace; there's means wrought, I tell

thee.

Francesca.   [*To Abberzanes*] Ay, sir, when?

Enter SEBASTIAN [*disguised*] *and* Gentleman.

Antonio. How now? What's he?

Isabella.   O, this is the man, sir,

    I entertained this morning for my service,   165

    Please you to give your liking.

Antonio.   Yes, he's welcome;

    I like him not amiss. [*To Sebastian*] Thou wouldst speak

       business,

    Wouldst thou not?

Sebastian.   Yes; may it please you, sir,

    There is a gentleman from the northern parts

    Hath brought a letter, as it seems in haste.   170

Antonio. From whom?

Gentleman.   Your bonny lady mother, sir.   [*Gives letter.*]

Antonio. You're kindly welcome, sir. How doth she?

Gentleman. I left her heal varray well, sir.

[*Antonio. Reads the*] *letter.* 'I pray, send your sister down with all

    speed to me; I hope it will prove much for her good in the   175

    way of her preferment. Fail me not, I desire you, son, nor let

    any excuse of hers withhold her. I have sent, ready furnished,

    horse and man for her.'

Abberzanes. [*To Francesca*] Now? Have I thought upon you?

Francesca.   [*To Abberzanes*] Peace, good sir;

    You're worthy of a kindness another time.   180

Antonio. Her will shall be obeyed. Sister, prepare yourself;

    You must down with all speed.

Francesca. [*Aside*]   I know down I must,

    And good speed send me.

Antonio.   'Tis our mother's pleasure.

Francesca. Good sir, write back again and certify her

    I'm at my heart's wish here. I'm with my friends   185

    And can be but well, say.

Antonio.   You shall pardon me, sister;
    I hold it no wise part to contradict her,
    Nor would I counsel you to't.
Francesca.   'Tis so uncouth
    Living i'th' country now I'm used to th' city
    That I shall ne'er endure't.
Abberzanes.   Perhaps, forsooth,   190
    'Tis not her meaning you shall live there long.
    I do not think but after a month or so
    You'll be sent up again; that's my conceit.
    However, let her have her will.
Antonio.   Ay, good sir,
    Great reason 'tis she should.
Isabella.   I am sorry, sister,   195
    'Tis our hard fortune thus to part so soon.
Francesca. The sorrow will be mine.
Antonio.   Please you, walk in, sir;
    We'll have one health into those northern parts,
    Though I be sick at heart.
Abberzanes.   Ay, sir, a deep one,
    [*To Francesca*] Which you shall pledge too.
                    Exeunt [ANTONIO, ISABELLA, *and* Gentleman].
Francesca.   [*To Abberzanes*] You shall pardon me;   200
    I have pledged one too deep already, sir.
Abberzanes. [*To Francesca*] Peace; all's provided for: thy wine's laid
        in,
    Sugar and spice; the place not ten mile hence.
    What cause have maids now to complain of men,
    When a farmhouse can make all whole again?   205
                    Exeunt [ABBERZANES *and* FRANCESCA.]

Sebastian. It takes; he's no content. How well she bears it yet!
    Hardly myself can find so much from her
    That am acquainted with the cold disease.
    O, honesty's a rare wealth in a woman!
    It knows no want, at least will express none,   210
    Not in a look. Yet I'm not throughly happy.
    His ill does me no good. Well may it keep me
    From open rage, and madness for a time,
    But I feel heart's grief in the same place still.
    What makes the greatest torment 'mongst lost souls?   215
    'Tis not so much the horror of their pains,
    Though they be infinite, as the loss of joys.
    It is that deprivation is the mother
    Of all the groans in hell, and here on earth
    Of all the red sighs in the hearts of lovers.   220
    Still she's not mine, that can be no man's else
    Till I be nothing, if religion
    Have the same strength for me as't has for others.
    Holy vows witness that our souls were married.

                Enter GASPERO *and* LORD GOVERNOR.

Gaspero. Where are you, sir? Come, pray, give your attendance;   225
    Here's my Lord Governor come.
Lord Governor.   Where's our new kindred?
    Not stirring yet, I think?
Gaspero.   Yes, my good lord.
    Please you walk near?
Lord Governor.   Come, gentlemen, we'll enter.
Sebastian. [*Aside*] I ha' done't upon a breach; this' a less venture.
                                                        [*Exeunt.*]

Scene ii

Enter ALMACHILDES.

Almachildes. What a mad toy took me to sup with witches!
          Fie of all drunken humours! By this hand,
          I could beat myself when I think on't. And the rascals
          Made me good cheer too; and to my understanding then
          Ate some of every dish, and spoiled the rest.   5
          But coming to my lodging, I remember
          I was as hungry as a tired foot-post.
          What's this?   [*Takes object from his pocket.*]
                    O, 'tis the charm her hagship gave me
          For my duchess' obstinate woman, wound about
          A threepenny silk ribbon of three colours.   10
          '*Necte tribus nodis ternos Amoretta colores*'—
          Amoretta! Why, there's her name indeed.
          '*Necte Amoretta*'—again, two bouts—
          '*Nodo et Veneris dic vincula necte*'—
          Nay, if *Veneris* be one, I'm sure there's no dead flesh in't.   15
          If I should undertake to construe this now,
          I should make a fine piece of work of it,
          For few young gallants are given to good construction
          Of anything, hardly of their best friends' wives,
          Sisters or nieces. Let me see what I can do now: 20
          '*Necte tribus nodis*'—Nick of the tribe of noddies—
          '*Ternos colores*'—that makes turned colours—
          '*Nodo et Veneris*'—goes to his venery like a noddy—
          '*Dic vincula*'—with Dick the vintner's boy.
          Here were a sweet charm now, if this were the meaning on't,   25
          and very likely to overcome an honourable gentlewoman. The

whoreson old hell-cat would have given me the brain of a cat
once in my handkercher—I bade her make sauce with't, with
a vengeance—and a little bone in the hithermost part of
a wolf's tail—I bade her pick her teeth with't, with a   30
pestilence.

Nay, this is somewhat cleanly yet and handsome:
A coloured ribbon? A fine, gentle charm;
A man may give't his sister, his brother's wife,
Ordinarily.

Enter AMORETTA.

        See, here she comes, luckily.   35

Amoretta. Blessed powers, what secret sin have I committed
    That still you send this punishment upon me?

Almachildes. 'Tis but a gentle punishment, so take it.   [*Seizes her.*]

Amoretta. Why, sir, what mean you? Will you ravish me?

Almachildes. What, in the gallery? And the sun peep in?   40
    There's fitter time and place.   [*Thrusts charm into her dress.*]
    [*Aside*]   'Tis in her bosom now.

Amoretta. Go! You're the rudest thing e'er came at court.

Almachildes. Well, well; I hope you'll tell me another tale
    Ere you be two hours older. A rude thing?
    I'll make you eat your word; I'll make all split else.   *Exit.*   45

Amoretta. Nay, now I think on't better, I'm to blame too.
    There's not a sweeter gentleman in court;
    Nobly descended too, and dances well.
    Beshrew my heart, I'll take him when there's time;
    He will be catched up quickly. The Duchess says   50
    She's some employment for him, and has sworn me
    To use my best art in't. Life of my joys,

There were good stuff! I will not trust her with him.
I'll call him back again. He must not keep
Out of my sight so long; I shall grow mad then.   55

Enter DUCHESS.

Duchess. [*Aside*] He lives not now to see tomorrow spent
    If this means take effect, as there's no hardness in't.
    Last night he played his horrid game again:
    Came to my bedside at the full of midnight,
    And in his hand that fatal, fearful cup,   60
    Waked me and forced me pledge him, to my trembling
    And my dead father's scorn. That wounds my sight
    That his remembrance should be raised in spite;
    But either his confusion or mine ends it.
    [*Aloud*] O, Amoretta, hast thou met him yet?   65
    Speak, wench; hast done that for me?
Amoretta.   What, good madam?
Duchess. Destruction of my hopes; dost ask that now?
    Didst thou not swear to me, out of thy hate
    To Almachildes, thou'dst dissemble him
    A loving entertainment, and a meeting   70
    Where I should work my will?
Amoretta.   Good madam, pardon me;
    A loving entertainment I do protest
    Myself to give him, with all speed I can too.
    But, as I'm yet a maid, a perfect one,
    As the old time was wont to afford, when   75
    There was few tricks and little cunning stirring,
    I can dissemble none that will serve your turn.
    He must have ev'n a right one and a plain one.

Duchess. Thou mak'st me doubt thy health. Speak; art thou well?

Amoretta. O, never better, if he would make haste   80

    And come back quickly; he stays now too long.

Duchess. [*Aside*] I'm quite lost in this woman.

                      [*The charm falls to the floor.*]

                                What's that fell

    Out of her bosom now? Some love-token?

Amoretta. Nay, I'll say that for him, he's the uncivil'st gentleman,

    And every way desertless.

Duchess. [*Aside*]   Who's that now   85

    She discommends so fast?

Amoretta.   I could not love him, madam,

    Of any man in court.

Duchess.   What's he now, prithee?

Amoretta. Who should it be but Almachildes, madam?

    I never hated man so deeply yet.

Duchess. As Almachildes?

Amoretta.   I am sick, good madam,   90

    When I but hear him named.

Duchess.   How is this possible?

    But now thou saidst thou loved'st him, and didst raise him

    'Bove all the court in praises.

Amoretta.   How great people

    May speak their pleasure, madam! But surely I

    Should think the worse of my tongue while I lived then.   95

Duchess. No longer have I patience to forbear thee,

    Thou that retain'st an envious soul to goodness.

    He is a gentleman deserves as much

    As ever fortune yet bestowed on man:

    The glory and prime lustre of our court.   100

Nor can there any but ourself be worthy of him;

And take you notice of that now from me,

Say you have warning on't. If you did love him,

You must not now.

Amoretta.   Let your grace never fear it.

Duchess. Thy name is Amoretta, as ours is;   105

'T has made me love and trust thee.

Amoretta.   And my faithfulness

Has appeared well i'th' proof still, has't not, madam?

Duchess. But if't fail now, 'tis nothing.

Amoretta.   Then it shall not.

I know he will not be long from flutt'ring

About this place, now he's had a sight of me;   110

And I'll perform

In all that I vowed, madam, faithfully.

Duchess. Then am I blessed both in revenge and love,

And thou shalt taste the sweetness.   *Exit.*

Enter ALMACHILDES.

Amoretta. [Aside]   What your aims be

I list not to enquire. All I desire   115

Is to preserve a competent honesty

Both for mine own and his use that shall have me,

Whose luck soe'er it be. O, he's returned already;

I knew he would not fail.

Almachildes. [Aside]   It works by this time

Or the Devil's in't, I think. I'll ne'er trust witch else,   120

Nor sup with 'em this twelvemonth.

Amoretta. [Aside]   I must soothe him now;

And 'tis great pain to do't against one's stomach.

Almachildes. Now, Amoretta?

Amoretta.   Now you're welcome, sir,
    If you'd come always thus.

Almachildes.   O, am I so?
    Is the case altered since?

Amoretta.   If you'd be ruled   125
    And know your times, 'twere somewhat, a great comfort.
    'Las, I could be as loving and as venturous
    As any woman—we're all flesh and blood, man—
    If you could play the game out modestly
    And not betray your hand. I must have care, sir;   130
    You know I have a marriage-time to come,
    And that's for life. Your best folks will be merry,
    But look to the main chance—that's reputation—
    And then do what they list.

Almachildes.   Wilt hear my oath?
    By the sweet health of youth, I will be careful   135
    And never prate on't, nor, like a cunning snarer,
    Make thy clipped name the bird to call in others.

Amoretta. Well, yielding then to such conditions
    As my poor bashfulness shall require from you,
    I shall yield shortly after.

Almachildes.   I'll consent to 'em;   140
    And may thy sweet humility be a pattern
    For all proud women living.

Amoretta.   They're beholden to you. *Exeunt.*

Scene iii

Enter ABBERZANES *and an* Old Woman [*with a baby*].

Abberzanes. So, so; away with him. I love to get 'em,
    But not to keep 'em. Dost thou know the house?
Old Woman. No matter for the house, I know the porch.
Abberzanes. There's sixpence more for that. Away; keep close.
                               [*Exit* Old Woman.]

    My tailor told me he sent away a maidservant   5
    Well ballast of all sides, within these nine days—
    His wife ne'er dreamed on't—gave the drab ten pound,
    And she ne'er troubles him—a common fashion.
    He told me 'twas to rid away a scape,
    And I have sent him this for't. I remember   10
    A friend of mine once served a prating tradesman
    Just on this fashion, to a hair in truth.
    'Tis a good ease to a man: you can swell a maid up
    And rid her for ten pound; there's the purse back again
    Whate'er becomes of your money or your maid.   15
    This comes of bragging now. It's well for the boy too;
    He'll get an excellent trade by't, and on Sundays
    Go like a gentleman that has pawned his rapier.
    He need not care what countryman his father was,
    Nor what his mother was when he was gotten.   20
    The boy will do well certain. 'Give him grace
    To have a quick hand and convey things cleanly;

Enter FRANCESCA.

    'Twill be his own another day. O, well said!
    Art almost furnished? There's such a toil always

127

To set a woman to horse, a mighty trouble.   25
The letter came to your brother's hands, I know,
On Thursday last by noon; you were expected there
Yesterday night.
Francesca.   It makes the better, sir.
Abberzanes. We must take heed we ride through all the puddles
'Twixt this and that now, that your safeguard there   30
May be most probably dabbled.
Francesca. [*Looks in mirror.*]   Alas, sir,
I never marked till now—I hate myself—
How monstrous thin I look!
Abberzanes.   Not monstrous neither;
A little sharp i'th' nose, like a country woodcock.
Francesca. Fie, fie, how pale I am! I shall betray myself.   35
I would you'd box me well and handsomely
To get me into colour.
Abberzanes.   Not I, pardon me;
That let a husband do when he has married you.
A friend at court will never offer that.
Come, how much spice and sugar have you left now   40
At this poor one month's voyage?
Francesca.   Sure not much, sir;
I think some quarter of a pound of sugar
And half an ounce of spice.
Abberzanes.   Here's no sweet charge!
And there was thirty pound, good weight and true,
Beside what my man stole when 'twas a-weighing,   45
And that was three pound more, I'll speak with' least.
The Rhenish wine, is't all run out in caudles too?
Francesca. Do you ask that, sir? 'Tis of a week's departure.

You see what 'tis now to get children, sir.

[*Enter* Boy.]

Boy. Your mares are ready both, sir.

Abberzanes.   Come, we'll up then.   50

    Youth, give my sister a straight wand; there's twopence.

Boy. I'll give her a fine whip, sir.

Abberzanes.   No, no, no;

    Though we have both deserved it.

Boy.   Here's a new one.

Abberzanes. Prithee talk to us of no whips, good boy;

    My heart aches when I see 'em. Let's away.   *Exeunt.*   55

Finis Actus Secundi.

ACT III

Scene i

Enter DUCHESS *leading* ALMACHILDES *blindfold.*

Almachildes. This' you that was a maid? How are you born
        To deceive men? I'd thought to have married you;
        I had been finely handled, had I not?
        I'll say that man is wise ever hereafter
        That tries his wife beforehand. 'Tis no marvel   5
        You should profess such bashfulness to blind one,
        As if you durst not look a man i'th' face,
        Your modesty would blush so. Why do you not run
        And tell the Duchess now? Go; you should tell all.
        Let her know this too: why, here's the plague now;   10
        'Tis hard at first to win 'em; when they're gotten
        There's no way to be rid on 'em; they stick
        To a man like bird-lime. My oath's out.
        Will you release me? I'll release myself else.
Duchess. Nay, sure I'll bring you to your sight again.   15
                                        [*Takes off his blindfold.*]
        Say, thou must either die or kill the Duke,
        For one of them thou must do.
Almachildes.   How, good madam?
Duchess. Thou hast thy choice, and to that purpose, sir,
        I've given thee knowledge now of what thou hast
        And what thou must do to be worthy on't.   20

130

You must not think to come by such a fortune
Without desert; that were unreasonable.
He that's not born to honour must not look
To have it come with ease to him; he must win't.
Take but into thine actions wit and courage,   25
That's all we ask of thee. But if through weakness
Of a poor spirit thou deniest me this,
Think but how thou shalt die, as I'll work means for't,
No murderer ever like thee; for I purpose
To call this subtle, sinful snare of mine   30
An act of force from thee. Thou'rt proud and youthful;
I shall be believed. Besides, thy wantonness
Is at this hour in question 'mongst our women,
Which will make ill for thee.
Almachildes.   I had hard chance
To light upon this pleasure that's so costly;   35
'Tis not content with what a man can do
And give him breath, but seeks to have that too.
Duchess. Well, take thy choice.
Almachildes.   I see no choice in't, madam,
For 'tis all death methinks.
Duchess.   Thou'st an ill sight then
Of a young man. 'Tis death if thou refuse it;   40
And say my zeal has warned thee. But consenting,
'Twill be new life, great honour and my love,
Which in perpetual bonds I'll fasten to thee.
Almachildes. How, madam?
Duchess.   I'll do't religiously;
Make thee my husband. May I lose all sense   45
Of pleasure in life else, and be more miserable

Than ever creature was; for nothing lives

But has a joy in somewhat.

Almachildes.   Then by all

The hopeful fortunes of a young man's rising,

I will perform it, madam.

Duchess. [*Kisses him.*]   There's a pledge then   50

Of a duchess' love for thee. And now trust me

For thy most happy safety. I will choose

That time shall never hurt thee. When a man

Shows resolution, and there's worth in him,

I'll have a care of him. Part now for this time,   55

But still be near about us till thou canst

Be nearer, that's ourself.

Almachildes. And that I'll venture hard for.

Duchess.   Good speed to thee.

                                        Exeunt.

Scene ii

Enter GASPERO *and* FLORIDA.

Florida. Prithee be careful of me, very careful now.

Gaspero. I warrant you; he that cannot be careful of a quean can be

          careful of nobody; 'tis every man's humour that. I should

          ne'er look to a wife half so handsomely.

Florida. O, softly, sweet sir! Should your mistress meet me now   5

          In her own house, I were undone for ever.

Gaspero. Never fear her. She's at her prick-song close;

          There's all the joy she has or takes delight in.

          Look, here's the garden-key. My master gave't me

And willed me to be careful; doubt not you on't.   10
Florida. Your master is a noble complete gentleman,
And does a woman all the right that may be.

Enter SEBASTIAN.

Sebastian. How now? What's she?
Gaspero.   A kind of doubtful creature.
        I'll tell thee more anon.   [*Exeunt* GASPERO *and* FLORIDA.]
Sebastian.   I know that face
        To be a strumpet's, or mine eye is envious   15
        And would fain wish it so where I would have it.
        I fail if the condition of this fellow
        Wears not about it a strong scent of baseness.
        I saw her once before here (five days since 'tis),
        And the same wary, panderous diligence   20
        Was then bestowed on her. She came altered then,
        And more inclining to the city-tuck.
        Whom should this piece of transformation visit,
        After the common courtesy of frailty,
        In our house here? Surely not any servant;   25
        They are not kept so lusty, she so low.
        I'm at a strange stand; love and luck assist me.
        The truth I shall win from him by false play.

Enter GASPERO.

        He's now returned. Well, sir, as you were saying—
        Go forward with your tale.
Gaspero.   What? I know nothing.   30
Sebastian. The gentlewoman.
Gaspero.   She's gone out at' back-door now.

Sebastian. Then farewell she, and you, if that be all.

Gaspero. Come, come, thou shalt have more. I have no power

     To lock myself up from thee.

Sebastian.   So methinks.

Gaspero. You shall not think; trust me, sir, you shall not.   35

     Your ear: she's one o'th' falling family,

     A quean my master keeps. She lies at Rutneys.

Sebastian. Is't possible? I thought I had seen her somewhere.

Gaspero. I tell you truth sincerely. She's been thrice here

     By stealth within these ten days, and departed still   40

     With pleasure and with thanks, sir; 'tis her luck.

     Surely I think if ever there were man

     Bewitched in this world, 'tis my master, sirrah.

Sebastian. Think'st thou so, Gasper?

Gaspero.   O, sir, too apparent.

Sebastian. [*Aside*] This may prove happy; 'tis the likeliest means   45

     That fortune yet e'er showed me.

Enter ISABELLA.

Isabella.   You're both here now,

     And strangers newly lighted. Where's your attendance?

Sebastian. [*Aside*] I know what makes you waspish. A pox on't!

     She'll every day be angry now at nothing.

               Exeunt [SEBASTIAN *and* GASPERO.]

Isabella. I'll call her stranger ever in my heart.   50

     She's killed the name of sister through base lust

     And fled to shifts. O, how a brother's good thoughts

     May be beguiled in woman! Here's a letter,

     Found in her absence, reports strangely of her

     And speaks her impudence. She's undone herself—   55

I could not hold from weeping when I read it—
Abused her brother's house and his good confidence.
'Twas done not like herself. I blame her much.
But if she can but keep it from his knowledge,
I will not grieve him first. It shall not come   60
By my means to his heart.

Enter GASPERO.

                        Now, sir, the news?
Gaspero. You called 'em strangers; 'tis my master's sister, madam.
Isabella. O, is't so? She's welcome. Who's come with her?
Gaspero. I see none but Abberzanes.   [*Exit.*]
Isabella.   He's enough
To bring a woman to confusion,   65
More than a wiser man or a far greater.
A letter came last week to her brother's hands
To make way for her coming up again
After her shame was lightened; and she writ there
The gentleman her mother wished her to,   70
Taking a violent surfeit at a wedding,
Died ere she came to see him. What strange cunning
Sin helps a woman to!

Enter ABBERZANES *and* FRANCESCA.

                  Here she comes now.
Sister, you're welcome home again.
Francesca.   Thanks, sweet sister.
Isabella. You've had good speed.
Francesca. [*Aside*]   What says she? [*Aloud*] I have made   75
All the best speed I could.

135

Isabella.   I well believe you.

    Sir, we're all much beholden to your kindness.

Abberzanes. My service ever, madam, to a gentlewoman.

    I took a bonny mare I keep and met her

    Some ten mile out of town—eleven, I think.   80

    'Twas at the Stump I met you, I remember,

    At bottom of the hill.

Francesca.   'Twas thereabout, sir.

Abberzanes. Full eleven then, by the rod, if they were measured.

Isabella. You look ill, methinks. Have you been sick of late?

    Truth, very bleak, doth she not? How think you, sir?   85

Abberzanes. No, no; a little sharp with riding; she's rid sore.

Francesca. I ever look lean after a journey, sister;

    One shall do that has travelled, travelled hard.

Abberzanes. Till evening I commend you to yourselves, ladies. *Exit.*

Isabella. And that's best trusting to if you were hanged.   90

    You're well acquainted with his hand went out now?

Francesca. His hand?

Isabella. I speak of nothing else. I think 'tis there.   *[Gives letter.]*

    Please you to look upon't; and when you've done,

    If you did weep, it could not be amiss,   95

    A sign you could say grace after a full meal.

    You had not need look paler, yet you do.

    'Twas ill done to abuse yourself and us,

    To wrong so good a brother and the thoughts

    That we both held of you. I did doubt you much   100

    Before our marriage-day, but then my strangeness,

    And better hope still, kept me off from speaking.

    Yet may you find a kind and peaceful sister of me

    If you desist here and shake hands with folly,

136

Which you ha' more cause to do than I to wish you.   105
As truly as I bear a love to goodness,
Your brother knows not yet on't, nor shall ever
For my part, so you leave his company.
But if I find you impudent in sinning,
I will not keep't an hour, nay, prove your enemy,   110
And you know who will aid me. As you've goodness,
You may make use of this; I'll leave it with you.   *Exit.*

Francesca. Here's a sweet churching after a woman's labour,
And a fine 'Give you joy'! Why, where the devil
Lay you to be found out? The sudden hurry   115
Of hast'ning to prevent shame brought shame forth.
That's still the curse of all lascivious stuff;
Misdeeds could never yet be wary enough.
Now must I stand in fear of every look,
Nay, tremble at a whisper. She can keep it secret?   120
That's very likely, and a woman too!
I'm sure I could not do't; and I am made
As well as she can be for any purpose.
'Twould never stay with me two days, I have cast it;
The third would be a terrible sick day with me,   125
Not possible to bear it. Should I then
Trust to her strength in't, that lies every night
Whispering the day's news in a husband's ear?
No; and I have thought upon the means. Blessed fortune,
I must be quit with her in the same fashion,   130
Or else 'tis nothing. There's no way like it
To bring her honesty into question cunningly.
My brother will believe small likelihoods,
Coming from me too. I lying now i'th' house

137

May work things to my will, beyond conceit too.   135

Disgrace her first, her tale will ne'er be heard;

I learned that counsel first of a sound guard.

I do suspect Gasper, my brother's squire there,

Had some hand in this mischief, for he's cunning,

And I perhaps may fit him.   140

Enter ANTONIO.

Antonio. Your sister told me you were come. Thou'rt welcome.

Francesca. Where is she?

Antonio.   Who? My wife?

Francesca.   Ay, sir.

Antonio.   Within.

Francesca. Not within hearing, think you?

Antonio.   Within hearing?

What's thy conceit in that? Why shak'st thy head so,

And look'st so pale and poorly?

Francesca.   I'm a fool indeed   145

To take such grief for others, for your fortune, sir.

Antonio. My fortune? Worse things yet? Farewell life then.

Francesca. I fear you're much deceived, sir, in this woman.

Antonio. Who? In my wife? Speak low; come hither, softly, sister.

Francesca. I love her as a woman you made choice of;   150

But when she wrongs you, natural love is touched, brother,

And that will speak, you know.

Antonio.   I trust it will.

Francesca. I held a shrewd suspicion of her lightness

At first, when I went down, which made me haste the sooner.

But more, to make amends, at my return now   155

I found apparent signs.

Antonio.   Apparent, say'st thou?

Francesca. Ay, and of base lust too; that makes th' affliction.

Antonio. There has been villainy wrought upon me then;

     'Tis too plain now.

Francesca.   Happy are they, I say still,

     That have their sisters living i'th' house with 'em,   160

     Their mothers, or some kindred; a great comfort

     To all poor married men. It is not possible

     A young wife can abuse a husband then;

     'Tis found straight. But swear secrecy to this, brother.

Antonio. To this and all thou wilt have.

Francesca.   Then this follows, sir.   165

                                [Whispers to him.]

Enter ISABELLA.

Antonio. I praise thy counsel well; I'll put't in use straight.

     See where she comes herself. Kind, honest lady,

     I must now borrow a whole fortnight's leave of thee.

Isabella. How, sir? A fortnight's?

Antonio. It may be but ten days; I know not yet.   170

     'Tis business for the state, and't must be done.

Isabella. I wish good speed to't then.

Antonio.   Why, that was well spoke.

     I'll take but a footboy; I need no more.

     The rest I'll leave at home to do you service.

Isabella. Use your own pleasure, sir.

Antonio.   Till my return   175

     You'll be good company, my sister and you.

Isabella. We shall make shift, sir.

Antonio.   I'm glad now she's come;

139

And so the wishes of my love to both.   *Exit.*

Enter SEBASTIAN.

Isabella. And our good prayers with you, sir.   [*Exit* FRANCESCA.]
Sebastian. [*Aside*]   Now, my fortune.
    [*Aloud*] By your kind favour, madam.
Isabella.   With me, sir?   180
Sebastian. The words shall not be many, but the faithfulness
    And true respect that is included in 'em
    Is worthy your attention, and may put upon me
    The fair repute of a just, honest servant.
Isabella. What's here to do, sir,   185
    There's such great preparation toward?
Sebastian. In brief, that goodness in you is abused, madam.
    You have the married life, but 'tis a strumpet
    That has the joy on't and the fruitfulness;
    There goes away your comfort.
Isabella.   How? A strumpet?   190
Sebastian. Of five years' cost and upwards, a dear mischief,
    As they are all of 'em. His fortnight's journey
    Is to that country, if it be not rudeness
    To speak the truth. I have found it all out, madam.
Isabella. Thou'st found out thine own ruin; for to my knowledge   195
    Thou dost belie him basely. I dare swear
    He's a gentleman, as free from that folly
    As ever took religious life upon him.
Sebastian. Be not too confident to your own abuse, madam.
    Since I have begun the truth, neither your frowns,   200
    The only curses that I have on earth
    Because my means depends upon your service,

Nor all the execration of man's fury
Shall put me off. Though I be poor, I'm honest,
And too just in this business. I perceive now   205
Too much respect and faithfulness to ladies
May be a wrong to servants.

Isabella.   Art thou yet
So impudent to stand in't?

Sebastian.   Are you yet so cold, madam,
In the belief on't? There my wonder's fixed,
Having such blessèd health and youth about you,   210
Which makes the injury mighty.

Isabella.   Why, I tell thee
It were too great a fortune for thy lowness
To find out such a thing; thou dost not look
As if thou'rt made for't. By the precious sweets of love,
I would give half my wealth for such a bargain   215
And think 'twere bought too cheap. Thou canst not guess
Thy means and happiness should I find this true.
First, I'd prefer thee to the lord, my uncle.
He's governor of Ravenna; all the advancements
I'th' kingdom flows from him. What need I boast that   220
Which common fame can teach thee?

Sebastian.   Then thus, madam:
Since I presume now on your height of spirit
And your regard to your own youth and fruitfulness,
Which every woman naturally loves and covets,
Accept but of my labour in directions.   225
You shall both find your wrongs, which you may right
At your own pleasure, yet not missed tonight
Here in the house neither. None shall take notice

Of any absence in you as I have thought on't.

Isabella. Do this, and take my praise and thanks for ever.   230

Sebastian. As I deserve, I wish 'em, and will serve you.   *Exeunt.*

Scene iii

Enter HECATE, [two] Witches, *and* FIRESTONE.

Hecate. The moon's a gallant; see how brisk she rides.

Stadlin. Here's a rich evening, Hecate.

Hecate.   Ay, is't not, wenches,
　　　To take a journey of five thousand mile?

Hoppo. Ours will be more tonight.

Hecate.   O, 'twill be precious!
　　　Heard you the owl yet?

Stadlin.   Briefly in the copse   5
　　　As we came through now.,

Hecate.   'Tis high time for us then.

Stadlin. There was a bat hung at my lips three times
　　　As we came through the woods, and drank her fill.
　　　Old Puckle saw her.

Hecate   You are fortunate still;
　　　The very screech-owl lights upon your shoulder   10
　　　And woos you, like a pigeon. Are you furnished?
　　　Have you your ointments?

Stadlin.   All.

Hecate.   Prepare to flight then;
　　　I'll overtake you swiftly.

Stadlin.   Hie thee, Hecate;
　　　We shall be up betimes.

Hecate.   I'll reach you quickly.

                    [*Exeunt* STADLIN *and* HOPPO.]

Firestone. [*Aside*] They're all going a-birding tonight. They talk of   15
    fowls i'th' air that fly by day; I am sure they'll be a company
    of foul sluts there tonight. If we have not mortality after it, I'll
    be hanged, for they are able to putrefy it, to infect a whole
    region. She spies me now.

Hecate. What, Firestone, our sweet son?   20

Firestone. [*Aside*] A little sweeter than some of you, or a dunghill
    were too good for me.

Hecate. How much hast here?

Firestone.   Nineteen, and all brave plump ones,
    Besides six lizard's and three serpentine eggs.

Hecate. Dear and sweet boy; what herbs hast thou?   25

Firestone. I have some marmartin and mandragon.

Hecate. Marmaritin and mandragora thou wouldst say.
    Here's panax too; I thank thee.

Firestone.   My pan aches, I am sure,
    With kneeling down to cut 'em.

Hecate.   And selago,
    Hedge-hyssop too. How near he goes my cuttings!   30
    Were they all cropped by moonlight?

Firestone.   Every blade of 'em,
    Or I am a moon-calf, mother.

Hecate.   Hie thee home with 'em.
    Look well to the house tonight; I am for aloft.

Firestone. [*Aside*] Aloft, quoth you? I would you would break your
    neck once, that I might have all quickly. [*Aloud*] Hark, hark,   35
    mother; they are above the steeple already, flying over your
    head with a noise of musicians.

Hecate. They are they indeed. Help, help me; I'm too late else.

Song.

In the air Come away, come away;

    Hecate, Hecate, come away.   40

Hecate. I come, I come, I come, I come,

    With all the speed I may,

    With all the speed I may.

    Where's Stadlin?

In the air Here.   45

[*Hecate.*] Where's Puckle?

In the air Here,

    And Hoppo too, and Hellwain too;

    We lack but you, we lack but you.

    Come away, make up the count.   50

Hecate. I will but 'noint, and then I mount.

Above There's one comes down to fetch his dues:

A spirit like a cat descends.

    A kiss, a coll, a sip of blood.

    And why thou stay'st so long

      I muse, I muse,   55

    Since the air's so sweet and good.

Hecate. O, art thou come?

    What news? What news?

[*Spirit.*] All goes still to our delight;

    Either come, or else   60

      Refuse, refuse.

Hecate. Now I am furnished for the flight.

Firestone. [*Aside*] Hark, hark, the cat sings a brave treble in her own
    language.

     Hecate. *Going up* Now I go, now I fly,   65
           Malkin, my sweet spirit, and I.
           O, what a dainty pleasure 'tis
           To ride in the air
           When the moon shines fair,
           And sing and dance, and toy and kiss.   70
           Over woods, high rocks and mountains,
           Over seas, our mistress' fountains,
           Over steep towers and turrets,
           We fly by night 'mongst troops of spirits.
           No ring of bells to our ears sounds,   75
           No howls of wolves, no yelps of hounds;
           No, not the noise of water's breach
           Or cannon's throat our height can reach.
                       [*Exeunt* HECATE *and* Spirit.]
    Above No ring of bells, etcetera.

Firestone. Well, mother, I thank your kindness: you must be   80
    gambolling i'th' air, and leave me to walk here like a fool and
    a mortal.   *Exit*.

               Finis Actus Tertii.

ACT IV

Scene i

Enter ALMACHILDES.

Almachildes. Though the fates have endued me with a pretty kind of
lightness, that I can laugh at the world in a corner on't, and
can make myself merry on fasting-nights to rub out a supper,
which were a precious quality in a young formal student, yet
let the world know there is some difference betwixt my jovial   5
condition and the lunary state of madness. I am not quite out
of my wits. I know a bawd from an aqua-vitae shop, a
strumpet from wildfire and a beadle from brimstone. Now
shall I try the honesty of a great woman soundly. She
reck'ning the Duke's made away, I'll be hanged if I be not   10
the next now. If I trust her as she's a woman, let one of her
long hairs wind about my heart and be the end of me, which
were a piteous lamentable tragedy and might be entitled *A
Fair Warning for All Hair-Bracelets.*
Already there's an insurrection   15
Among the people. They are up in arms,
Not out of any reason but their wills
(Which are in them their saints), sweating and swearing,
Out of their zeal to rudeness, that no stranger,
As they term her, shall govern over them.   20
They say they'll raise a duke among themselves first.

Enter DUCHESS.

146

Duchess. O, Almachildes, I perceive already
    Our loves are born to crosses! We're beset
    By multitudes, and, which is worse, I fear me
    Unfriended too of any. My chief care   25
    Is for thy sweet youth's safety.
Almachildes. [*Aside*]   He that believes you not
    Goes the right way to heaven, o' my conscience.
Duchess. There is no trusting of 'em; they are all as barren
    In pity as in faith. He that puts confidence
    In them dies openly to the sight of all men,   30
    Not with his friends and neighbours in peace private,
    But as his shame, so his cold farewell is,
    Public and full of noise. But keep you close, sir,
    Not seen of any, till I see the way
    Plain for your safety. I expect the coming   35
    Of the Lord Governor, whom I will flatter
    With fair entreaties, to appease their wildness,
    And before him take a great grief upon me
    For the Duke's death, his strange and sudden loss.
    And when a quiet comes, expect thy joys.   40
Almachildes. [*Aside*] I do expect now to be made away
    'Twixt this and Tuesday night; if I live Wednesday,
    Say I have been careful and shunned spoon-meat.   *Exit.*
Duchess. This fellow lives too long after the deed;
    I'm weary of his sight. He must die quickly,   45
    Or I've small hope of safety. My great aim's
    At the Lord Governor's love. He is a spirit
    Can sway and countenance; these obey and crouch.
    My guiltiness had need of such a master,
    That with a beck can suppress multitudes   50

And dim misdeeds with radiance of his glory,
Not to be seen with dazzled, popular eyes.

Enter LORD GOVERNOR [*attended.*]

And here behold him come.
Lord Governor.   Return back to 'em;
    Say we desire 'em to be friends of peace
    Till they hear farther from us.   [*Exeunt* Attendants.]
Duchess.   O my lord!   55
    I fly unto the pity of your nobleness,
    The grieved'st lady that was e'er beset
    With storms of sorrows or wild rage of people.
    Never was woman's grief for loss of lord
    Dearer than mine to me.
Lord Governor.   There's no right done   60
    To him now, madam, by wrong done to yourself;
    Your own good wisdom may instruct you so far.
    And for the people's tumult, which oft grows
    From liberty or rankness of long peace,
    I'll labour to restrain as I've begun, madam.   65
Duchess. My thanks and prayers shall ne'er forget you, sir,
    And, in time to come, my love.
Lord Governor.   Your love, sweet madam?
    You make my joys too happy. I did covet
    To be the fortunate man that blessing visits,
    Which I'll esteem the crown and full reward   70
    Of service present and deserts to come.
    It is a happiness I'll be bold to sue for
    When I have set a calm upon these spirits
    That now are up for ruin.

Duchess.   Sir, my wishes

    Are so well met in yours, so fairly answered   75

    And nobly recompensed, it makes me suffer

    In those extremes that few have ever felt:

    To hold two passions in one heart at once,

    Of gladness and of sorrow.

Lord Governor.   Then as the olive

    Is the meek ensign of fair fruitful peace,   80

    So is this kiss, of yours.   [*Kisses her.*]

Duchess.   Love's power be with you, sir.

Lord Governor. [*Aside*] How she's betrayed her! May I breathe no

    longer

    Than to do virtue service and bring forth

    The fruits of noble thoughts, honest and loyal.

    This will be worth th' observing; and I'll do't.   *Exit.*   85

Duchess. What a sure happiness confirms joy to me

    Now in the times of my most imminent dangers!

    I looked for ruin, and increase of honour

    Meets me auspiciously. But my hopes are clogged now

    With an unworthy weight: there's the misfortune.   90

    What course shall I take now with this young man?

    For he must be no hindrance. I have thought on't:

    I'll take some witch's counsel for his end;

    That will be sur'st. Mischief is mischief's friend.   *Exit.*

Scene ii

Enter SEBASTIAN *and* FERNANDO.

Sebastian. If ever you knew force of love in life, sir,

Give to mine pity.

Fernando. You do ill to doubt me.

Sebastian. I could make bold with no friend seemlier
Than with yourself, because you were in presence
At our vow-making.

Fernando. I'm a witness to't. 5

Sebastian. Then you best understand, of all men living,
This is no wrong I offer, no abuse
Either to faith or friendship; for we're registered
Husband and wife in heaven, though there wants that
Which often keeps licentious man in awe 10
From starting from their wedlocks, the knot public.
'Tis in our souls knit fast; and how more precious
The soul is than the body, so much judge
The sacred and celestial tie within us
More than the outward form, which calls but witness 15
Here upon earth to what is done in heaven.
Though I must needs confess the least is honourable—
As an ambassador sent from a king
Has honour by the employment, yet there's greater
Dwells in the king that sent him; so in this. 20

Enter FLORIDA.

Fernando. I approve all you speak, and will appear to you
A faithful, pitying friend.

Sebastian. Look, there is she, sir,
One good for nothing but to make use of;
And I'm constrained to employ her to make all things
Plain, easy and probable. For when she comes 25
And finds one here that claims him, as I've taught

150

Both this to do't and he to compound with her,
'Twill stir belief the more of such a business.
Fernando. I praise the carriage well.
Sebastian.   Hark you, sweet mistress,
I shall do you a simple turn in this;   30
For she disgraced thus, you are up in favour
For ever with her husband.
Florida.   That's my hope, sir;
I would not take the pains else. Have you the keys
Of the garden-side, that I may get betimes in
Closely and take her lodging?
Sebastian.   Yes, I have thought upon you;   35
Here be the keys.
Florida.   Marry and thanks, sweet sir.
Set me a-work so still.
Sebastian. [*Aside*]   Your joys are false ones;
You're like to lie alone. You'll be deceived
Of the bedfellow you look for, else my purpose
Were in an ill case. He's on his fortnight's journey;   40
You'll find cold comfort there. A dream will be
Even the best market you can make tonight.
[*Aloud*] She'll not be long now; you may lose no time neither.
If she but take you at the door, 'tis enough.
When a suspect doth catch once, it burns mainly.   45
There may you end your business, and as cunningly
As if you were i'th' chamber, if you please
To use but the same art.
Florida.   What need you urge that
Which comes so naturally I cannot miss on't?
What makes the Devil so greedy of a soul   50

But 'cause he's lost his own, to all joys lost?

So 'tis our trade to set snares for other women

'Cause we were once caught ourselves.   [*Exit.*]

Sebastian.   A sweet allusion

Hell and a whore it seems are partners then

In one ambition. Yet thou'rt here deceived now: 55

Thou canst set none to hurt or wrong her honour;

It rather makes it perfect. Best of friends

That ever love's extremities were blessed with,

I feel mine arms with thee and call my peace

The offspring of thy friendship. I will think   60

This night my wedding-night; and with a joy

As reverend as religion can make man's,

I will embrace this blessing. Honest actions

Are laws unto themselves, and that good fear

Which is on others forced grows kindly there.   65

                                    [*Knocking within.*]

Fernando. Hark, hark, one knocks. Away, sir; 'tis she certainly.

It sounds much like a woman's jealous 'larum.

                                    [*Exit* SEBASTIAN.]

Enter ISABELLA.

Isabella. By your leave, sir.

Fernando.   You're welcome, gentlewoman.

Isabella. [*Aside*] Our ladyship then stands us in no stead now.

        [*Aloud*] One word in private, sir.   [*Whispers to him.*]

Fernando.   No, surely, forsooth,   70

There is no such here; you've mistook the house.

Isabella. O, sir, that have I not. Excuse me there,

I come not with such ignorance; think not so, sir.

'Twas told me at the ent'ring of your house here

By one that knows him too well.

Fernando.   Who should that be?   75

Isabella. Nay, sir, betraying is not my profession.

But here I know he is; and I presume

He would give me admittance, if he knew on't,

As one on's nearest friends.

Fernando.   You're not his wife, forsooth?

Isabella. Yes, by my faith, am I.

Fernando.   Cry you mercy then, lady.   80

Isabella. [*Aside*] She goes here by the name on's wife—good stuff!

But the bold strumpet never told me that.

Fernando. We are so oft deceived that let out lodgings,

We know not whom to trust. 'Tis such a world;

There are so many odd tricks nowadays   85

Put upon housekeepers.

Isabella.   Why, do you think I'd wrong

You or the reputation of your house?

Pray show me the way to him.

Fernando.   He's asleep, lady,

The curtains drawn about him.

Isabella.   Well, well, sir,

I'll have that care, I'll not disease him much.   90

Tread you but lightly. [*Aside*] O, of what gross falsehood

Is man's heart made of! Had my first love lived

And returned safe, he would have been a light

To all men's actions, his faith shined so bright.

                    Exeunt [FERNANDO *and* ISABELLA.]

                    Enter SEBASTIAN.

Sebastian. I cannot so deceive her, 'twere too sinful; 95

There's more religion in my love than so.

It is not treacherous lust that gives content

T'an honest mind; and this could prove no better.

Were it in me a part of manly justice,

That have sought strange hard means to keep her chaste 100

To her first vow, and I t'abuse her first?

Better I never knew what comfort were

In woman's love than wickedly to know it.

What could the falsehood of one night avail him

That must enjoy for ever or he's lost? 105

'Tis the way rather to draw hate upon me;

For, known, 'tis as impossible she should love me

As youth in health to dote upon a grief,

Or one that's robbed and bound t'affect the thief.

No, he that would soul's sacred comfort win 110

Must burn in pure love like a seraphin.

Enter ISABELLA.

Isabella. Celio?

Sebastian.   Sweet madam.

Isabella.   Thou'st deluded me;

There's nobody.

Sebastian.   How? I wonder he would miss, madam,

Having appointed too. 'Twere a strange goodness

If heaven should turn his heart now by the way. 115

Isabella. O, never, Celio!

Sebastian.   Yes, I ha' known the like.

Man is not at his own disposing, madam;

The blessed powers have provided better for him,

154

Or he were miserable. He may come yet;
   'Tis early, madam. If you would be pleased   120
   To embrace my counsel, you should see this night over,
   Since you've bestowed this pains.
Isabella.   I intend so.
Sebastian. [*Aside*] That strumpet would be found, else she should go.
   I curse the time now I did e'er make use
   Of such a plague. Sin knows not what it does.   *Exeunt*.   125

Scene iii

Enter FRANCESCA *in her chamber*.

Francesca. 'Tis now my brother's time, even much about it;
   For though he dissembled a whole fortnight's absence,
   He comes again tonight; 'twas so agreed
   Before he went. I must bestir my wits now
   To catch this sister of mine and bring her name   5
   To some disgrace first, to preserve mine own.
   There's profit in that cunning. She cast off
   My company betimes tonight by tricks and sleights,
   And I was well contented. I am resolved
   There's no hate lost between us; for I know   10
   She does not love me now but painfully,
   Like one that's forced to smile upon a grief
   To bring some purpose forward; and I'll pay her
   In her own metal. They're now all at rest,
   And Gasper there, and all. List. Fast asleep;   15
   He cries it hither. I must disease you straight, sir.
   For the maidservants and the girls o'th' house,

I spiced them lately with a drowsy posset;

They will not hear in haste. [*Knocking within*] My brother's

   come.

O, where's this key now for him? Here 'tis, happily.   20

But I must wake him first. Why, Gasper! Gasper!

Enter GASPERO.

Gaspero. What a pox gasp you for?

Francesca. [*Aside*]   Now I'll throw't down.

Gaspero. Who's that called me now? Somebody called Gasper?

Francesca. O, up, as thou'rt an honest fellow, Gasper!

Gaspero. I shall not rise tonight then. What's the matter?   25

   Who's that? Young mistress?

Francesca.   Ay. Up, up, sweet Gasper.

   My sister hath both knocked and called this hour,

   And not a maid will stir.

Gaspero.   They'll stir enough sometimes.

Francesca. [*Knocking*] Hark, hark again! Gasper! O, run, run

     prithee!

Gaspero. Give me leave to clothe myself.

Francesca.   Stand'st upon clothing   30

   In an extremity? [*Knocking*] Hark, hark again!

   She may be dead ere thou com'st. O, in quickly!

                     [*Exit* GASPERO.]

   He's gone. He cannot choose but be took now

   Or met in his return; that will be enough.

Enter ANTONIO.

   Brother? Here, take this light.

Antonio.   My careful sister.   35

Francesca. Look first in his own lodging ere you enter.

                                                [*Exit* ANTONIO.]

Antonio. [*Within*] O abused confidence! Here's nothing of him

    But what betrays him more.

                      [*Enter* ANTONIO.]

Francesca.   Then 'tis too true, brother.

Antonio. I'll make base lust a terrible example;

    No villainy e'er paid dearer.

Francesca.   Help! Hold, sir!   40

Antonio. I'm deaf to all humanity.   [*Exit. Noise within.*]

Francesca.   List, list.

    A strange and sudden silence after all.

    I trust he's spoiled 'em both—too dear a happiness.

    O, how I tremble between doubts and joys!

                      [*Enter* ANTONIO.]

Antonio. There perish both; down to the house of falsehood   45

    Where perjurous wedlock weeps. O perjurous woman!

    She'd took the innocence of sleep upon her

    At my approach and would not see me come,

    As if she'd lain there like a harmless soul

    And never dreamed of mischief. What's all this now?   50

    I feel no ease; the burden's not yet off

    So long as th' abuse sticks in my knowledge.

    O, 'tis a pain of hell to know one's shame!

    Had it been hid and done, it'd been done happy;

    For he that's ignorant lives long and merry.   55

Francesca. [*Aside*] I shall know all now. [*Aloud*] Brother.

Antonio.   Come down quickly,

For I must kill thee too.

Francesca.   Me?

Antonio.   Stay not long;

    If thou desir'st to die with little pain,

    Make haste I'd wish thee, and come willingly.

    If I be forced to come, I shall be cruel   60

    Above a man to thee.

Francesca.   Why, sir! My brother!

Antonio. Talk to thy soul, if thou wilt talk at all;

    To me thou'rt lost for ever.

Francesca.   This is fearful in you,

    Beyond all reason, brother. Would you thus

    Reward me for my care and truth shown to you?   65

Antonio. A curse upon 'em both, and thee for company!

    'Tis that too diligent, thankless care of thine

    Makes me a murderer, and that ruins truth

    That lights me to the knowledge of my shame.

    Hadst thou been secret, then had I been happy   70

    And had a hope, like man, of joys to come.

    Now here I stand, a stain to my creation,

    And, which is heavier than all torments to me,

    The understanding of this base adultery;

    And that thou told'st me first, which thou deserv'st   75

    Death worthily for.

Francesca.   If that be the worst, hold, sir;

    Hold, brother. I can ease your knowledge straight,

    By my soul's hopes I can. There's no such thing.

Antonio. How?

Francesca.   Bless me but with life, I'll tell you all.

    Your bed was never wronged.

Antonio.   What? Never wronged?   80

Francesca. I ask but mercy as I deal with truth now.

    'Twas only my deceit, my plot, and cunning

    To bring disgrace upon her, by that means

    To keep mine own hid, which none knew but she.

    To speak truth, I'd a child by Abberzanes, sir.   85

Antonio. How? Abberzanes?

Francesca.   And my mother's letter

    Was counterfeited to get time and place

    For my delivery.

Antonio.   O, my wrath's redoubled!

Francesca. At my return she could speak all my folly,

    And blamed me, with good counsel. I, for fear   90

    It should be made known, thus rewarded her,

    Wrought you into suspicion without cause,

    And at your coming raised up Gasper suddenly,

    Sent him but in before you by a falsehood,

    Which to your kindled jealousy I knew   95

    Would add enough. What's now confessed is true.

Antonio. The more I hear, the worse it fares with me.

    I ha' killed 'em now for nothing, yet the shame

    Follows my blood still. Once more, come down.

    Look you, my sword goes up. Call Hermio to me.   100

    Let the new man alone; he'll wake too soon

    To find his mistress dead, and lose a service.

                          [*Exit* FRANCESCA.]

Already the day breaks upon my guilt;

                  Enter HERMIO.

I must be brief and sudden. Hermio.

159

Hermio.   Sir.

Antonio. Run, knock up Abberzanes speedily.   105

     Say I desire his company this morning

     To yonder horse-race, tell him; that will fetch him.

     O, hark you, by the way—   [*Whispers.*]

Hermio.   Yes, sir.

Antonio.   Use speed now

     Or I will ne'er use thee more. [*Aside*] And perhaps

     I speak in a right hour. My grief o'erflows;   110

     I must in private go, and vent my woes.   *Exeunt.*

Finis Actus Quarti.

ACT V

Scene i

Enter ANTONIO *and* ABBERZANES.

Antonio. You are welcome, sir.

Abberzanes. I think I'm worthy on't,
For look you, sir, I come untrussed, in truth.

Antonio. [*Aside*] The more's the pity, honester men go to't,
That slaves should scape it. [*Aloud*] What blade have you got
    there?

Abberzanes. Nay, I know not that, sir. I am not acquainted greatly   5
    with the blade. I am sure 'tis a good scabbard, and that
    satisfies me.

Antonio. 'Tis long enough indeed, if that be good.

Abberzanes. I love to wear a long weapon; 'tis a thing
    commendable.   10

Antonio. I pray, draw it, sir.

Abberzanes. It is not to be drawn.

Antonio. Not to be drawn?

Abberzanes. I do not care to see't.
    To tell you truth, sir, 'tis only a holiday thing to wear by a
    man's side.

Antonio. Draw it, or I'll rip thee down from neck to navel,   15
    Though there's small glory in't.

Abberzanes. Are you in earnest, sir?

Antonio. I'll tell thee that anon.

Abberzanes.   Why, what's the matter, sir?

Antonio. [*Aside*] What a base misery is this in life now!

    This slave had so much daring courage in him

    To act a sin would shame whole generations,   20

    But hath not so much honest strength about him

    To draw a sword in way of satisfaction.

    [*Aloud*] This shows thy great guilt, that thou dar'st not fight.

Abberzanes. Yes, I dare fight, sir, in an honest cause.

Antonio. Why, come then, slave; thou'st made my sister a whore.   25

Abberzanes. Prove that an honest cause and I'll be hanged.

Antonio. So many starting-holes? Can I light no way?

    Go to, you shall have your wish, all honest play.

    [*Calls offstage*] Come forth thou fruitful wickedness, thou
        seed

    Of shame and murder.

[Enter FRANCESCA.]

               Take to thee in wedlock   30

    Baseness and cowardice, a fit match for thee.

    Come, sir, along with me.

Abberzanes.   'Las, what to do?

    I am too young to take a wife, in truth.

Antonio. But old enough to take a strumpet though.

    You'd fain get all your children beforehand,   35

    And marry when you've done; that's a strange course, sir.

    This woman I bestow on thee. What dost thou say?

Abberzanes. I would I had such another to bestow on you, sir.

Antonio. Uncharitable slave, dog, coward as thou art,

    To wish a plague so great as thine to any!   40

Abberzanes. To my friend, sir, where I think I may be bold.

Antonio. Down, and do't solemnly. [*They kneel.*] Contract yourselves
    With truth and zeal or ne'er rise up again.
    I will not have her die i'th' state of strumpet,
    Though she took pride to live one. Hermio, the wine.   45

                [*Enter* HERMIO.]

Hermio. 'Tis here, sir. [*Aside*] Truth, I wonder at some things
    But I'll keep honest.
Antonio.   So, here's to you both now,   [*Drinks.*]
    And to your joys, if't be your luck to find 'em;
    I tell you, you must weep hard if you do.
    Divide it 'twixt you both. [*They drink.*] [*Aside*] You shall not
        need   50
    A strong bill of divorcement after that
    If you mislike your bargain. [*Aloud*] Go, get in now;
    Kneel and pray heartily to get forgiveness
    Of those two souls whose bodies thou hast murdered.

         [*Exeunt* ABBERZANES *and* FRANCESCA.]

    Spread, subtle poison. Now my shame in her   55
    Will die when I die; there's some comfort yet.
    I do but think how each man's punishment
    Proves still a kind of justice to himself.
    I was the man that told this innocent gentlewoman,
    Whom I did falsely wed and falsely kill,   60
    That he that was her husband first by contract
    Was slain i'th' field; and he's known yet to live.
    So did I cruelly beguile her heart,
    For which I'm well rewarded; so is Gasper,
    Who, to befriend my love, swore fearful oaths   65
    He saw the last breath fly from him. I see now

'Tis a thing dreadful t'abuse holy vows,
And falls most weighty.

Hermio.   Take comfort, sir;
You're guilty of no death; they're only hurt,
And that not mortally.

Antonio.   Thou breath'st untruths.   70

Enter GASPERO.

Hermio. Speak, Gasper, for me then.

Gaspero.   Your unjust rage, sir,
Has hurt me without cause.

Antonio.   'Tis changed to grief for't
How fares my wife?

Gaspero.   No doubt, sir, she fares well,
For she ne'er felt your fury. The poor sinner
That hath this seven year kept herself sound for you,   75
'Tis your luck to bring her into th' surgeon's hands now.

Antonio. Florida?

Gaspero.   She; I know no other, sir.
You were ne'er at charge yet but with one light horse.

Antonio. Why, where's your lady? Where's my wife tonight then?

Gaspero. Nay, ask not me, sir. Your struck doe within   80
Tells a strange tale of her.

Antonio.   This is unsufferable!
Never had man such means to make him mad.
O, that the poison would but spare my life
Till I had found her out!

Hermio.   Your wish is granted, sir.
Upon the faithfulness of a pitying servant,   85
I gave you none at all; my heart was kinder.

Let not conceit abuse you; you're as healthful,

For any drug, as life yet ever found you.

Antonio. Why, here's a happiness wipes off mighty sorrows.

The benefit of ever-pleasing service   90

Bless thy profession.

Enter LORD GOVERNOR [*attended*].

O, my worthy lord,

I've an ill bargain; never man had worse.

The woman that, unworthy, wears your blood

To countenance sin in her, your niece, she's false.

Lord Governor. False?

Antonio.   Impudent-adulterous.

Lord Governor.   You're too loud,   95

And grow too bold too with her virtuous meekness.

Enter FLORIDA.

Who dare accuse her?

Florida.   Here's one dare and can.

She lies this night with Celio, her own servant;

The place, Femando's house.

Lord Governor.   Thou dost amaze us.

Antonio. Why, here's but lust translated from one baseness   100

Into another. Here I thought to have caught 'em,

But lighted wrong by false intelligence,

And made me hurt the innocent. But now

I'll make my revenge dreadfuller than a tempest;

An army should not stop me, or a sea   105

Divide 'em from my revenge.   *Exit.*

Lord Governor.   I'll not speak

To have her spared if she be base and guilty.

If otherwise, heaven will not see her wronged;

I need not take care for her. Let that woman

Be carefully looked to, both for health and sureness.   110

[*To her*] It is not that mistaken wound thou wear'st

Shall be thy privilege.

Florida.   You cannot torture me

Worse than the surgeon does; so long I care not.

              [*Exeunt* FLORIDA *and* GASPERO *attended.*]

[*Lord Governor.*] If she be adulterous I will never trust

Virtues in women; they're but veils for lust.   *Exit* [*attended.*]   115

Hermio. To what a lasting ruin mischief runs!

I had thought I had well and happily ended all

In keeping back the poison, and new rage now

Spreads a worse venom. My poor lady grieves me.

'Tis strange to me that her sweet-seeming virtues   120

Should be so meanly overtook with Celio,

A servant; 'tis not possible.

         Enter ISABELLA *and* SEBASTIAN [*disguised.*]

Isabella.   Good morrow, Hermio.

My sister stirring yet?

Hermio.   How? Stirring, forsooth!

Here has been simple stirring. Are you not hurt, madam?

Pray, speak; we have a surgeon ready.   125

Isabella. How, a surgeon?

Hermio.   Hath been at work these five hours.

Isabella. How he talks!

Hermio.   Did you not meet my master?

Isabella. How, your master? Why, came he home tonight?

166

Hermio. Then know you nothing. Madam,

    Please you but walk in, you shall hear strange business.   130

Isabella. [*To Sebastian*] I'm much beholden to your truth now, am I

      not?

    You've served me fair: my credit's stained for ever.

                    Exeunt [ISABELLA *and* HERMIO.]

Sebastian. This is the wicked'st fortune that e'er blew.

    We're both undone for nothing. There's no way

    Flatters recovery now, the thing's so gross.   135

    Her disgrace grieves me more than a life's loss.   *Exit.*

Scene ii

Enter DUCHESS, HECATE, FIRESTONE.

Hecate. What death is't you desire for Almachildes?

Duchess. A sudden and a subtle.

Hecate.   Then I have fitted you.

    Here lie the gifts of both, sudden and subtle:

    His picture made in wax and gently molten

    By a blue fire kindled with dead men's eyes   5

    Will waste him by degrees.

Duchess.   In what time, prithee?

Hecate. Perhaps in a moon's progress.

Duchess.   What? A month?

    Out upon pictures! If they be so tedious,

    Give me things with some life.

Hecate.   Then seek no further.

Duchess. This must be done with speed, dispatched this night,   10

    If it may possible.

Hecate.   I have it for you;

    Here's that will do't. Stay but perfection's time,

    And that's not five hours hence.

Duchess.   Canst thou do this?

Hecate. Can I?

Duchess.   I mean so closely.

Hecate.   So closely

    Do you mean too?

Duchess.   So artfully, so cunningly.   15

Hecate. Worse and worse; doubts and incredulities,

    They make me mad. Let scrupulous greatness know:

    Cum volui, ripis ipsis mirantibus, amnes

    In fontes rediere suos; concussaque sisto,

    Stantia concutio cantu freta; nubila pello,   20

    Nubilaque induco; ventos abigoque vocoque;

    Vipereas rumpo verbis et carmine fauces;

    Et silvas moveo; jubeoque tremiscere montes,

    Et mugire solum, manesque exire sepulchris.

    Teque, luna, traho. Can you doubt me then, daughter,   25

    That can make mountains tremble, miles of woods walk,

    Whole earth's foundation bellow, and the spirits

    Of the entombed to burst out from their marbles,

    Nay, draw yon moon to my involved designs?

Firestone. [*Aside*] I know as well as can be when my mother's mad   30

    and our great cat angry, for one spits French then and th'

    other spits Latin.

Duchess. I did not doubt you, mother.

Hecate.   No? What did you?

    My power's so firm, it is not to be questioned.

Duchess. Forgive what's past. And now I know th' offensiveness   35

168

That vexes art, I'll shun th' occasion ever.

Hecate. Leave all to me and my five sisters, daughter.

It shall be conveyed in at howlet-time.

Take you no care; my spirits know their moments.

Raven or screech-owl never fly by th' door   40

But they call in (I thank 'em) and they lose not by't;

I give 'em barley soaked in infants' blood.

They shall have *semina cum sanguine,*

Their gorge crammed full, if they come once to our house;

We are no niggard.   [*Exit* DUCHESS.]   45

Firestone. [*Aside*] They fare but too well when they come hither;
they ate up as much t'other night as would have made me a
good conscionable pudding.

Hecate. Give me some lizard's brain; quickly, Firestone.

Where's grannam Stadlin and all the rest o'th' sisters?   50

[*Enter* STADLIN *and four other* Witches.]

Firestone. All at hand, forsooth.

Hecate. Give me some marmaritin, some bear-breech. When?

Firestone. Here's bear-breech and lizard's brain, forsooth.

Hecate. Into the vessel;

And fetch three ounces of the red-haired girl   55

I killed last midnight.

Firestone.   Whereabouts, sweet mother?

Hecate. Hip; hip or flank. Where is the acopus?

Firestone. You shall have acopus, forsooth.

Hecate. Stir, stir about, whilst I begin the charm.

A Charm Song, About a Vessel

Black spirits and white, red spirits and grey,   60

Mingle, mingle, mingle, you that mingle may.

Titty, Tiffin,

Keep it stiff in.

Firedrake, Puckey,

Make it lucky.   65

Liard, Robin,

You must bob in.

Round, around, around, about, about;

All ill come running in, all good keep out.

1 Witch. Here's the blood of a bat.   70

Hecate. Put in that; O, put in that!

2 Witch. Here's libbard's bane.

Hecate. Put in again.

1 Witch. The juice of toad, the oil of adder.

2 Witch. Those will make the younker madder.   75

Hecate. Put in; there's all; and rid the stench.

Firestone. Nay, here's three ounces of the red-haired wench.

All.   Round, around, around, etcetera.

Hecate. So, so, enough. Into the vessel with it;

There 't hath the true perfection. I am so light   80

At any mischief. There's no villainy

But is a tune methinks.

Firestone. [*Aside*] A tune? 'Tis to the tune of damnation then, I

warrant you, and that song hath a villainous burden.

Hecate. Come, my sweet sisters; let the air strike our tune,   85

Whilst we show reverence to yon peeping moon.

Here they dance The Witches' Dance *and exeunt.*

170

Scene iii

Enter LORD GOVERNOR, ISABELLA, [SEBASTIAN,
disguised,] FLORIDA, FRANCESCA, ABBERZANES,
GASPERO [*and* Servants.]

Isabella. My lord, I have given you nothing but the truth
    Of a most plain and innocent intent.
    My wrongs being so apparent in this woman,
    A creature that robs wedlock of all comfort
    Where'er she fastens, I could do no less   5
    But seek means privately to shame his folly.
    No further reached my malice; and it glads me
    That none but my base injurer is found
    To be my false accuser.
Lord Governor.   This is strange
    That he should give the wrongs, yet seek revenge.   10
    [*To Sebastian*] But, sirrah, you; you are accused here doubly:
    First, by your lady for a false intelligence
    That caused her absence, which much hurts her name,
    Though her intents were blameless; next, by this woman
    For an adulterous design and plot   15
    Practised between you to entrap her honour,
    Whilst she for her hire should enjoy her husband.
    Your answer.
Sebastian.   Part of this is truth, my lord,
    To which I'm guilty in a rash intent,
    But clear in act, and she most clear in both,   20
    Not sanctity more spotless.

[*Enter*] HERMIO.

Hermio.   O, my lord!

Lord Governor. What news breaks there?

Hermio.   Of strange destruction.

    Here stands the lady that within this hour

    Was made a widow.

Lord Governor.   How?

Hermio.   Your niece, my lord.

    A fearful, unexpected accident   25

    Brought death to meet his fury: for my lord

    Ent'ring Fernando's house like a raised tempest,

    Which nothing heeds but its own violent rage,

    Blinded with wrath and jealousy, which scorn guides,

    From a false trap-door fell into a depth   30

    Exceeds a temple's height, which takes into it

    Part of the dungeon that falls threescore fathom

    Under the castle.

Lord Governor.   O, you seed of lust,

    Wrongs and revenges wrongful, with what terrors

    You do present yourselves to wretched man   35

    When his soul least expects you!

Isabella.   I forgive him

    All his wrongs now, and sign it with my pity.

Florida. O my sweet servant!   [*Swoons.*]

Lord Governor.   Look to yon light mistress.

Gaspero. She's in a swoon, my lord.

Lord Governor.   Convey her hence.

                         [*Servants remove Florida.*]

    It is a sight would grieve a modest eye   40

    To see a strumpet's soul sink into passion

    For him that was the husband of another.

[*To Sebastian*] Yet all this clears not you.

Sebastian.   Thanks to heaven

    That I am now of age to clear myself then.

                            [*Discovers himself.*]

Lord Governor. Sebastian?

Sebastian.   The same, much wronged, sir.

Isabella.   Am I certain   45

    Of what mine eye takes joy to look upon?

Sebastian. Your service cannot alter me from knowledge;

    I am your servant ever.

Lord Governor.   Welcome to life, sir.

    Gasper, thou swor'st his death.

Gaspero.   I did indeed, my lord,

    And have been since well paid for't: one forsworn mouth   50

    Hath got me two or three more here.

Sebastian.   I was dead, sir,

    Both to my joys and all men's understanding

    Till this my hour of life. For 'twas my fortune

    To make the first of my return to Urbin

    A witness to that marriage, since which time   55

    I have walked beneath myself and all my comforts,

    Like one on earth whose joys are laid above.

    And though it had been offence small in me

    To enjoy mine own, I left her pure and free.

Lord Governor. The greater and more sacred is thy blessing;   60

    For where heaven's bounty holy groundwork finds,

    'Tis like a sea encompassing chaste minds.

Enter DUCHESS.

Hermio. The Duchess comes, my lord.

Lord Governor.   Be you then all witnesses

    Of an intent most horrid.

Duchess. [Aside]   One poor night

    Ever Almachildes now.   65

    Better his meaner fortunes wept than ours

    That took the true height of a princess' spirit

    To match unto their greatness. Such lives as his

    Were only made to break the force of fate

    Ere it came at us, and receive the venom.   70

    'Tis but a usual friendship for a mistress

    To lose some forty years' life in hopeful time,

    And hazard an eternal soul for ever.

    As young as he has done, and more desertful.

Lord Governor. Madam.   75

Duchess. My lord.

Lord Governor. This is the hour that I've so long desired.

    The tumult's full appeased. Now may we both

    Exchange embraces with a fortunate arm

    And practise to make love-knots, thus.

Duchess.   My lord?   80

        [The dead figure of the] Duke is discovered.

Lord Governor. Thus, lustful woman and bold murd'ress, thus!

    Blessed powers,

    To make my loyalty and truth so happy.

    Look thee, thou shame of greatness, stain of honour;

    Behold thy work and weep before thy death,   85

    If thou be'st blessed with sorrow and a conscience,

    Which is a gift from heaven and seldom knocks

    At any murderer's breast with sounds of comfort.

    See this thy worthy and unequalled piece,

A fair encouragement for another husband.   90
Duchess. [*Kneels*.] Bestow me upon death, sir. I am guilty,
  And of a cruelty above my cause:
  His injury was too low for my revenge.
  Perform a justice that may light all others
  To noble actions. Life is hateful to me,   95
  Beholding my dead lord. Make us an one
  In death, whom marriage made one of two living
  Till cursèd fury parted us. My lord,
  I covet to be like him.
Lord Governor.   No, my sword
  Shall never stain the virgin brightness on't   100
  With blood of an adult'ress.
Duchess.   There, my lord,
  I dare my accuser and defy the world,
  Death, shame and torment. Blood I am guilty of,
  But not adultery, not the breach of honour.
Lord Governor. No? [*Calls offstage*] Come forth, Almachildes.

Enter ALMACHILDES.

Duchess. [*Aside*]   Almachildes? 105
  Hath time brought him about to save himself
  By my destruction? I am justly doomed.
Lord Governor. Do you know this woman?
Almachildes. I have known her better, sir, than at this time.
Lord Governor. But she defies you there.   110
Almachildes. That's the common trick of them all.
Duchess. Nay, since I am touched so near, before my death then,
  In right of honour's innocence, I am bold
  To call heaven and my woman here to witness.

My lord, let her speak truth, or may she perish.   115

Enter AMORETTA.

Amoretta. Then, sir, by all the hopes of a maid's comfort
            Either in faithful service or blessed marriage,
            The woman that his blinded folly knew
            Was only a hired strumpet, a professor
            Of lust and impudence, which here is ready   120
            To approve what I have spoken.
Almachildes.   A common strumpet?
            This comes of scarves; I'll nevermore wear
            An haberdasher's shop before mine eyes again.
Lord Governor. My sword is proud thou art lightened of that sin;
            Die then a murd'ress only.
Duke. [*Rising*]   Live a duchess,   125
            Better than ever loved, embraced and honoured.
Duchess. My lord!
Duke. Nay, since in honour thou canst justly rise,
            Vanish all wrongs, thy former practice dies.
            I thank thee, Almachildes, for my life,   130
            This lord for truth, and heaven for such a wife,
            Who, though her intent sinned, yet she makes amends
            With grief and honour, virtue's noblest ends.
            What grieved you then shall nevermore offend you:
            Your father's skull with honour we'll inter   135
            And give the peace due to the sepulchre.
            And in all times may this day ever prove
            A day of triumph, joy and honest love.   *Exeunt.*

Finis Actus Quinti.

176

Textual Collation

I.i.

ACT I] *Scott; Actus Primus: MS.*

Scene i] *Scott; Sce^a. Prim^a. MS.*

15. Perhaps, ... credit,] *MS subst.;* Perhaps ... credit, *Corbin & Sedge.*

23. S.D.] *Scott; E^{xt} MS.*

32.] *Corbin & Sedge add S.D. 'Noise of preparations for a banquet' before* A.

38. S.D.] *Dyce; placed after* hither *Corbin & Sedge.*

I'll ... straight] *As aside Corbin & Sedge.*

Duke's] *Dyce;* King's *MS.*

41. he's] *MS subst.* (h'as); has *Steevens*

42. fellow: ... feast-time] *Dyce;* ffellow, ... ffeast-time *MS;* fellow ... feast-time; *Steevens.*

45.1. S.D.] *So placed MS; after* comes *l. 46 Dyce.*

46. Aside] *Scott pres.; Dyce begins aside at* Alas.

48. spleen,] *MS;* spleene *Steevens.*

75.1. S.D.] *So placed MS; at l. 76.1 Dyce.*

76. S.D.] *Dyce.*

78. sir!] *Scott;* Sir? *MS.*

Almachildes!] *Scott; Almachildes? MS;* Almachildes!—*Dyce.*

87.1 S.D.] *Dyce.*

91. charms] *Steevens;* Charmes, *MS.*

96.1. S.D.] *So placed Dyce; at l. 91.1 MS. Corbin & Sedge add 'and* Attendants *with a banquet' to this S.D.*

101. much:] *This ed.;* much *MS;* much, *Steevens;* much. *Corbin & Sedge.*

111. S.D.] *Scott subst., placed after* period.

113.] *Corbin & Sedge add S.D. 'To the skull' before* Fie.

116. Marry ... that] *As aside Corbin & Sedge.*

Marry, I] *Steevens;* mary' I *MS.*

123. country; thou; that beauty] *MS subst.;* country: thou; that beauty *Scott;* country, thou, that beauty, *Dyce;* country, thou; that beauty *Corbin & Sedge.*

125. S.D.] *Corbin & Sedge.*

126. *Aside] Corbin & Sedge.*

127. fate] *MS;* face *Steevens.*

132. S.D.] *Scott, placed before* Sir *l. 131; placed as in this ed. Dyce.*

133.1. S.D.] *Dyce, placed after* must *l. 134; placed as in this ed. Corbin & Sedge.*

134. *To Francesca] Corbin & Sedge.*

Aside] Scott.

137. S.D.] *Corbin & Sedge.*

138. *Aside] Dyce; Scott marks only l. 138 as aside.*

141. since] *MS;* set *or* sure *conjs. Corbin & Sedge.*

144. S.D.] *Dyce.*

149.1. *Exeunt] MS; no S.D. in Dyce.*

all but GASPERO] *Corbin & Sedge.*

150. S.D.] *MS; Exeunt Dyce.*

I.ii.

Scene ii] *Scott; Sce^a. 2^a. MS.*

0.1-2. *Enter ... fitting] MS;* 'Hoppo, Stadlin' *added to MS S.D. Scott;* 'Enter Hecate' *Dyce.*

8. Hellwain] *Scott;* Hellwin *MS.*

Puckle] *Dyce;* Prickle *MS.*

9. S.D.] *Dyce.*

10. S.D.] *Dyce.*

11. seeton] *MS;* suet *conj. Scott;* seething *Dyce.*

12. S.D.] *Dyce.*

17.] *Dyce, who adds 'with a dish'.*

18. There,] *Scott;* there *MS.*

18.] *Dyce adds S.D. 'Giving the dead body of a child' after* brat.

21. air,] *MS;* air. *Scott.*

22. o'er] *Corbin & Sedge, conj. Greg & Wilson;* or *MS;* on *Steevens.*

31-2. incubus? ... Stadlin?] *MS;* Incubus; ... Stadlin. *Scott.*

33. Whelpley's] *This ed.;* Wlelplies *MS;* Whelplies *Steevens;* Whelply's *Scott;* Whelplie's *Dyce.*

40. *eleoselinum* lately,] *Dyce; Eleoselinum* lately *MS;* Eleoselinum—lately *Steevens.*

41. *populeas] Dyce; Populeus MS.*

42. black] *Steevens;* back *MS.*

43. *acarum] Dyce subst.; Acharum MS.*

44. *Pentaphyllon] Dyce; Dentaphillon MS.*

45. *somniferum] This ed.; Somnificum MS.*

46. Hecate?] *MS;* Hecate. *Dyce.*

50. S.D.] *Dyce.*

54. charmings] *MS;* churnings *Steevens.*

61. soap] *MS;* soupe *Steevens;* sup *Dyce;* sop *Corbin & Sedge.*

62. those] *MS;* these *Steevens.*

64. dewed-skirted] *MS;* dew-skirted *Dyce.*

68. S.D.] *So placed MS; at l. 67.1 Steevens.*

69.] *Dyce adds S.D. 'Gives dish' after* ware.

84. portion] *MS;* potion *conj. Corbin & Sedge.*

86. nineteen,] *MS subst.;* nineteen *Dyce.*

87. *Aside*] *Scott.*

91. villainy.] *Steevens;* Villany? *MS.*

92. *Aside*] *Scott.*

villain] *MS;* 'Villainie *is a possible reading' Greg & Wilson.*

101. all, ... that.] *MS subst.;* all; ... that *Ellis.*

106.1. S.D.] *So placed MS; at l. 109.1 Dyce.*

107. S.D.] *Scott subst.;* 'Kneels' *Corbin & Sedge.*

Silens,] *Greg & Wilson;* Silence. *MS;* silence! *Scott;* Sylvans, *Dyce.*

111. *Aside*] *Scott pres.*

113. religious] *MS;* religion's *Steevens.*

117. wretched] *MS;* th'wretched'st *conj. Greg & Wilson.*

123. S.D.] *Scott pres.*

127. mile] *MS;* mile, *Steevens.*

129. as] *Dyce;* and *MS.*

160.1. S.D.] *Corbin & Sedge subst.;* 'Giving serpent-skins, &c. to *Sebastian'*

Dyce.

182. *Aside*] *Dyce.*

grant you, ... powers,] *MS subst.;* grant, you ... powers *Dyce;* graunt (you ... Powres,) *conj. Greg & Wilson.*

186.1. S.D.] *Scott.*

196.1. S.D.] *So placed Scott; in right-hand margin, linked by a dash to white space above line (*Coverd ... (Mother)*) MS; after* be *l. 196 Steevens.*

200. *Aside*] *Dyce.*

213. sea-lamprey] *Dyce;* Stalamprey *MS.*

218. *Aside*] *Dyce.*

223.] *Dyce adds S.D. 'Gives marchpane' after* you.

224. me.] *MS;* me? *Bullen.*

225.] *Dyce adds S.D. 'Gives other pieces of marchpane' after* son.

235.1-2. S.D.] *MS;* 'MALKIN, *a* Spirit *like' added to this S.D. after 'enter'* Corbin & Sedge.

236. Fiddle?] *MS;* Fidle's *Steevens.*

237. fox-skin?] *MS;* fox-skin. *Steevens.*

238.1. Come] *MS;* come, *Dyce.*

all but FIRESTONE] *Dyce subst.*

II.i.

ACT II] *Scott;* Actus Secundus. *MS.*

Scene i] *Scott;* Sce^a. pri^a. *MS.*

1. sir.] *MS;* Sir, *Steevens.*

11.] *S.H.* 'An.' *erased in MS.*

28. brother lately?] *The two words are separated in the MS by two dashes,*

between which two letters have been erased, and the query mark falls within the second word (Brother— —latel?y); Drees & de Vocht suggest —of—late? as the original reading.

46. once] *MS;* our *Steevens.*

62. *Aside] Scott.*

95. *Aside] Scott.*

98. *Aside] Scott; Dyce begins aside at* But *(misreading of MS* And) *l. 99.*

104. *Aside] This ed.; Scott begins aside at* I'm *l. 106.*

107. *Aside] Dyce; Scott begins aside at* I'll.

108-9. sir— ... opinion— ... way— ... sir,] *This ed.;* Sir, ... opinion, ... way, ... (Sir) *MS;* sir, ... opinion, ... way; ... sir, *Scott;* sir,— ... opinion, ... way, ... sir: *Dyce.*

113. *Aside] Dyce.*

120. *Aside] Scott.*

126. S.D.] *Scott.*

135. S.D.] *Scott; placed after* reward.

137. *Aside] Dyce.*

139. *Enter* ABBERZANES] *So placed Scott; in right-hand margin, linked by a dash to white space above l. 139 (that ... comes) MS; at l. 138.1 Steevens; at l. 141.1 Dyce.*

and Servants] *Scott subst.; Dyce adds 'carrying baked meats and bottles' to this S.D.*

142. into th'] *Steevens;* into'th' *MS.*

143. sir?] *MS;* sir— *Dyce.*

145. S.D.] *Dyce.*

150. *Aside] Scott pres.*

160. *Aside] Dyce.*

To ... Abberzanes] *Scott pres.*

163. *To Francesca*] *Corbin & Sedge subst.*

To Abberzanes] *Corbin & Sedge subst.*

163.1. S.D.] *So placed MS; after* thee *l. 163 Steevens.*

disguised] *Scott, who adds 'as a Servant'; Corbin & Sedge add 'as* CELIO' *to this S.D.*

165. service,] *MS;* service; *Scott.*

167. S.D.] *Dyce pres.*

168. sir,] *MS;* sir; *Scott.*

170. letter, ... seems] *MS;* letter, ... seems, *Steevens.*

171. S.D.] *Dyce subst.*

174. *Antonio*] *Scott; no S.H. in MS.*

Reads the] *Scott subst.*

179. *To Francesca*] *Corbin & Sedge.*

Now?] *MS;* Now, *Scott.*

To Abberzanes] *Corbin & Sedge subst.*

182. *Aside*] *Dyce.*

183. good speed send] *Steevens;* good-speed'send *MS.*

189. to th'] *Steevens;* to'th' *MS.*

198. into] *MS;* unto *Dyce.*

199. at heart] *Steevens;* at'hart *MS.*

199.] *Steevens adds S.D. 'Exit' after* heart.

200. *To Francesca*] *Dyce pres.*

Exeunt] *So placed MS; after* heart *l. 199 Scott.*

ANTONIO, ISABELLA] *Scott subst.*

and Gentleman] *Dyce.*

205.1. ABBERZANES *and* FRANCESCA] *Scott.*

206. he's no] *Steevens subst.* (h'as no); ha's no *MS;* he's not *Scott;* has no *Dyce.*

213. rage,] *MS;* rage *Dyce.*

224.1.] *MS; Dyce adds 'attended by Gentlemen' to subst. this S.D.; Corbin & Sedge add 'with* Attendants. SEBASTIAN *retires' to this S.D.*

228.] *Corbin & Sedge add 'Exeunt all but* SEBASTIAN' *after* enter.

229. I ha'] *Steevens;* I'ha' *MS.*

229.1. S.D.] *Scott; 'Exit' Corbin & Sedge.*

II.ii.

Scene ii] *Scott; Sce^a. 2^a. MS.*

8. S.D.] *This ed.; 'Pulls out the charm' placed after l. 7 Scott; 'Takes from his pocket a ribbon' Dyce.*

9. wound about] *MS;* roound-about *Steevens.*

11.] *Scott adds S.D.* 'Reads' *before 'Necte'.*

12. Amoretta] *Steevens; Amoretta (possibly as Latin as in previous line) MS.*

29. hithermost] *Dyce;* hethermost *MS;* nethermost *Corbin & Sedge.*

33. ribbon?] *MS;* ribbon, *Dyce.*

35. S.D.] *So placed Scott; in right-hand margin, linked by a dash to l. 34 MS; at l. 34.1 Steevens; at l. 35.1 Dyce.*

38. S.D.] *Scott subst.*

41. *Thrusts ... dress] This ed.; 'As he embraces her, he thrusts the ribbon into her bosom' Dyce.*

Aside] Scott.

42. court.] *MS;* court? *Ellis.*

46. better,] *Steevens;* better: *MS.*

48-9. well. ... heart,] *Steevens;* well ... hart; *MS.*

55.1. S.D.] *In right-hand margin next to l. 55 without dash.*

56. *Aside] Dyce.*

65. S.D.] *Scott pres.*

him yet?] *Steevens;* him, yet *MS.*

71. Good] *MS;* Good, *Steevens.*

72-3. A ... too] *As aside Scott pres.*

72. entertainment I] *Question mark erased between these two words in MS.*

74.] *Close parentheses mark erased after* one, *then written again in MS.*

80-1. if ... long] *As aside Scott pres.*

82. *Aside] Scott pres.*

The ... floor] *Dyce subst.;* 'She drops the charm' *Scott, placed at l. 81.1; so placed this ed.*

83. love-token?] *Dyce;* Love-token. *MS.*

83.] *Corbin & Sedge add S.D.* 'Picks up ribbon' *after* love-token.

84-5. Nay ... desertless] *As aside Scott.*

85. *Aside] Scott.*

now] *Dyce;* now? *MS.*

107. has't not] *Steevens;* ha'st-not *MS.*

114. *Exit] So placed MS; after* be *l. 118 Scott.*

Enter ALMACHLDES] *So placed MS; at l. 117.1 Dyce; after* be *l. 118 Corbin & Sedge.*

119. *Aside] Dyce.*

120. in't, ... think.] *Steevens subst.;* in't: ... thinck: *MS.*

121. *Aside*] *Dyce.*

123. Amoretta?] *MS;* Amoretta,— *Scott.*

125. ruled] *Scott;* rude *MS.*

126. somewhat, ... comfort.] *Steevens;* somewhat: ... Comfort: *MS;* somewhat; ... comfort *Ellis.*

II.iii.

Scene iii] *Scott;* Ṣce*ᵃ*. *3ᵃ*. *MS.*

0.1. *with a baby*] *Scott subst.*

4.1. S.D.] *Scott.*

6. sides,] *MS;* sides *Dyce.*

8-9. him— ... fashion. ... 'twas] *MS subst.* (him: ... fashion: ... 'twas); him. ... fashion ... 'twas, *Scott.*

13. up] *MS;* up, *Steevens.*

17. on] *Steevens;* one *MS.*

21-2. certain. ... cleanly;] *MS subst.;* certain, ... cleanly, *Corbin & Sedge.*

21. 'Give] *MS;* Give *Scott.*

22.1. S.D.] *So placed MS; after* day *l. 23 Corbin & Sedge.*

31. S.D.] *Corbin & Sedge.*

32. now— ... myself—] *Dyce;* now: ... myself, *MS.*

46. with' least] *MS subst.* (with'least); with 'least *Steevens;* with th' least *Scott;* with least *Dyce.*

49.1. S.D.] *Scott.*

III.i.

ACT III] *Scott; Actus Tercius MS.*

Scene i] *Scott; Sce^a. pri^a. MS.*

1-2. born ... men?] *MS;* born ... men! *Scott;* born? ... men! *Ellis.*

10.] *Corbin & Sedge add S.D. 'Attempts to free himself' after* too.

15. sure] *MS;* sure, *Dyce.*

15.1. S.D.] *Scott subst. ('Unbinds his eyes').*

16. Say,] *MS;* Say *Corbin & Sedge.*

21. to] *Steevens;* to. *MS.*

25. into] *MS;* unto *Dyce.*

actions wit and courage,] *Steevens;* Actions, Wit, and Courage *MS.*

33. women,] *MS;* women *Ellis.*

35. pleasure] *Steevens;* pleasure, *MS.*

39.] *'Enter Gaspero' erased in right-hand margin, linked by a dash to l. 39 (for ... me-thincks) MS.*

50. S.D.] *Corbin & Sedge, placed after* thee *l. 51.*

III.ii.

Scene ii] *Scott; Sce^a. 2^a. MS.*

12.1. S.D.] *MS; Corbin & Sedge add 'as* CELIO' *to thi S.D.*

14. S.D.] *Scott.*

22. city-tuck] *MS;* city-truck *conj. Bullen.*

28.1. S.D.] *So placed MS; at l. 27.1 Steevens.*

29.] *Corbin & Sedge add S.D. 'To Gaspero' before* Well.

saying—] *Scott;* saying *MS;* saying, *Steevens.*

30. What?] *MS;* What, *Corbin & Sedge.*

31. gentlewoman.] *Steevens;* Gentlewoman *MS;* gentlewoman? *Corbin & Sedge.*

33. Come, come,] *Steevens;* Come: come, *MS;* Come, come: *Scott.*

37. Rutneys] *MS;* Rutney's *Scott.*

42. think] *MS;* think, *Scott.*

45. *Aside] Scott.*

46. S.D.] *MS; Dyce adds 'with a letter' to this S.D.*

47. lighted.] *This ed.;* lighted: *MS;* lighted! *Dyce.*

48. *Aside] Dyce.*

on't!] *Scott;* on't *MS;* on't, *Corbin & Sedge.*

49.1. SEBASTIAN *and* GASPERO] *Scott.*

55-6. herself— ... it—] *Scott subst.;* herself. ... it; *MS.*

61. S.D.] *So placed Scott; in text at bottom of page below l. 59 MS; at l. 59.1 Steevens.*

news?] *MS;* news. *Bullen.*

64. S.D.] *Scott.*

65. confusion,] *Dyce;* Confusion *MS.*

73. S.D.] *So placed Scott; in right-hand margin linked by a dash to end of l. 72 MS; at l. 72.1 Steevens; at l. 73.1 Dyce.*

75. *Aside] Scott.*

90. And ... hanged] *As aside Dyce.*

93. S.D.] *Dyce subst.; 'Showing the letter' Scott.*

102. still,] *MS;* still *Dyce.*

114. fine] *Steevens;* five *MS.*

114.] *Corbin & Sedge add S.D. 'Addressing the letter' before* Why.

121. likely,] *MS;* likely *Corbin & Sedge.*

124. days, ... it;] *This ed.;* daies; ... it *MS;* daies; ... it. *Steevens;* days— ... it— *Dyce.*

129. means. ... fortune,] *Corbin & Sedge;* means: ... fortune; *MS;* means: ... fortune! *Steevens.*

134. I ... house] *Dyce;* I ... house, *MS;* I, ... house, *Corbin & Sedge.*

143. Not within] not' within *MS.*

149. hither,] *MS;* hither; *Scott.*

154-5. sooner. ... amends,] *Steevens;* sooner ... amends, *MS;* sooner, ... amends; *Corbin & Sedge.*

159. still,] *Steevens;* still *MS.*

165.1. S.D.] *Dyce subst.;* 'They whisper' *Scott.*

165.2. S.D.] *So placed MS; after* have *l. 165 Steevens; after* herself *l. 167 Dyce.*

169. sir?] *MS;* sir, *Dyce.*

178. S.D.] *So placed MS;* 'Exit Antonio' *placed after* sir *l. 179 Dyce.*

178.1. S.D.] *So placed MS; after* sir *l. 179 Steevens. Corbin & Sedge add* 'as CELIO' *to this S.D.*

179. *Exit* FRANCESCA] *Scott, placed at end of l. 166; after* herself *l. 167 Dyce.*

Aside] *Scott pres.*

193-4. country, ... truth.] *Corbin & Sedge;* Cuntry, ... truth, *MS;* cuntry: ... truth, *Steevens.*

197. gentleman,] *MS;* gentleman *Steevens.*

209. on't? ... fixed,] *MS;* on't; ... fixed; *Ellis.*

220. that] *Steevens;* that. *MS.*

230. this,] *MS;* this *Corbin & Sedge.*

III.iii.

Scene iii] *Scott; Sce^a. 3^a. MS.*

0.1. *two]* This ed.*; 'Stadlin, Hoppo, *and other' Scott;* 'STADLIN, HOPPO, three other' *Corbin & Sedge.*

and FIRESTONE] *MS;* 'Enter Firestone' *Scott, placed at l. 14.1;* 'Firestone in the back-ground' *Dyce;* 'carrying eggs, herbs, etc.' *added to this S.D. Corbin & Sedge.*

9. still;] *Steevens subst.;* still *MS.*

11. you,] *MS;* you *Scott.*

14.1. S.D.] *This ed.;* 'They ascend' *Scott;* 'Exeunt all the Witches except Hecate' *Dyce.*

21. *Aside] Dyce.*

24. lizard's] *Corbin & Sedge*; lizards *MS.*

28. S.H.] *So placed Greg & Wilson; to left of text between lines* heer's ... thee / My ... sure *MS; before* Here's *Steevens.*

34. *Aside] Scott.*

35.] *Corbin & Sedge add S.D.* 'Music in the air' *after* quickly.

38. they] *MS; omitted Scott;* there *Corbin & Sedge.*

38.1. *Song] So placed Scott; before* Come *l. 39 MS.*

39. S.D.] *MS, placed to right of text between ll. 39-40, linked by a brace to ll. 39-40;* 'above' *added to this S.D. and placed at l. 38.2 Scott;* 'above' *added after* 'Song' *Dyce;* 'Voice. Above' *Ellis;* 'Voices' *added before this S.D. Corbin & Sedge.*

45. S.D.] *MS, placed to immeditate right of and linked by a brace to l. 45;* 'Above' *placed as in this ed. Scott;* 'Voice above' *Dyce;* 'Voice' *added before this S.D. Corbin & Sedge.*

46. S.H.] *Scott.*

47. S.D.] *MS, placed to right of text at l. 49, linked by a brace to ll. 48-50; to right of text between ll. 48-9, linked by a brace to ll. 47-50 Steevens; 'Above' placed as in this ed. Scott; 'Voice above' Dyce; 'Voices' added before this S.D. Corbin & Sedge.*

51.] *Corbin & Sedge add S.D. 'HECATE anoints herself' after* mount.

52. Above] *MS, placed to right of text at l. 53, linked by a brace to ll. 52-4; placed as in this ed. Scott; 'Voice above' Dyce; 'MALKIN' added before this S.D. Corbin & Sedge.*

52.1. A ... descends] *So placed this ed.; two lines (A ... like / a ... descends) to left of text at ll. 53-4, linked by a brace to white space between ll. 53-4 MS; after l. 51 Steevens; after l. 53 Corbin & Sedge.*

56. good.] *MS;* good? *Scott.*

59. S.H.] *Scott;* 'Malkin' *Corbin & Sedge.*

62.] *Corbin & Sedge add S.D. 'MALKIN sings' after* flight.

63. hark,] *MS;* hark? *Corbin & Sedge.*

65. S.D.] *MS; 'Ascending with the Spirit' Scott; 'with MALKIN' added to this S.D. Corbin & Sedge.*

70. kiss.] *MS subst.(;);* kiss *Bullen.*

73. steep] *MS;* steeples, *Ellis, conj. Dyce.*

79. S.D.] *MS, placed to immediate right of l. 79, linked by a brace to l. 79; placed as in this ed. Scott; 'Voices' added before this S.D. Dyce.*

IV.i.

ACT IV] *Scott;* Actus Quartus. *MS.*

Scene i] *Scott;* Sce^a. pri^a. *MS.*

12. her as] *MS;* her, as *Dyce.*

21.1. S.D.] *So placed Steevens; in right-hand margin at top of MS page, linked by a dash to white space above l. 22.*

26. *Aside*] *Dyce.*

32. shame, ... is,] *MS;* shame ... is *Corbin & Sedge.*

41. *Aside*] *Dyce.*

43. I have been] *Steevens;* I haue'byn *MS;* I'haue byn *conj. Greg & Wilson.*

46. aim's] *Steevens;* Aymes *MS.*

50. multitudes] *MS;* multitudes, *Steevens;*

51. misdeeds] *Dyce;* Misse-deedes, *MS.*

glory,] *Steevens;* Glory. *MS.*

52.1. S.D.] *So placed MS; at l. 55 after* come *Dyce.*

attended] *Dyce, who adds 'by Gentlemen'.*

53.] *Scott adds S.D. 'Speaking within' before* Return.

55. S.D.] *Dyce, subst.*

81. kiss,] *MS;* kisse *Steevens.*

S.D.] *Corbin & Sedge.*

81.] '—*Exit' erased after* sir *MS.*

82. *Aside*] *Scott.*

88.] *The word* horro^r *crossed out after* of *MS.*

IV.ii.

Scene ii] *Scott;* Sce^a. 2^a. *MS.*

1. love] *Steevens;* Love. *MS.*

15. form,] *MS;* form *Corbin & Sedge.*

20.1. S.D.] *So placed MS; after* friend *l. 22 Scott.*

29.] *Corbin & Sedge add S.D. 'To Florida' before* Hark.

36.] *Dyce adds S.D. 'Giving keys' after* keys.

37. Aside] *Scott pres.*

43. S.D.] *This ed.; 'To her' Corbin & Sedge.*

53. S.D.] *Scott.*

55. now:] *Steevens poss. (now,); Dyce subst. (now;); now* MS.

57.] *Corbin & Sedge add 'Embracing* FERNANDO' *before* Best.

59. feel] MS; feede *or* fill *conj. Greg & Wilson;* feed *Corbin & Sedge.*

65.1. S.D.] *Dyce; 'Knocking at the door' Scott.*

67.1. S.D.] *Scott; placed at end of l. 66 Dyce.*

67.2. S.D.] *So placed Steevens; in text and right-hand margin, linked by a dash to white space between l. 67 and l. 68 (by ... Sir)* MS.

69. Aside] *Scott.*

70. sir.] *Steevens;* Sir.— *MS.*

Whispers to him] Scott subst.

81. Aside] *Dyce.*

84. world;] *MS subst. (world,);* world *Ellis.*

86. Why,] *Scott;* why? *MS.*

90. care,] *MS;* care *Dyce.*

much.] *MS;* much, *Steevens.*

91. Aside] *Dyce.*

94.1. FERNANDO *and* ISABELLA] *Dyce subst.; 'Exit' Steevens.*

94.2.] *MS; Corbin & Sedge add 'as* Celio' *to this S.D.*

98. better.] *Steevens;* better, *MS.*

104.] *A two-letter word, possibly* me, *crossed out after* avail *MS.*

112, 113.] *S.H. 'Seb.' altered from 'Fer.' MS.*

112. madam.] *MS;* madam? *Scott.*

116.] *'S' altered from 'F' in S.H. 'Seb.' MS.*

123. *Aside] Corbin & Sedge.*

IV.iii.

Scene iii] *Scott; Sce^a. 3^a. MS.*

0.1. *in her chamber] MS;* 'above' *Scott;* omitted *Bullen;* 'above' *added to this S.D. Corbin & Sedge.*

4-7. now ... own. ... cunning.] *MS subst.;* now. ...own: ... cunning. *Ellis.*

15.] *Corbin & Sedge add S.D.* 'Snoring within' *after* List.

17. maidservants] *Scott;* Maides-Servants *MS.*

19. S.D.] *This ed.;* 'Noise within' *Dyce.*

21.1. S.D.] *So placed Steevens; in right-hand margin, linked by a dash to white space above l. 22 (*What ... for*) MS; omitted Scott; at l. 26.1 Dyce. Corbin & Sedge add* 'below' *to this S.D.*

22.] *Scott adds S.D.* 'within' *before* What.

23.] *Dyce adds S.D.* 'within' *before* Who's.

Gasper?] *MS;* 'Gasper'. *Corbin & Sedge.*

25.] *Dyce adds S.D.* 'within' *before* I.

26. Ay] *Scott subst.;* I *MS.*

29. again! Gasper!] *MS subst. (*agen: *Gasper:);* agen! Gasper, *Steevens;* again, Gasper! *Corbin & Sedge.*

32.1. S.D.] *Dyce.*

34.1. S.D.] *So placed MS; at l. 33.1 Steevens. Corbin & Sedge add* 'above' *to this S.D.*

36. his] *Steevens;* her *MS (*'er *apparently written over* is' *Greg & Wilson).*

36.1. S.D.] *Scott subst., who adds 'and re-enter below'.*

37. S.D.] *Dyce.*

38. S.D.] *Scott subst., placed after l. 36.*

39.] *Dyce adds S.D. 'within' before* I'll.

40. S.H.] *MS; 'Flo.' Dyce.*

Dyce adds S.D. 'within' before Help.

41.] *Dyce adds S.D. 'within' before* I.

Exit] *Scott.*

44.1. S.D.] *Scott subst., who adds 'below'; 'Re-entering with his sword drawn' placed after* weeps *l. 46 Dyce; 'below' added after 're-entering' to Dyce S.D. Corbin & Sedge.*

45.] *Dyce adds S.D. 'within' before* There.

56. *Aside*] *Dyce.*

57-8. long; ... pain,] *Steevens subst.;* long ... paine *MS.*

63-4. you, ... brother.] *Scott subst. (*you! ... brother:*);* you ... (Brother,) *MS;* you: ... (Brother) *Steevens.*

68. ruins] *MS (*Ruynes*);* ruinous *Dyce.*

82. plot, ... cunning] *MS;* plot ... cuñing, *Steevens.*

85. truth] *Steevens, subst.;* troth' *MS.*

87. time] *Steevens;* time, *MS.*

90. me,] *MS;* me *Corbin & Sedge.*

100.] *Dyce adds S.D. 'Sheathing sword' after* up.

102.1. S.D.] *Scott; 'above' added to this S.D. and placed after* soon *l. 101 Dyce; Dyce S.D. after* alone *l. 101 Corbin & Sedge.*

103.1. S.D.] *So placed MS; after* Hermio *l. 104 Corbin & Sedge.*

104. sudden.] *MS;* sodaine, *Steevens.*

108. S.D.] *Scott.*

111. go,] *MS;* go *Dyce.*

V.i.

ACT V] *Scott; Actus Quintus. MS.*

Scene i] *Scott; Sce^a. pri^a. MS.*

0.1. ANTONIO] *Scott, conj. Steevens; Sebastian MS.*

1, 3. *Antonio] Scott subst., conj. Steevens pres.; Seb. MS.*

18. *Aside] Corbin & Sedge.*

now!] *MS subst.;* now *Ellis.*

29. S.D.] *Corbin & Sedge subst.*

30. S.D.] *Scott. So placed Corbin & Sedge; at l. 28.1 Scott; after* me *l. 32 Dyce.*

39. slave, dog, ... art,] *This ed.;* Slave: Dog: ... art *MS;* slave; dog, ... art *Steevens;* slave! Dog! ... art, *Corbin & Sedge.*

42. S.D.] *Corbin & Sedge.*

45.1. S.D.] *Scott, who adds 'with a cup'; Dyce adds 'with wine' to this S.D.*

46. *Aside] Dyce.*

47.] *Scott adds S.D. 'Exit' after* honest.

S.D.] *Scott; 'They drink' Dyce.*

50. *They drink] Corbin & Sedge.*

54.1. S.D.] *Scott.*

63. her] er *altered from* is *MS;* his *Steevens.*

68.] *Scott adds S.D. 'Enter* Hermio' *after* weighty.

70.1. S.D.] *So placed MS; after* mortally *l. 70 Steevens; after* then *l.71 Scott. Corbin & Sedge add 'wounded' to MS S.D.*

72. for't] *Steevens;* fo't *MS.*

91. S.D.] *So placed Scott; in right-hand margin, linked by a dash to white space between ll. 89-90 MS; at l. 89.1 Steevens.*

attended] Dyce, who adds 'by Gentlemen'.

96.1. S.D.] *So placed MS; after* adulterous *l. 95 Scott. Corbin & Sedge add 'wounded' to this S.D.*

113.1. S.D.] *Dyce subst.; 'She is carried off' Scott.*

114. *Lord Governor*] *Steevens subst.; no S.H. in MS.*

115. *attended] This ed.; 'with Gentlemen' Dyce.*

122. *disguised*] *Corbin & Sedge subst.*

128. Why,] *Scott;* why *MS.*

129. nothing. Madam,] *MS;* nothing, Madam? *Steevens.*

131. S.D.] *Scott.*

132.1. ISABELLA *and* HERMIO] *Scott.*

135. now, ... gross.] *Dyce subst.;* now; ... grosse *MS;* now: ... gross. *Scott.*

V.ii.

Scene ii] *Scott; Sce*ᵃ*. 3*ᵃ*. MS;* SCEᵃ. 2ᵃ. *Steevens.*

0.1. S.D.] *MS; Corbin & Sedge add 'A cauldron in the centre' to this S.D.*

3. both,] *MS;* both *Corbin & Sedge.*

8. pictures! ... tedious,] *Steevens subst.;* pictures, ... tedious *MS;* pictures, ... tedious! *Dyce.*

14. closely.] *MS;* closely? *Corbin & Sedge.*

15. cunningly.] *Steevens;* cuñingly *MS;* cunningly? *Corbin & Sedge.*

23. *tremiscere*] *Steevens; trenniscere MS.*

25. *Teque*] *MS;* Te quoque *Steevens.*

30. *Aside*] *Dyce.*

42. infants' blood] *Steevens;* Infants-Blood *MS;* infant's blood *Corbin & Sedge.*

45. S.D.] *Scott.*

49.] *Dyce adds S.D.* 'Firestone *brings the different ingredients for the charm, as* Hecate *calls for them' after* Firestone.

50.1. S.D.] *This ed.;* '*Enter* Stadlin, Hoppo, *and other Witches' at l. 51.1 Dyce; Corbin & Sedge add 'three' before 'other' to Dyce S.D.*

59.1. *About a Vessel*] *MS;* '*The Witches going about the Cauldron' Scott.*

66. Liard] *Steevens;* Liand *MS.*

73. again] *MS;* a grain *Corbin & Sedge.*

78. *All.*] *Steevens;* 'all' *written within text at beginning of line and not set off to left of text as all other S.H.s on MS page;* 'All the Witches' *Dyce.*

80. There] *MS;* There, *Steevens.*

83. *Aside*] *Dyce.*

86.1. *Here they dance*] *MS;* '*Here they daunce.' Steevens; omitted Scott.*

V.iii.

Scene iii] *Scott; Sce^a. 4^a. MS; SCE^a 3^a. Steevens.*

0.1-3. S.D.] *MS, which adds 'Hermio' after* GASPERO *(see also collation at l. 21); Dyce omits* FRANCESCA *and* ABBERZANES *from this S.D.*

SEBASTIAN] *Scott;* 'Antonio' *erased after* ISABELLA *MS.*

disguised] *Corbin & Sedge subst. ('as* CELIO').

and Servants] *Dyce.*

11. S.D.] *Corbin & Sedge.*

21. S.D.] *So placed Scott; at l. 0.2 after* GASPERO *MS.*

24. How?] *MS;* Who? *conj. Dyce.*

26. for ... lord] *MS;* for, ... lord, *Steevens.*

33. lust,] *Dyce;* Lust *MS;* lust! *Scott.*

38. S.D.] *Scott.*

39.1. S.D.] *Dyce, placed after* another *l. 42.*

43. S.D.] *Scott.*

44.1. S.D.] *Scott subst., placed at l. 43 before* Thanks; *placed as in this ed. Dyce.*

51.] *Scott adds S.D. 'Showing his wounds' after* here.

54. Urbin] *MS;* Ravenna *Corbin & Sedge.*

62.1. S.D.] *So placed MS; after* lord *l. 63 Dyce, who adds 'and* Amoretta' *to this S.D. (see also collation at l. 115.1).*

64. *Aside*] *Dyce.*

65. Ever] *MS;* Ends *Corbin & Sedge.*

65.] *lacuna after* now *conj. Dyce.*

70. us,] *MS;* us *Corbin & Sedge.*

74. done] *MS;* done['t] *Dyce.*

80.1. S.D.] *So placed MS; after* thus *Steevens.*

The ... the] *This ed.;* 'Draws a curtain, and discovers the Duke laid out as a corpse' *Scott;* 'A curtain is drawn, and the Duke discovered on a couch, as if dead' *Dyce.*

84. thee] *MS;* there *Scott.*

greatness, ... honour;] *Corbin & Sedge, subst.;* Greatnes: ... Hono^r, *MS.*

85-8. death, ... comfort.] *This ed.;* death ... Comfort *MS;* death. ... comfort, *Steevens;* death! ... comfort. *Scott;* death, ... comfort, *Corbin & Sedge.*

91. S.D.] *Corbin & Sedge, placed before* My *l. 27.*

94. Perform] *Steevens;* performes *MS.*

96. an] *MS;* as *conj. Corbin & Sedge.*

103. torment.] *Steevens subst.;* Torment, *MS.*

115.1. S.D.] *So placed MS; at l. 114.1 Scott; after* lord *l. 63 Dyce.*

125. S.D.] *Scott; Dyce adds 'and embracing her' to this S.D.*

Explanatory Notes

[Dramatis Personae]

1. *Ravenna*] The Italian setting is characteristic for both the court love intrigue of the Sebastian/Isabella/Antonio plot and for the revenge section of the Duchess/Duke/Almachildes plot. See Fredson Bowers, *Elizabethan Revenge Tragedy 1587-1642* (Princeton, 1940), pp. 47-54.

2, 13. *The Persons*] listed side by side on MS title page: see photographic reproduction, p. 88. The characters are equally divided between the sexes, which is unusual in the plays of the period.

9. fantastical] (1) foppish or showy in attire: see *O.E.D.2*, fantastic, a. and sb., A.4b; (2) impulsive, arbitrary: see *O.E.D.2*, fantastic, a. and sb., A.4b; (3) improvident: see *O.E.D.2*, fantastic, a. and sb., B.2.

17. *FRANCESCA*] close homonym of Frances Carr, an historical influence upon the play's action: see Introduction, pp. 21-3, 31 and 43.

20. *HECATE*] pronounced *Hek*-at, 'the Ancient Goddess of witchcraft ... particularly associated with the moon, and with other moon goddesses Diana, Artemis and Selene, with whom she was identified': Valiente, p. 168. The name suggests sexual excess: cf. *M.W.M.M.*, I.ii.2, 'He-cats an' courtesans stroll most i' th' night'. 'Cat' was also a cant term for a prostitute: cf. *W.B.W.*, I.ii.105-7 and n. (Revels).

[Dedication]

1. *Thomas Holmes*] not convincingly identified, but for a discussion of likely candidates see Wayne H. Phelps, 'Thomas Holmes, Esquire: The Dedicatee of Middleton's *The Witch*', *N.&Q.*, 225 (1980), pp. 152-4.

4-5. *recovered ... difficulty*] Perhaps Middleton had trouble retrieving the prompt-book from the playhouse or company who owned it.

5. *ignorantly ill-fated*] probably indicating either (1) a failure on stage, or (2) a political mistake of writing material that paralleled court scandal too closely: see Anne Lancashire, '*The Witch*: Stage Flop or Political Mistake?', in Kenneth Friedenreich, ed., "*Accompaninge the players*": *Essays Celebrating Thomas Middleton, 1580-1980* (New York, 1983), pp. 161-81, and Introduction, pp. 25-6 and 37-9.

6. *Witches ... condemned*] a reference to the act of 1604: see Introduction, p. 37.

7. *imprisoned obscurity*] perhaps an indication of supression?

I.i.

3-4. *She ... angels*] For the contract, or betrothal, to have the force that Sebastian claims for it here and throughout the play, it must have been the verbal marriage agreement between both parties known as *sponsalia per verba de praesenti,* rather than the verbal agreement known as *sponsalia per verba de futuro.* 'A *de praesenti* contract had almost the force of marriage, though the couple did not have the full legal status of husband and wife; it was indissoluble, and could annul a subsequent marriage by one of the parties, even if celebrated publicly in church and then consummated. The *de futuro* form was more conditional, and could be broken off by mutual consent, though it was made binding if the couple had intercourse.': N.W. Bawcutt, ed., William Shakespeare, *MM* (Oxford, 1991), p. 7. See also *Shakespeare's England*, pp. I, 407-8, Ernest Schanzer, 'The Marriage-Contracts in *Measure for Measure*', *Sh.S. 13* (1960), 81-9, and Karl P. Wentersdorf, 'The Marriage Contracts in *Measure for Measure*', *Sh.S. 32* (1979), 129-44. The 'pre-contract' is a favourite Middleton plot device: cf. *H.K.K.*, I.ii.142-5ff, especially II.i.6-11, *R.G.*, I.i.73-80 (Revels), and *F.Q.*, I.i.195-6. Cf. also Tourneur, *A.T.*, I.ii.99-102 (Revels) and Webster, *The*

Duchess of Malfi, I.i.478-9 and n. (Revels).

5. *remedy*] (1) cure; (2) legal redress: cf. *P.*, IV.iii.59. There is often such secondary legal meaning in Middleton; cf. *possession* l. 6.

8. *proves*] turns out to be.

fast'ning] joining in a (marriage) contract with (Antonio): see *O.E.D.*2, fasten, vb., 5b.

11. *fair-spoken*] (1) courteous; (2) smooth-tongued.

mild] gentle and conciliatory in disposition or behaviour: *O.E.D.*2, a., 1d.

12. *devil in a sheep-skin*] proverbial: cf. Tilley, W614, 'A wolf in a lamb's (sheep's) skin'.

13. *Clapped it up*] settled the marriage hastily: see *O.E.D.*2, clap, vb.[1], 13b. Cf. *M.W.M.M.*, IV.v.116, *T.C.O.O.*, III.i.241, especially II.i.281-2: 'my intent was to have clapped it [a marriage] up suddenly', and Shakespeare, *Shr*, II.i.321: 'Was ever match clapped up so suddenly?'.

14. *over-loves him*] loves him excessively.

15. *credit*] good name, honour or reputation: *O.E.D.*2, sb., 5b.

16. *Performance*] to act the part or role.

18. *You ... labour*] proverbial: Tilley, L9, 'You lose your labor'.

19. *mine*] my (unemphatic usage: see Abbott, 237).

21. *employments*] uses or purposes to which I am now devoted: see *O.E.D.*2, employments, 2b.

in] for: *O.E.D.*2, prep. 22d notes this usage only in negative sentences.

22-3. *unless ... years*] The comparison of death to sleep was commonplace: cf. Tilley, S526 and S527.

23. *these seven years*] proverbial for 'for a long time': see Tilley, Y25, 'This seven years'. The phrase occurs in well over half of the plays in the Middleton canon.

24.] probably proverbial: cf. Tilley, G450, 'That grief is light which is capable of counsel'.

can] i.e. that can: omission of the relative pronoun (Abbott, 244).

25-6. *Wrongs ... deeply*] probably proverbial: cf. Tilley, L480, 'Great love great sorrow (grief)'.

27. *sensible*] sensitive, feeling.

28. *unbelievèd*] unbelievable, incredible: *O.E.D.2*, 2.

30. *In truth*] truly, indeed.

31. *His ... life-blood*] For symptoms of love-melancholy, including sighing, see Burton, *The Anatomy of Melancholy*, Pt. 3, Sec. 2, Memb. 3.

32. *A ... too!*] Fernando's exclamation is probably a recognition of what is already on stage, not, as in Corbin & Sedge, a cue for a S.D.

banquet] 'a course of sweetmeats, fruit, and wine, served either as a separate entertainment, or as a continuation of the principal meal, but in the latter case usually in a different room': *O.E.D.2*, sb.¹, 3.

towards] at hand.

32-3. *riot ... scene*] The personification of 'riot' is an inheritance of the vice figure of the same name from earlier plays: see, for instance, *The Interlude of Youth* (Revels).

33. *still*] always, invariably.

36. *sirrah*] a term of address usually applied to men or boys, expressing contempt or assumption of authority.

37. *Prithee*] (I) pray thee.

38. *rid ... straight*] get rid of him (Fernando) immediately. The interview with Florida (ll. 52-68) requires privacy.

risen] i.e. from the main meal of the marriage-feast.

40. *less*] least.

40-1. *he ... enough*] proverbial: cf. Tilley, L163, 'He that eats least eats most' and E158, 'Enough is as good as a feast'.

41. *he's*] he has.

42. *fellow*] This is 'the customary title of address to a servant or other person of humble station' (*O.E.D.2*, sb., 10a), but because Gaspero is

referring to his social superior, Fernando, the term becomes an insult.

43. *pledged*] drunk to a health or toast which has been proposed: see *O.E.D.2*, pledge, vb., 5a.

44. *Malaga*] a white wine exported from a seaport of the same name in the south of Spain.

black-jack] a large leather jug for beer, etc. coated externally with tar.

45. *sticks ... water-rat*] possibly proverbial.

water-rat] literally, an aquatic rodent, but here, figuratively, a water-thief or pirate. This may be another impertinence because the term was used contemptuously of a sailor or boatman.

47. *grace*] 'the divine influence which operates in men to regenerate and sanctify, to inspire virtuous impulses, and to impart strength to endure trial and resist temptation': *O.E.D.2*, sb., 11b. Florida's tears do not indicate repentance for prostitution; cf. Tilley, W328, 'Whoredom and grace can never bide in one place'.

48. *spleen*] violent ill-temper, usually debilitating: cf. *Pur.*, V.iv.54, *F.Q.*, II.i.237, and *O.L.*, V.i.423.

madness] ungovernable anger: *O.E.D.2*, 3 cites 1665 as the earliest date of this usage, but see also *O.E.D.2*, mad, 5.

50. *man*] i.e. Lord Governor

52. *Why*] 'used interjectionally, before a sentence or clause ... as an expression of surprise (sometimes only momentary or slight; sometimes involving protest), either in reply to a remark or question, or on perceiving something unexpected': *O.E.D.2*, 7a.

needs not] is not necessary.

52-4. *for ... too*] Cf. Tilley, M695, 'They who marry where they do not love will love where they do not marry' (earliest recorded usage is 1658).

54. *keep*] i.e. privately as his mistress. Keeping a mistress is an indication of substantial moral weakness: cf. *R.T.*, I.iii.104 (Revels) and *C.M. in C.*, IV.i.242 (Revels).

How] 'elliptical for "How is it?" or "How say you?" and used interjectionally, the modern equivalent being "What?" or "What!"': *O.E.D.2*, adv. (sb.³), 4a.

56. *traded*] in the trade (of prostitution): see Partridge, trade, vb. and n.) and Tourneur, *A.T.*, IV.iv.29 (Revels).

60. *comfortable*] encouraging, reassuring: *O.E.D.2*, A.1.

61. *Beshrew*] curse (often, as here, used in imprecatory expressions with weakened force: see *O.E.D.2*, 3b).

miss] do without: *O.E.D.2*, vb.¹, 14c. Cf. Shakespeare, *Tmp*, I.ii.314: 'We cannot miss him. He does make our fire'.

62. *perfumers*] either (1) one engaged to fumigate rooms, or (2) one engaged in making or selling perfumes.

65. *Please you*] i.e. if it may please you (a standard courteous qualification to a request: see *O.E.D.2*, please, vb., 3c and 6b, c).

66. *venison*] The metre requires the pronunciation 'venson', which is the flesh of deer, boar, hare or any other game animal killed in the chase or by hunting and used as food.

parsnip pie] *O.E.D.2* cites this as the earliest recorded usage of the phrase: see parsnip, 3.

67. *suckets*] succades, sweetmeats of candied fruit or vegetable products.

68. *take 'em kindly*] (1) accept them pleasantly or as a kindness: see *O.E.D.2*, kindly, adv., 4a, which cites 1622 as the earliest recorded usage; (2) 'bawdy innuendo; *take it* = "to accept amorous advances"': Corbin & Sedge (presumably quoting Partridge). Cf. *T.C.O.O.*, III.i.58 and *M.D.B.W.*, III.ii.29.

69. *She's*] She has.

your] 'used more of less vaguely of something the person ... addressed may be expected to possess, or have to do with in some way' and 'often expressing contempt': *O.E.D.2*, 5 and 5b.

complement] personal accomplishment, quality.

to a tittle] to the smallest particular: see *O.E.D.2*, tittle, sb., 2b.

70-5.] The image is one of the prostitute as a rooming-house occupied by several lodgers: cf. Middleton, *M.C.*, Satire V, p. 131.

74. *Marry*] a common ejaculation of the period used as an exclamation of asseveration, surprise, indignation, etc.; originally, 'By Mary', a mild oath.

termers] those who resorted to London in term, each of the periods (usually three or four in the year) appointed for the sitting of certain courts of law, for business at a court of law, amusements, intrigues or dishonest practices: see *O.E.D.2*, term, sb., 5 and termer, 1. They were notoriously dissolute: see *F. of L.*, II.i.15-16.

75.1. severally] They obviously must meet on stage: see l. 77.

77. *fates*] in later Greek and Roman mythology, the three goddesses, Clotho, Lachesis and Atropos, supposed to determine the course of human life.

79. *I'll ... mouth*] i.e. with a kiss; proverbial: Dent, M1264.1, 'To stop one's mouth with a kiss'.

83. *maid of honour*] 'an unmarried lady, usually of noble birth, who attends upon a queen or princess': *O.E.D.2*, 1. The setting of the play demands that Amoretta attend a duchess, a rank in Ravenna equivalent to queen in England.

84. *Amsterdam*] 'It became the refuge of all sorts of Puritan sectaries, who took refuge there from the persecutions of Elizabeth's reign': Sugden, p. 17.

85. *Geneva*] 'During the Marian persecution in England many of the British Protestants emigrated to G[eneva]': Sugden, p. 216—another Protestant stronghold like Amsterdam.

85-6. *she ... Queenhithe*] a popular legend associated with Elinor, queen of Edward I: cf. the title-page of Peele, *Edward I* (1593), which promises

entertainments including 'the sinking of Queene Elinor, who sunck | *at*
Charingcross, and rose againe at Potters— | hith, now named Queenehith'.
The legend is also referred to in *A.F.Q.L.*, V.ii.33-4.

88. *venery*] the practice or pursuit of sexual pleasure.

tail] (1) end; (2) pudendum: Partridge.

89. *headstrong*] drunk (this meaning not in *O.E.D.2*).

90. *company*] i.e. the wedding-party.

90-6. *I ... Conclusions*] Witches were commonly thought to be skilled in
love charms: cf. *F. of L.*, II.iii.83-9, II.iv.130-5, *S.M.T.*, II.iii.67-8 (Revels),
and Shakespeare, *Oth*, I.iii.60-4.

91. *charms*] any material things that possess magical power, including
words, sentences, verses, chants, incantations, talismen and amulets.

tricks] sexual stratagems: Partridge, trick.

92. *fall backwards*] i.e. in a standard female position for sexual
intercourse: Partridge, and cf. Shakespeare, *Rom*, I.iii.44-5.

93. *a country house*] Malone claims that this was a specific country
house at Brentford (see Edmond Malone, ed., *The Plays and Poems of
William Shakspeare*, II (London, 1821), p. 428), but the preceding indefinite
article points to a general rather than to a specific practice.

94. *firedrake*] will-o'-the wisp. For use as image of moral entrapment
cf. Wilkins, *The Miseries of Enforced Marriage*, ed., Glenn H. Blayney
(M.S.R., Oxford, 1964 for 1963), ll. 2744-5, where Scarborrow comments
on the role of divines 'Who should be lamps to comfort out our way, / And
not like Firedrakes to lead men astray'.

94-5. *whoreson kind / Girls*] i.e. sexually willing young women
(literally, 'types of girls who will produce illegitimate sons').

95-6. *try / Conclusions*] experiment, see what will come of it: see
O.E.D.2, conclusion, 8b. Cf. *S.G.*, II.i.99 and Shakespeare, *Ham*, III.iv.179.

98. *Bacchus*] Greek god of wine.

104. *goodness*] virtue, moral excellence: a stronger meaning than current usage.

105. *So ... rightly*] If you comprehend (my actions) as you say, then you interpret (them) correctly.

106. *health*] toast drunk in a person's honour.

107. *round*] to each in turn.

110. *shrink*] refuse (to drink).

111. Produces ... skull] Skulls were popular stage properties: cf. *1H.W.*, IV.i.0.2ff, *R.T.*, I.i.0.1ff, III.v.42.1ff (Revels), Tourneur, *A.T.*, IV.iii.77ff (Revels), and Shakespeare, *Ham*, V.i.74.1ff.

full period] full stop.

112. *soldier's cup*] The skull is a spoil of war: see I.i.117-21.

115. *For*] because of: *O.E.D.2*, prep. and conj., A.21b.

117. *Our ... us*] the royal plural.

118. *trophy*] memorial of a victory in war.

120. *steel*] sword.

121. *bravely*] courageously, valiantly.

thee] i.e. the Duchess.

125. *straight*] immediately, without delay.

126. *bride-cup*] a cup or bowl handed round at a wedding: see *Shakespeare's England*, II, p. 147.

127. *the fate on't*] what it portends; literally, the fate of it. *O.E.D.2*'s earliest example of fate = portent is 1850 (fate, sb., 3c); therefore, Steevens's emendation is possible, but on't = of it (Abbott, 182), which allows the retention of the MS reading. Also cf. *N.W.N.H.*, V.i.50 and *F.Q.*, I.i.295.

129. *fails*] errs.

130. *The ... fresher*] proverbial: cf. Tilley, R176, 'As fresh as a rose'.

rose'] contraction of *rose is*: see Kökeritz, p. 278.

130-1. *the ... pleasing*] proverbial: cf. Tilley, S979, 'The rising, not the setting, sun is worshiped by most men'.

132. *first moving*] Antonio's compliment equates the royal couple to the *primum mobile*, the outermost sphere in Ptolemaic cosmology, which is responsible for the continuing movement of the universe.

134. *This'*] contraction of *This is*: see Kökeritz, p. 278.

139. *surfeits*] excesses (usually of eating and/or drinking).

141. *since*] (1) i.e. since the time he did this; (2) now (*O.E.D.*2, A.1c cites Udall as the only writer to use the word in this manner).

145. *round*] the walk or circuit performed by the watch among the sentinels of a garrison or camp, especially during the night.

150. *ne'er tossed pike*] (1) i.e. is inexperienced as a soldier (a pike is a battle weapon consisting of a long wooden shaft with a pointed head of iron or steel); (2) i.e. is sexually inexperienced (as yet, with his wife): see Partridge, pike = penis.

I.ii.

0.1. *S.D.*] The MS S.D. points to a group performance of Hecate's opening chant.

other witches] i.e. the four named in l. 8.

properties] They must include at least the body of a dead child (see l. 18) and snakes or snake-skins (see ll. 15, 158-9 and, possibly, l. 62).

habits fitting] appropriate clothing or dress.

1-7. *Titty ... devil-dam*] These lines are written in italic in the MS, as are the songs at III.iii.39-79 and V.ii.60-78, and thus probably indicate a delivery other than regular speech. They could be a formal invocation (see Corbin & Sedge, p. 222, n. 1-7), a song (see J.M. Nosworthy, *Shakespeare's Occasional Plays: Their Origin and Transmission* (London, 1965), p. 34) or a dance. If they are a song or a dance, no music has yet been found for them. Cf. Scot, p. 542: 'Now, how *Brian Darcies* he spirits and shee spirits, Tittie and Tiffin, Suckin and Pidgin, Liard and Robin, &c: his white spirits and blacke spirits, graie spirits and red spirits, diuell tode and diuell lambe, diuels cat and diuels dam, agree herewithall, or can stand consonant with the word of GOD, or true philosophie, let heauen and earth iudge.'

9. *vessel*] the cauldron, which we see again at V.i.50.1ff; cf. *Mac*, IV.i.0.1ff. For the history of the connection of the cauldron and witchcraft dating from the days of Ancient Greece, see Valiente, pp. 57-8.

10. *gallops*] boils: see *O.E.D.2*, gallop, vb.^{2}, which cites this example as earliest usage.

flames blue] a sign that spirits are present: see Opie & Tatem, p. 150 and Valiente, p. 136. Cf. V.ii.5.

11. *seeton*] (1) possibly 'a thread, piece of tape, or the like, drawn through a fold of skin so as to maintain an issue or opening for discharges, or drawn through a cavity to keep this from healing up': see *O.E.D.2*, seton, 1; (2) 'a substance presumably having the property of turning the flames more blue': Corbin & Sedge; (3) echoing 'Seyton', a character in *Macbeth*?

12. *The ... azure*] an allusion to the superstition that fairies pinched sluttish maids: cf. Shakespeare, *Wiv*, V.v.43-5.

14-16. *Send ... hour*] Cf. Scot, p. 255-6: 'But they that take vpon them to worke these mysteries and miracles, doo indeed (after rehearsall of these and such like words and charmes) take vp euen in their bare hands, those snakes and vipers, and sometimes put them about their necks, without receiuing anie hurt thereby, to the terror and astonishment of the beholders, which naturallie both feare and abhorre all serpents....

Iames Sprenger, and *Henrie Institor* affirme, that serpents and snakes, and their skins exceed all other creatures for witchcraft: in so much as witches doo vse to burie them vnder mens threshholds, either of the house or stalles, whereby barrennes is procured both to woman and beast: yea and that the verie earth and ashes of them continue to haue force of fascination.'

16. *squeeze*] presumably, a way of skinning.

17. *Why, when*] an exclamation of impatience, common in both the contested and uncontested plays in the Middleton canon: cf. *B.M.C.*,

IV.iii.25, *Y.T.*, iii.38, *Pur.*, IV.ii.118, *A.F.Q.L.*, II.iii.27, and *M.D.B.W.*, V.i.17.

18-29. *There ... everything*] Cf. Scot, p. 41: 'Then he teacheth them to make ointments of the bowels and members of children, whereby they ride in the aire, and accomplish all their desires. So as, if there be anie children vnbaptised, or not garded with the signe of the crosse, or orizons; then the witches may and doo catch them from their mothers sides in the night, or out of their cradles, or otherwise kill them with their ceremonies; and after buriall steale them out of their graues, and seeth them in a caldron, vntill their flesh be made potable. Of the thickest whereof they make ointments, whereby they ride in the aire; but the thinner potion they put into flaggons, whereof whosoeuer drinketh, obseruing certeine ceremonies, immediatlie becommeth a maister or rather a mistresse in that practise and facultie.' Also cf. quotation from Scot at I.ii.38-45n. For further description of ointments and transvection see Valiente, pp. 142-7 and Robbins, pp. 364-8 and 511-14.

21. *'nointed*] anointed.

23. *pricks*] (1) dots, ticks: *O.E.D.2*, sb., 2a; (2) small marks used in writing, such as punctuation marks: *O.E.D.2*, sb., 3a; (3) upright tapering spikes, applied to various things: *O.E.D.2*, sb., 16.

stops] (1) marks or points of punctuation; (2) full stops, periods.

25. *Like*] i.e. seem like.

26. *leek*] obsolete form of 'like': *O.E.D.2*.

29-30. *What ... incubus*] Cf. Scot, pp. 74-5: 'Howbeit *M. Mal.* proceedeth, affirming that All witches take their beginning from such filthie actions, wherein the diuell, in likenes of a prettie wench, lieth prostitute as *Succubus* to the man, and reteining his nature and seede, conueieth it vnto the witch, to whome he deliuereth it as *Incubus*.'

29. *coll*] embrace, hug.

use] copulate with: Partridge.

31. *incubus*] 'a feigned evil spirit or demon (originating in personified represenations of the nightmare), supposed to descend upon persons in their sleep, and especially to seek carnal intercourse with women': *O.E.D.*2, 1. Female incubi were also able to summon male lovers to them as here: see Valiente, pp. 197-202, particularly p. 199, which mentions this passage, and Robbins pp. 254-9.

33. *Whelpley*] a town or village in Wiltshire in the Frustfield hundred: see *Villare Anglicum: or A View of the Townes of England* (London, 1656), Z8v and J.E.B. Gover, Allan Mawer and F.M. Stenton, *The Place-Names of Wiltshire*, English Place-Name Society, XVI (Cambridge, 1939). Nothing of the town exists today beyond a farm, but it must have been fairly substantial because the remains of 'St. Leonard's Chapel' are still in evidence.

34. *black ... yellow*] a possible fashion reference to Mrs. Turner's execution in 1615? She invented the style of wearing yellow bands, which was copied by many people, including her hangman, presumably as a joke, when she was executed: see Alexander Dyce, ed., *The Works of Thomas Middleton*, III (London, 1840), p. 422, and Carew W. Hazlitt, ed., *A Select Collection of Old English Plays*, ed. Robert Dodsley, XI (London, 1875), pp. 328-9. Cf. *M.D.B.W.*, V.i.104-5, *F.Q.*, IV.iv.189, and *Wid.*, V.i.52-3. See Introduction, pp. 23-4 for discussion of the implications that this possible reference may have on dating *Witch*.

36. *mounting*] (1) time of ascending into the air; (2) time of copulating: see Partridge, mount.

38-45. *Where ... oleum*] Cf. Scot, p. 184: 'The receipt is as followeth.

R. The fat of yoong children, and seeth it with water in a brasen vessell, reseruing the thickest of that which remaineth boiled in the bottome, which they laie vp and keepe, vntill occasion serueth to vse it. They put herevnto *Eleoselinum, Aconitum, Frondes populeas*, and Soote.

Another receipt to the same purpose.

R. *Sium, acarum vulgare, pentaphyllon,* the bloud of a flitter-mouse, *solanum somniferum, & oleum.* They stampe all these togither, and then they rubbe all parts of their bodies exceedinglie, till they looke red, and be verie hot, so as the pores may be opened, and their flesh soluble and loose. They ioine herewithall either fat, or oile in steed thereof, that the force of the ointment maie the rather pearse inwardly, and so be more effectuall. By this means (saith he) in a moone light night they seeme to be carried in the aire, to feasting, singing, dansing, kissing, culling, and other acts of venerie, with such youthes as they loue and desire most....'

40. eleoselinum] water parsley or smallage; wild parsley: see Gerarde, pp. 862 and 867.

41. Aconitum] winter wolf's bane. 'This herbe is counted to be very dangerous and deadly ... for which ... there was neuer founde his antidote or remedie ... this plant is the most poisonest herbe of all others': Gerarde, p. 819.

frondes populeas] poplar leaves.

42. *black*] The 'black/back' confusion appears elsewhere in the Middleton canon: cf. *S.G.*, IV.i.123 and *O.L.*, III.ii.226, where in both cases 'black' is the original quarto reading yet 'back' seems to be required for sense. There is, however, no other example in Middleton, as here, of the phrase 'back in the mouth', but 'black in the mouth' occurs twice: *P.*, I.vi.67-70: 'the poor pipe was the last man he took leave of in this world, who fell in three pieces before him, and seemed to mourn inwardly, for it looked as black i' th' mouth as my [newly deceased] master'; *O.L.*, III.ii.46-7: '*Sim.* Now, by this hand, he's almost black i'the mouth, indeed. / *First Court.* He should die shortly, then.' In both these cases, 'black in the mouth' seems to refer to a physiological state indicating early decomposition after death. Such a meaning fits perfectly here, thus the joke is deepened beyond the obvious play on 'soot' (l. 41). Cf. also *M.D.B.W.*, V.ii.18-19.

43. sium] yellow watercress.

acarum vulgaro] presumably, *acarum vulgare*, common myrtle, but Gerarde defines *vulgaro* as asarabacca. 'The leaves draw foorth by vomit thicke, phlegmaticke, and cholericke humours, and withall mooue the belly, and in this they are more forceable, and of greater effect then the rootes themselues': p. 689.

44. Pentaphyllon] cinquefoil, five-leaved grass: Lewis and Short, *A Latin Dictionary* (Oxford, 1897).

flitter-mouse] bat.

45. Solanum somniferum] deadly nightshade or belladonna. 'It would certainly produce hallucinations, with a considerable amount of general vascular excitement': Ellis.

et oleum] and oil.

48-67. *And ... youths*] Cf. Scot, p. 8: 'And further, in tract of time the witch waxeth odious and tedious to hir neighbors; and they againe are despised and despited of hir: so as sometimes she cursseth one, and sometimes another; and that from the maister of the house, his wife, children, cattell, &c. to the little pig that lieth in the stie.'

48. *picture*] either (1) the portrait or likeness of a person, or (2) a representation in the solid, especially a statue or effigy: *O.E.D.2*, sb., 2d.

53. *barm*] 'The froth that forms on the top of fermenting malt liquors, which is used to leaven bread, and to cause fermentation in other liquors': *O.E.D.2*, sb.^{2}, 1a.

54. *charmings*] variant form of 'churnings', the agitations of milk or cream in a churn so as to make butter: see *O.E.D.2*, churn, vb.

55. *brew-locks*] (1) 'perhaps a variant of "brew-lead", a leaden vessel used in brewing': Corbin & Sedge, but see also *O.E.D.2*, brew, vb., 7; (2) perhaps the air locks which ensure a successful brewing.

batches] (1) bakings of bread; (2) quantities of dough for each baking.

forspoke] bewitched, charmed: see *O.E.D.2*, forspeak, 1.

56. *breedings*] hatchings, productions of young.

be meet with] be even or quits with, be revenged upon: see *O.E.D.2*, meet, a. and adv., A.2b.

60. *evensong*] a church service celebrated towards sunset.

62. *milch-kine*] cows kept for milking.

64. *dewed-skirted*] perhaps a sign of slovenliness: cf. *W.B.W.*, II.ii.112-14 (Revels): 'She must be neither slut nor drab, / Nor go too splay-foot with her shoes, / To make her smock lick up the dews.'

66. *syllabubs*] drinks or dishes made of milk (frequently as drawn from the cow) or cream, curdled by the admixture of wine, cider or other acid, and often sweetened and flavoured: see *O.E.D.2*, sillabub, 1.

69. *ware*] (1) goods? (2) food: this meaning is not in *O.E.D.2*, but can be derived from sb.³, 4d.

71. *twelve o'clock*] the most ominous hour of the day: cf. *R.T.*, I.iii.66-70 (Revels): 'Well, if anything / Be damn'd, it will be twelve o'clock at night, / That twelve will never 'scape; / It is the Judas of the hours, wherein / Honest salvation is betray'd to sin.'

72. *one ... dozen*] referring to a 'baker's dozen', as l. 75 makes clear.

75. *unconscionable*] unscrupulous, harsh.

76-7. *sixscore ... hundred*] Hecate is thus 117 years old.

78. *cast*] chance, opportunity: *O.E.D.2*, sb., 4.

79. *The ... eaten*] i.e. from the Tree of the Knowledge of Good and Evil in the Garden of Eden.

80. *costermonger's*] apple-seller's.

81-2. *some ... him*] (1) i.e. because, proverbially, the tailor makes the man: cf. Tilley, T23 and Shakespeare, *Lr*, II.ii.53-4. (2) The phrase contains bawdy meaning through the puns 'tail' = 'pudendum' and 'prick' = 'penis': see Hilda Hulme, 'Three Notes', *J.E.G.P.*, 57 (1958), 722-4, and Partridge, prick, n., prick, vb., and prick out.

81-2. *pricked down*] (1) noted down or recorded in writing; (2) punning on (tailor's) needle marking a name or item in a list by making a 'prick' through or against it.

83. *shed*] (1) part with (it): *O.E.D.2*, vb.¹, 1d; (2) spill (it): *O.E.D.2*, vb.¹, 5a.

84. *hour*] See ll. 16 and 37.

89. *posset*] a drink composed of hot milk curdled with ale, wine or other liquor, often with sugar, spices, etc.

92-3. *How ... straight*] probably proverbial: cf. Tilley, T110, 'Set a thief (fool) to catch a thief (fool)' and T115, 'A thief knows a thief and a wolf knows a wolf'.

93. *nosed*] keen-scented: *O.E.D.2*, 1b cites this example as earliest usage.

96. *Nightmare*] 'a female spirit or monster supposed to beset people and animals by night, settling upon them when they are asleep and producing a feeling of suffocation by its weight': *O.E.D.2*, sb., 1.

98-103. *And ... mothers*] Cf. Scot, p. 44: '*Psellus* addeth herevnto, that certeine magicall heretikes, to wit; that *Eutychians*, assemblie themselues euerie good fridaie at night; and putting out the candles, doo commit incestuous adulterie, the father with the daughter, the sister with the brother, and the sonne with the mother; and the ninth moneth they returne and are deliuered; and cutting their children in peeces, fill their pots with their bloud; then burne they the carcases, and mingle the ashes therewith, and so preserue the same for magicall purposes.' Incest in Middleton always points to moral depravity: cf. *P.*, II.iii.33-8, *R.T.*, I.ii.130-3, I.iii.56-66 (Revels), and *H.K.K.*, III.i.74-5.

100. *Make shift*] do your best, be content: see *O.E.D.2*, shift, sb., 6d.

104. *six ounces*] Mulryne suggests that 'This may have been a conventional amount': cf. *W.B.W.*, II.ii.71-2 (Revels): 'How he sweats is the foolish zeal of fatherhood / After six ounces an hour', and see n.

107-10. *Urchins ... Puckle*] Cf. Scot, p. 153: '... and they [our mothers] haue so fraied vs with bull beggars, spirits, witches, vrchens, elues, hags, fairies, satyrs, pans, faunes, sylens, kit with the cansticke, tritons, centaurs, dwarfes, giants, imps, calcars, coniurors, nymphes, changlings, *Incubus*, Robin good-fellowe, the spoorne, the mare, the man in the oke, the hell waine, the fierdrake, the puckle, Tom thombe, hob gobblin, Tom tumbler, boneles, and such other bugs, that we are afraid of our owne shadowes.... For right graue writers report, that spirits most often and speciallie take the shape of women appearing to monks, &c: and of beasts, dogs, swine, horsses, gotes, cats, haires; of fowles, as crowes, night owles, and shreeke owles; but they delight most in the likenes of snakes and dragons.'

107. *Urchins*] 'a dialect name for a hedgehog, and small bogies or pixies often took hedgehog form': Briggs, p. 420.

Elves] 'in England it was the smaller trooping faries who were called elves, and the name was particularly applied to small fairy boys', but in Scotland elves 'stole humans away, destroyed their cattle and avenged any injuries done to them': Briggs, p. 122.

Hags] (1) 'ugly old women who had given themselves to witchcraft'; (2) supernatural old women 'such as those who haunted the Fen country'; (3) giant-like old women 'who seem to have been the last shadows of a primitive nature goddess': Briggs, p. 216.

Satyrs] 'woodland gods or demons, in form partly human and partly bestial, supposed to be the companions of Bacchus': *O.E.D.*2, satyr, 1a—they were particularly lustful.

Pans] presumably followers of Pan, 'a Greek rural diety, represented as having the head, arms, and chest of a man, while his lower parts were those of a goat, of which he sometimes also bore the horns and ears': *O.E.D.*2, Pan, sb.^{2}, 1—also particularly lustful.

Fauns] rural dieties who were 'at first represented like men with horns and the tail of a goat, afterwards with goat's legs like the Satyrs, to whom they were assimilated in lustful character': *O.E.D.2*, faun, 1.

Silens] the Greek *Silini* or wood-gods; a species of satyrs: *O.E.D.2*, silen, 1.

107-8. *Kit ... candlestick*] (1) Jack-o'-lantern: *O.E.D.2*, Kit, sb.[5], cites Scot and this as the only examples of the usage; (2) will o' the wisp: Briggs, p. 254.

108. *Tritons*] 'inferior sea-deities, or imaginary sea-monsters, of semi-humna form': *O.E.D.2*, Triton[1], 1.

Centaurs] fabulous creatures 'with the head, trunk and arms of a man, joined to the body and legs of a horse': *O.E.D.2*, centaur, 1.

Dwarfs] 'stunted and grotesque figures in English fairy-lore': Briggs, p. 115.

Imps] small devils, off-shoots of Satan: Briggs, p. 232.

109. *Spoorn*] a special kind of spectre or phantom: *O.E.D.2*, which quotes Scot and this as examples.

Mare] i.e. Nightmare: see II.i.96n.

Man i'th' oak] 'a spirit supposed to inhabit an oak': *O.E.D.2*, man, sb.[1], 18 again cites Scot and this as the only examples of the usage; see also Briggs, pp. 313-14.

Hellwain] Hecate's sister witch.

110. *Firedrake*] See I.i.94n.

Puckle] (1) Hecate's sister witch; (2) a kind of bugbear: *O.E.D.2*, sb.,[1].

A ... hus] Cf. Scot, p. 244: [a charm] *'Against the toothach.* Scarifie the gums in the greefe, with the tooth of one that hath beene slaine. Otherwise: *Glabes galbat, galdes galdat.* Otherwise: *A ab hur hus*, &c.'

114. *disease*] (1) uneasiness, disquiet, trouble: *O.E.D.2*, sb., 1a.

121. *supper-time*] about 5:30 p.m.: see *Shakespeare's England*, II, p. 134.

122. *all ... suppers*] proverbial.

127. *firk*] drive, force or move sharply and suddenly off, out or up: cf. *F. of L.*, II.iv.193-4, *O.L.*, II.i.258, and *G. of C.*, III.i.380.

a thousand mile] proverbial for 'an extreme distance': cf. *Pur.*, III.ii.89-90 and *R.T.*, IV.iii.16 (Revels).

128. *ointments*] See Scot quotation at I.ii.18-29n.

131. *bravely*] excellently, well: *O.E.D.*2, 3.

sworn] i.e. in the compact with the Devil: cf. Scot, p. 40: '... the diuell exhorteth them to obserue their fidelitie vnto him, promising them long life and prosperitie'. See also Introduction, p. 35.

135-50. *Is't ... ground*] Cf. Scot, p. 222: 'It is constantlie affirmed in *M. Mal.* that *Stafus* vsed alwaies to hide himselfe in a monshoall, and had a disciple called *Hoppo*, who made *Stadlin* a maister witch, and could all when they list inuisiblie transferre the third part of their neighbours doong, hay, corne, &c: into their owne ground, make haile, tempests, and flouds, with thunder and lightning; and kill children, cattell, &c: reueale things hidden, and many other tricks, when and where they list.'

135. *confound*] defeat, overthrow.

138. *barks*] any small sailing vessels.

139. Anno Domini] literally, in the year of (our) Lord, and here indicating the date of building.

142. *chambered*] shut up, enclosed: see *O.E.D.*2, chamber, vb., 1.

154. *starve up generation*] destroy the process of procreation.

159. *serpents*] Christian icons of evil: see Introduction, pp. 57-8.

160-4. *So ... duty*] Cf. Scot, p. 223: '... yea men and women themselues are by their [witches'] imprecations so afflicted with externall and inward paines and diseases, that men cannot beeget, nor women bring foorth anie children, nor yet accomplish the dutie of wedlocke, denieng the faith which they in baptisme professed, to the destruction of their owne soules, &c.' Cf. also Scot, p. 77: 'They also affirme, that the vertue of generation is impeached by witches, both inwardlie, and outwardlie: for intrinsecallie they represse the courage, and they stop the passage of the mans seed, so as it may not descend to the vessels of generation: also they hurt extrinsecallie, with images, hearbs, &c.'

161. *knots*] traditionally hindered conception: see Opie & Tatem, p. 221.

164-8. *I ... way*] Cf. Scot, p. 117: '*Pythagoras* and *Democritus* giue vs the names of a great manie magicall hearbs and stones, whereof now, both the vertue, and the things themselues also are vnknowne: as *Marmaritin*, whereby spirits might be raised: *Archimedon*, which would make one bewraie in his sleepe, all the secrets in his heart: *Adincantida*, *Calicia*, *Meuais*, *Chirocineta*, &c: which had all their seuerall vertues, or rather poisons. But all these now are worne out of knowledge: marrie in their steed we haue hogs turd and cheruill, as the onelie thing whereby our witches worke miracles.'

167. *sort*] end in coming or leading to a specified result.

168-72. *More ... sunset*] Cf. Scot, p. 124: 'Besides these, manie other follies there be to this purpose proposed to the simple; as namelie the garments of the dead, candels that burne before a dead corps, and needels wherwith dead bodies are sowne or sockt into their sheetes: and diuerse other things, which for the reuerence of the reader, and in respect of the vncleane speach to be vsed in the description thereof, I omit...'.

168. *instance*] cite as an example in illustration or proof.

170. *socks up*] sews a corpse into a shroud: *O.E.D.2*, vb.[1], cites this as an example of the usage.

171. *privy gristle*] penis?: not in *O.E.D.2*. '"A privy gristle", etc., as given by Middleton, was, I presume, one of the things which, "for the reverence of the reader", Scot omits, though whence the former got it I know not': Brinsley Nicholson, ed., *The Discoverie of Witchcraft*, by Reginald Scot (London, 1886), p. 550. Cf. *M.W.M.M.*, III.ii.82-5: ''tis but a surfeit of gristles: — — ha, ha, I have fitted her: an old knight and a cock a' th' game still: I have not spurs for nothing, I see', and, possibly, *N.W.N.H.*, I.i.244.

See also I.ii.168-72n above.

176-80. *Well ... disjoint*] Cf. Scot, pp. 283-4: 'If all this will not serue, then set *Iobs* patience before your eies. And neuer thinke that a poore old woman can alter supernaturallie the notable course, which God hath appointed among his creatures.'

176. *jars*] discords.

178. *scurf*] (1) a morbid condition of the skin, especially of the head, characterized by the separation of branny scales, without inflamation; (2) any incrustation upon the surface of a body, a scab.

our master] i.e. the Devil.

179. *patient miracle*] i.e. Job.

182. *dispose*] control, direct.

186. *first oath*] See I.ii.131n[2].

188. *bravest*] fineliest dressed, most handsome.

189. *fineliest*] (1) most completely: see *O.E.D.*2, finely, 1; (2) most splendidly: see *O.E.D.*2, finely, 6a.

190. *pipkin*] a small earthenware or metal pot or pan, used chiefly in cookery.

191. *tumbling-cast*] somersault, fall: *O.E.D.*2, tumbling-, and see I.ii.199n[2].

191-2. *struck up ... heels*] (1) tripped; cf. *R.G.*, II.i.368 (Revels); (2) i.e. in conventional female position for sexual intercourse. Mulholland notes that 'Wanton behaviour in women is frequently associated with light heels': *R.G.*, IV.ii.83n (Revels); cf. *1H.W.*, I.ii.20 and *C.M. in C.*, III.ii.187-8 (Revels).

193. *Hoyday*] obsolete form of 'heydey', 'an exclamation denoting frolicsomeness, gaiety, surprise, wonder, etc.': *O.E.D.*2, hey-day, heyday, int. Both forms are common throughout the Middleton canon.

195. *honesty*] (1) respectability; (2) reputation; (3) sexual virtue: Partridge; (4) chastity.

196. *covered*] (1) clothed; (2) i.e. as a stallion copulates with a mare: see *O.E.D.2*, vb.¹, 6a; cf. *Oth*, I.i.113.

199. *flat*] dull, uninteresting, lifeless.

tumblers] copulators: cf. *C.M. in C.*, I.ii.68 (Revels), *O.L.*, II.ii.43, and *W.B.W.*, IV.ii.106 and n. (Revels), where Mulryne quotes Shakespeare, *Ham*, IV.v.60-3 to support 'tumble' = 'copulate'.

202. *incubus*] See I.ii.31n.

203. *Goody*] goodwife: a term of civility formerly applied to a (married) woman in humble life. Cf. *R.G.*, II.i.237 (Revels) for similar ironic usage.

206-16. *Thou ... pismires*] Cf. Scot, p. 124: 'The toies, which are said to procure loue, and are exhibited in their poison loouing cups, are these: the haire growing in the nethermost part of a woolues taile, a woolues yard, a little fish called *Remora*, the braine of a cat, of a newt, or of a lizzard: the bone of a greene frog, the flesh thereof being consumed with pismers or ants; the left bone whereof ingendereth (as they saie) loue; the bone on the right side, hate.'

207. *thou'rt ... think*] proverbial: Tilley, W585, 'I think you are a witch [A comment made on a good guess, or the like ...]'.

211. *remora*] 'the sucking-fish (*Echeneis remora*), believed by the ancients to have the power of staying the course of any ship to which it attached itself: *O.E.D.2*, 1.

212. *suck-stone*] sucking fish: see *O.E.D.2*, suck-

213. *sea-lamprey*] (1) same as remora: see *O.E.D.2*, sea, 23d, sea-lamprey, a.; (2) a marine lamprey *Petromyzon marinus*: see *O.E.D.2*, sea, 23d, sea-lamprey, b.; (3) possibly 'penis'; cf. *The Duchess of Malfi*, I.i.336-7 (Revels): 'And women like that part which, like the lamprey, / Hath ne'er a bone in't'.

216. *pismires*] ants.

217. *Pismires ... chamber-pot*] The humour rests upon the pun, 'piss' = 'to urinate'.

223. *toad*] appropriate gift because (1) toads were often familiars of witches: see Valiente, p. 124-5; (2) toads were proverbially poisonous: see Tilley, T360, 'Full as a toad of poison'; cf. *R.G.*, III.iii.161-2 (Revels) and *G. at C.*, IV.ii.76.

marchpane] marzipan, a paste of pounded almonds, sugar, etc., made into cakes, etc. Mulryne points out that '"Marchpane" is a native English form, "marzipan" a German introduction'; he also gives a contemporary recipe: *W.B.W.*, III.ii.189n^2 (Revels).

224. *fitted*] (1) supplied or provided with what is suitable or necessary: see *O.E.D.2*, fit, vb.^{1}, 11; (2) i.e. displayed an aptitude for love-making: see Partridge, fitness; (to) fit. See also III.ii.140n.

225. *paddock-brood*] toad or frog offspring.

226. *handkercher*] variant form of handkerchief. For the practice of using handkerchiefs to pocket edible delicacies, cf. *W.B.W.*, III.ii.186-7 (Revels): 'I'll step but up, and fetch two handkerchiefs / To pocket up some sweetmeats', and *C.M. in C.*, III.ii.50-4 (Revels). Parker also quotes John Taylor, 'The Prayse of Cleane Linen', *Works* (London, 1630), p. 168: 'At Christening-banquets & at funerals, / At Weddings (Comfit-makers festivals) / A *Handkerchiefe* doth filch most manifold, / And shake & steale as much as it can hold.'

227. *berayed*] dirtied, befouled: see *O.E.D.2*, beray, 1.

wet sucket] fruit preserved in syrup.

228. *spit*] expectorated—used figuratively here. Toad saliva was thought to be venomous: *O.E.D.2*, sb.^{2}, 2 quotes '1590 *Pasquil's Apol.* I.B.iij Hath the Toade no poyson before he spits it?' See also I.ii.223n.

232. *pickled spiders*] an example of particularly mean fare: cf. *G. at C.*, III.i.371-2: 'Your food shall be blackberries, and upon gaudy-days / A pickled spider'.

233. *meat*] food in general.

235.1. cat] (1) probably a witch: cf., for instance, Scot, p. 91: 'Item, he saith, that diuerse witches at *Vernon*, turned themselues into cats, and both committed and receiued much hurt', and see Opie & Tatem, pp. 57-8; (2) possibly a familiar: see Valiente, pp. 55-7.

236. Cat and Fiddle] 'The "Cat and Fiddle" was evidently a large messuage at one time, and probably extended from Mitre Court westwards to about the position of No. 39 Fleet Street': Kenneth Rogers, *The Mermaid and Mitre Taverns in Old London* (London, 1928), pp. 141-2.

ordinary] 'an eating-house or tavern where public meals are provided at a fixed price': *O.E.D.2*, sb., 14b.

239. *to ... Devil*] Cf. *R.T.*, V.i.49 (Revels): 'let him reel to hell'.

240. *I'll be hanged*] proverbial: cf. Dent, HH4.1, 'Hang me if, And be hanged if, I'll see you hanged first (etc.)'.

240-1. *if ... him*] possibly proverbial: cf. Tilley, L91, 'Laugh and be fat'.

II.i.

2. *was*] i.e. who was.

4. *wont*] accustomed.

6. *parts*] personal qualities.

8-9. *You'll ... you*] Cf. *M.W.M.M.*, I.i.157-8: 'Your base mechanic fellow can spy out / A weakness in a lord, and learns to flout'.

9. *The ... you*] The entire phrase modifies 'all' of the previous line: 'even the best servant a man can maintain' will flout.

13. *pearl*] probably an aphrodisiac, certainly an expensive ingredient for restorative medicine; cf. *M.W.M.M.*, II.vi.49-51, *Y.F.G.*, IV.viii.16, and *C.M. in C.*, V.ii.25 (Revels).

cullis] a strong broth of meat, fowl, etc. boiled and strained; it is clearly an aphrodisiac here: cf. *M.W.M.M.*, IV.ii.26 and *G. at C.*, II.ii.22.

14. *a consumption*] any wasting disease, not just tuberculosis.

and] but.

14-16. *I ... goldsmith*] William Clowes, *A Profitable and Necessarie Booke of Obseruations* (London, 1596), p. 161 recommends chicken broth as part of a cure for syphilis; he also recommends gold mixed with quicksilver (mercury) as a cure (p. 197). Gaspero's facetious hope is that Antonio has not been infected with syphilis from only one night's sexual activity with Isabella.

18-19. *Pray ... well*] The surgeon and the apothecary might be needed if the infection was in an advanced stage. William Clowes demonstrates the prevalence of syphilis in his first medical publication, *A Short and Profitable Treatise Touching the Cure of the Disease Called (Morbus Gallicus)* (London, 1579), where he notes that fifteen out of every twenty people admitted to St. Bartholomew's Hospital were found to be suffering from the disease (B.ii.v). The statistic decreased to ten out of every twenty by the time Clowes rewrote his treatise: see *A Profitable and Necessarie Booke of Obseruations*, p. 150.

18. *pothecary*] aphetic form of 'apothecary'.

20. *As ... see*] proverbial: Dent, F55.11, 'As far as I can see (i.e. it appears to me)'.

sojourner] guest or visitor, sometimes of close acquaintance: cf. *W.B.W.*, II.ii.173 and n. (Revels).

21. *four-nobles-a-week*] i.e. Florida, persumably because it cost Antonio four nobles (6s 8d in 1614) per week to keep her as his mistress.

22. *panada*] bread boiled to a pulp and flavoured with sugar, nutmeg, etc.

25-6. *Your ... you*] May you have the good fortune to receive all that you want and subconsciously (i.e. erotically) hope for. Single women proverbially could not keep their minds off sexual intercourse: cf. Tilley, D590, 'If dreams and wishes were true there would hardly be found a maid in all the nunneries of Christendom'.

26. *come upon*] (1) descend to: see *O.E.D.2*, come, vb., 48a and d; (2) coit with: see Partridge, come over.

33. *porridge*] i.e. the cullis that Antonio ordered Gaspero to prepare at ll. 11-13.

34-61.] A mixture of verse and prose in a single speech is fairly common in Middleton: cf., for instance, *R.G.*, IV.i.130-46 (Revels).

36. *make merry*] enjoy sex: see quotations in *O.E.D.2*, merry, adj., 3 and Rubinstein, merry.

friend] a lover or paramour of either sex.

seven year] See I.i.23 and n.

38. *as ... rocking*] as a young girl who has just come from the cradle, and thus a virgin. For omission of the relative pronoun see Abbott, 244.

39. *first hour*] very beginning (of the affair).

40. *time*] end of the period of pregnancy, moment to give birth. This specific meaning is not in *O.E.D.2*, but is derived from sb., 7b(a).

41. *scholar*] Francesca means 'student', but 'scholar' also means 'whore': cf. *M.W.M.M.*, I.i.184-5, where the Courtesan says, 'Mother, I am too deep a scholar grown / To learn my first rules now'.

42. *account*] reckoning, calculation.

43. *venturing*] (1) adventuring, daring; (2) gambling, as in risking investment in a shipping venture or voyage, a sense which continues throughout this speech. (3) There is also an unconscious irony here: a 'venturer' is a prostitute (see *O.E.D.2*, venture, sb., 8 and venturer, 3; see also Rubinstein, (ad)venture and cf. *M.T.*, I.i.9; *Pur.*, II.i.12-13, and *T.C.O.O.*, IV.iv.147-8).

45. *I'll be hanged*] See I.ii.240n.

46-50. *When ... custards*] The journey of the friend sounds like one from the city to a brothel of Southwark. He is a lover who visits for sexual gratification; his actions are clandestine; he travels by water; and he brings food with him (brothel-keepers were forbidden by law to sell 'any victuals':

Stow, II, p. 55). Cf. *R.T.*, II.ii.139-40 (Revels): 'This woman in immodest thin apparel / Lets in her friend by water'. The goods the friend brings have aphrodisiacal qualities: see l. 51 and ns.

50. *chewets*] dishes made of various kinds of meat or fish, chopped fine, mixed with spices and fruits, baked, fried or boiled: *O.E.D.2*, chewet[1].

curran] currant.

custards] open pies containing pieces of meat or fruit covered with a preparation of broth or milk, thickened with eggs, sweetened and seasoned with spices, etc.: see *O.E.D.2*, custard, 1a. Eggs were thought to have aphrodisiacal qualities: cf. *F. of L.*, V.i.9-21, particularly 17-19, *T.C.O.O.*, III.i.94, and *F.Q.*, III.i.160-2: 'Is coward a more stirring meat than bastard, my masters? / Put in more eggs, for shame, when you get children, / And make it true court-custard.'

51. *egg-pies*] another name for the custards.

meat] food in general, not only flesh, as aphrodisiac. See Partridge, eat, for sexual associations.

help forward] urge (me) to proceed immodestly.

54. *junkets*] (1) feasts; (2) sweetmeats, confections; (3) merrymakings accompanied with feasting: see *O.E.D.2*, junket, sb., 4.

54-5. *he ... sake*] See II.i.142-5 for examples of benefits to Antonio.

57. *provide*] make provision, take due measures.

58. *credit*] reputation.

60. *powder up*] to sprinkle with salt or powdered spice for preserving: see *O.E.D.2*, powder, vb.[1], 2a.

61. *East Indian voyage*] tenuously identified as either the Trade's Insurance (Frank Sullivan, 'Thomas Middleton's *The Witch*', Ph.D. dissertation, Yale University, 1939, p. 126) or 'the voyage captained by Nicholas Downton which set sail for the East early in 1614' (Paul Yachnin, '"This Great Game": The Opportunism of Thomas Middleton', Ph.D. thesis, University of Toronto, 1983, pp. 105-6), but see Introduction, pp. 19-20 and

23.

63. *'Morrow*] i.e. good morrow, good morning.

64. Aside] An aside is required here because the relationship between the two women is not an intimate one, and thus Isabella would not be inclined to share a secret of her marital sex life with Francesca.

75. *gamester*] (1) gambler; (2) one addicted to amorous sport, a lewd person: *O.E.D.*2, 5, and cf. *N.W.N.H.*, II.iii.174, *A.F.Q.L.*, I.i.85-9, and Massinger, *The Picture*, I.ii.26-7 (*Plays and Poems*, eds. Philip Edwards and Colin Gibson, III (Oxford, 1976)): 'Thou was at twelue a gamester, and since that / Studied all kinds of females'.

77. *surfeiter*] (1) glutton; (2) one given to sexual excess, a libertine: *O.E.D.*2 and Partridge.

77-88. *He ... fiddlers*] Middleton's characters often criticize smokers: cf. *B.B.*, pp. 10 and 42-3; *F.H.T.*, pp. 72-3.

78. *leave tobacco*] quit smoking. Yachnin, '"This Great Game"', p. 106, thinks that this hit, coupled with the East Indian voyage reference at II.i.61, 'possibly is intended to stand for the Virginian Company', but hits at tobacco are common in Middleton: cf. *B.M.C.*, II.ii.338-44, *IH.W.*, II.i.83, *F.Q.*, IV.i.206-44, and *A.F.Q.L.*, I.i.324-5.

80. *toy*] (1) a thing of little or no importance; (2) amorous sport: *O.E.D.*2, sb., 1 and Partridge; (3) possibly 'penis' (not in *O.E.D.*2).

81. *knights' ... town*] a typical reference to James I's traffic in knighthoods, but not as vicious as most: cf. Chapman, Jonson and Marston, *Eastward Ho!* (Revels), IV.i.197-8. Perhaps the joke is aimed at the pretensions of the new aristocratic wives?

86. *pipers*] (1) those who smoke tobacco in a pipe: *O.E.D.*2, piper^2, 2 gives 1632 as the earliest date of this usage; (2) musical bawdiness, as with 'fiddlers' at l. 88, because pipe=penis: see Partridge, pipe.

87-8. *statute ... fiddlers*] the *Act for the Punishment of Rogues, Vagabondes and Beggers* of 7 July 1604 (1 Jac. I, c. 7), which included

'Minstrels wanderinge abroad'. There were at least two previous such acts: 29 June 1572 (14 Eliz. c. 5) and 9 February 1598 (39 Eliz. c. 4). See Chambers, pp. 269-71, 324-5 and 336-7 for extracts from all three acts.

88. *fiddlers*] (1) those who play the fiddle, especially for money like buskers; (2) cheats; (3) those who take liberties with women: see *O.E.D.2*, fiddle, vb., 5, which gives 1632 as the earliest date of a similar usage, and see also Henke, fiddler. Mulholland notes that '*Fiddle* and cognate terms commonly carried bawdy significations': *R.G.*, II.i.64-5n (Revels). Cf. *N.W.N.H.*, I.i.292-3 and John Taylor, *Works* (London, 1630), p. 119: 'And there he spied / The pamper'd prodigal on cock-horse ride; / There was his fare, his fiddlers, and his whores.'

offices] services.

95. *near ... to*] closely she touches: see *O.E.D.2*, adv.^{2}, 12b.

98. *pride*] (1) a feeling of elation of high satisfaction; (2) sexual desire, especially in female animals: *O.E.D.2*. sb., B.11; (3) denotes 'insurgent penis': see Partridge. Pride was often associated with women: cf. *R.T.*, I.iii.73 (Revels): 'Ladies know Lucifer fell, yet still are proud.'

102. *now and then*] provebial: Dent, NN5.1.

105. *Quicker*] (1) speedier; (2) more mentally active, cleverer; (3) more fertile: see *O.E.D.2*, quick, sb.^{1}, A.4b and II.i.43-5.

108-9. *Why ... sir,*] Isabella begins her sentence four times; she gets Antonio's attention only on the final attempt.

114. *bit*] morsel, i. e. her unborn child.

stay my stomach] (1) stave off my hunger: see *O.E.D.2*, stay, vb.^{1}, 29; (2) arrest (or check) my sexual appetite: see Partridge, stomach: cf. *C.M. in C.*, I.i.140-1 (Revels).

115. *broke ... sinner*] 'referring to the injunction of fasting until after morning service': Corbin & Sedge.

117. *lower*] shorter.

118. *lawn*] 'linen of extreme fineness and, hence, expense' (Linthicum, pp. 88-9), and so a substantial bet, but cf. Tilley, L120, 'The finest lawn (cloth) will be soonest stained' for possible irony.

125. *But ... means*] i.e. because of Antonio's impotence: see II.i.208 and n^2.

126. *fault*] 'bawdy quibble on the meaning "crack, flaw"': Corbin & Sedge.

126.1. Song] See Appendix B for music.

127-34.] The entire song is bawdy, from young women only 'professing' maidenhood (l. 127) to the conclusion which identifies the middle state, i.e. married and thus legitimately sexually active, as best. For 'middle' = 'sexual parts', see Partridge, favours, and cf. Tilley, W689, 'Of women and fish the middle is best', *B.M.C.*, II.ii.64, *M.W.M.M.*, IV.iii.33, and *N.W.N.H.*, II.i.108-9.

135-6. *grumble ... musician*] Musicians presumably often begged for more money than they were paid: cf. Shakespeare, *Rom*, IV.iv.123-71.

137-9.] Cf. Tilley, T80, 'We learn by teaching'.

137. *tricks*] (sexually) provocative behaviour. This meaning is not in *O.E.D.2*, but see trick, sb., 7 and Partridge, trick.

138. *spoils*] corrupt: cf. *Wid.*, V.i.209: 'This house is able to spoil any maid'. See Abbott, 333 for this third person plural verb form.

140-1. *He ... I*] The watermen are Thames boatmen who made a living transporting people and goods on the river (Stow, I, p. 12 estimates that they numbered about 3000 in 1603), and Abberzanes employs them: see II.i.46-50 and n. and II.i.153 and n.

142. *bakemeats*] pastries, pies.

144. *canary-bottles*] bottles of a light sweet wine from the Canary Islands.

152. *bag and baggage*] proverbial: Dent BB1. *O.E.D.2*, bag, sb., 19 cites this as the earliest example of depreciative usage expressing 'the

absolute character of any one's departure: to clear out completely, "and a good riddance too!'"

153. *Why ... married*] Abberzanes obviously procured women for Antonio.

155. *idle*] frivolous, trifling.

156. *travail*] labour.

157.] probably proverbial: cf. Tilley K50, 'One kindness is the price of another' and T616, 'One good turn asks (requires, deserves) another'.

office] something done toward any one, a service?

158. *What*] an exclamation used to express surprise or astonishment and to introduce or call attention to a statement: *O.E.D.2*, B.1 and 2.

163. *means*] a course of action: see *O.E.D.2*, mean, sb.², 10c for plural form with singular sense and construction.

wrought] planned, devised.

when] possibly also used elliptically as an exclamation of impatience: *O.E.D.2*, 1b.

164. *How now*] elliptical for 'How is it now?' and often, as here, used interjectionally: see *O.E.D.2*, how, adv. (sb.³), 4b.

165. *entertained*] retained, hired.

service,] Retaining the MS punctuation allows for the possibility that Isabella's conclusion ('Please ... liking') to the sentence is a conditional dependent clause, rather than an independent clause.

166. *Please you*] See I.i.65n.

167. *I ... amiss*] I do not think that there is anything wrong with him (see *O.E.D.2*, amiss, B.2).

169. *northern parts*] Scotland, as becomes clear from the following words of Scottish dialect (see ll. 171 and 173 and ns.). Although the play is set in Ravenna, Middleton is writing for a London audience, for which the north meant Scotland. Jacobean playwrights often set their plays nominally on the continent and then used English costumes, place names and

references.

171. *bonny*] comely, beautiful: Scottish dialect.

173. *heal*] health: Scottish dialect.

varray] very: Scottish spelling.

174-8.] Letters read aloud are common in Middleton: cf., for example, *P.*, II.ii.87ff, *T.C.O.O.*, III.ii.17-19, and *M.D.B.W.*, IV.ii.150ff.

174. *down*] used to express the direction from the capital to the distant parts of a country: *O.E.D.2*, adv., 2.

176. *preferment*] that which is done towards the promotion of the marriage of a daughter: *O.E.D.2*, 2.

177. *ready furnished*] thoroughly or completely equipped: see *O.E.D.2*, ready, A.16b, and furnished, 2c.

182. *must down*] (1) i.e. must go down: see *O.E.D.2*, down, adv., 23 for ellipsis of the verb; (2) i.e. into the country: see l. 174n; (3) i.e. into a childbed (not in *O.E.D.2*); (4) i.e. into bed for sex, a common meaning in Middleton: cf., for example, *T.C.O.O.*, II.i.66-9, *N.W.N.H.*, IV.i.70-1, and *O.L.*, II.i.137-40.

183. *And ... me*] and may good fortune come to me (see *O.E.D.2*, send, vb.^{1}, 7a). 'Good speed' describes the successful delivery of a child in *C.M. in C.*, III.ii.20 (Revels).

184. *certify*] assure.

186. *You ... me*] proverbial: Dent, PP2.1, 'You shall pardon me (for that)'.

188-90. *'Tis ... endure't*] London, and in particular the court, was the centre of fashionable life; the country lagged behind. The court culture of James I was significantly different from Elizabeth I's in that it was 'usually created in or near the capital, or at least by men who usually resided there', rather than 'formed in the provinces as often as in London and its environs': R. Malcolm Smuts, *Court Culture and the Origins of a Royalist Tradition in Early Stuart England* (Philadelphia, 1987), p. 56. But see Kevin Sharpe,

Criticism and Compliment: The Politics of Literature in the England of Charles I (Cambridge, 1987), pp. 11-22 for the opposing view that city and court cultures were inseparable under James I.

193. *up*] i.e. back to Ravenna. This usage, 'at or in a place of importance, specifically London', predates the earliest citation date in *O.E.D.2* by over two hundred years: see adv.², 8d.

conceit] personal opinion.

198. *into*] to.

199. *sick at heart*] deeply affected by inward sorrow: see *O.E.D.2*, sick, a. and sb., 4 and *O.E.D.2*, heart sb., 31. Cf. *R.G.*, I.ii.149 (Revels) and *C.M. in C.*, V.ii.22-3 (Revels).

deep] (1) large: *O.E.D.2*, a., 11b; (2) solemn; cf. *B.M.C.*, II.ii.310.

200. *pledge*] See I.i.43n.

You ... me] See II.i.186n.

201. *pledged ... deep*] (1) become surety to or for someone too profoundly; (2) pawned myself to someone too far; (3) drunk once too often; (4) bawdy, with 'deep' describing distance of sexual penetration.

202-5.] Becoming pregnant in the city and delivering clandestinely in the country occurs in *F. of L.*: see IV.ii.52-4, V.ii.71-3. There is also a secret birth in *F.Q.*, II.ii.189-92 within the city.

203. *ten mile*] perhaps a conventional distance from the city to insure secrecy: cf. *Wid.*, III.iii.107-8.

205. *whole*] (1) sound; (2) intact, unimpaired, with sexual innuendo: cf. *R.G.*, II.i.305-6 (Revels) and *Pur.*, III.v.340-3: 'twas told me she lost her maidenhead at Stonie-stratford; now if youle do but so much as coniure fort, and make all whole agen —'.

206. *takes*] succeeds, i.e. the witchcraft that he has used to make Antonio impotent: see I.ii.153-64. The earliest citation in *O.E.D.2* for this usage is 1622: see take, vb., B.11.

he's] he has.

content] sexual satisfaction. Although *O.E.D.2*, sb.^{2}, 1 does not give this specific definition, it does admit the meaning through its illustrations of the usage of the word.

208. *That*] who: see Abbott, 260.

cold disease] i.e. state of enforced abstinence (see Partridge, cold).

210. *want*] deficiency.

211. *throughly*] completely; archaic spelling of 'thoroughly'.

220. *red*] violent, passionate.

224.] See I.i.3-4 and n.

225. *attendance*] 'the action or condition of waiting upon, accompanying, or escorting a person, to do him service': *O.E.D.2*, 3.

227. *stirring*] (1) awake and moving about: see *O.E.D.2*, stir, vb., 5; (2) copulating: see Partridge, stir and IV.iii.28: cf. *Pur.*, V.ii.5-6: 'who would haue thought you to be so rare a stirrer'.

229. *I ... venture*] 'Sebastian reminds himself that the courage he needs to sustain his present role is less than he has shown formerly in military action': Corbin & Sedge. A breach is 'a gap in a fortification made by a battery': *O.E.D.2*, sb., 7c. The form 'ha' done't' seems to have been a common contraction: cf., for instance, *Y.T.*, iv.68 (Revels) and Tourneur, *A.T.*, IV.iv.16 (Revels).

II.ii.

1. *toy*] fantastic notion, whim: *O.E.D.2*, sb., 4; common in Middleton: cf., for example, *P.*, IV.i.3.

2. *humours*] temporary states of mind or feeling: see *O.E.D.2*, humour, sb., 5.

3. *rascals*] rogues, but rarely, as here and uniquely in Middleton, applied to a woman. The earliest usage in reference to a woman cited in *O.E.D.2* is 1624: see rascal, sb., 3c.

4. *Made ... cheer*] feasted me well and made me merry: see *O.E.D.2*, cheer, sb.¹, 6.

5. *Ate*] MS spelling 'Eat' is usual for the past tense and possibly pronounced 'et', but cf. John Milton, *Paradise Lost*, ed. Merritt Y. Hughes (New York), Book IX, ll. 780-1, 'So saying, her rash hand in evil hour / Forth reaching to the Fruit, she pluck'd, she eat', and n.

6-7. *But ... foot-post*] Cf. Scot, p. 42: 'You must also vnderstand, that after they haue delicatlie banketted with the diuell and the ladie of the fairies; and haue eaten vp a fat oxe, and emptied a butt of malmesie, and a binne of bread at some noble mans house, in the dead of the night, nothing is missed of all this in the morning.... and yet at their returne home they are like to starue for hunger; as *Spineus* saith.'

7. *foot-post*] a postman or messenger who travels on foot.

9-10. *wound ... colours*] The charm is presumably the Latin which is written on the ribbon; thus there is no need for Steevens's emendation.

11-14. 'Necte ... necte'] The quotation is taken from Virgil's *Eclogue VIII*, ll. 77-8, with Amoretta substituted for Amaryllis. Pvblivs Virgilivs Maro, *The Bvcoliks*, trans. A[braham]. F[leming]. (London, 1589), p. 25 renders the lines 'O Amaryll knit in three knots those [twisted] colours three, / O Amaryll knit by and by, and say I knit the knots / Of Venus [to procure and cause kindnesse and loue againe:]'. See Introduction, pp. 33-4 for further discussion of Middleton's source here.

13. *bouts*] attempts, i.e. at Amoretta. A bout is 'a "round" of any kind of exercise, a turn or spell of work; as much of an action as is performed at one time': *O.E.D.2*, bout, sb.², 2a. Almachildes seems to think that the charm has two chances to work because it names Amoretta twice. He may also be playing on the bawdy suggestion of the term (sexual encounter), which is common in Middleton: cf., for example, *R.G.*, IV.ii.94 (Revels), *C.*, V.i.126 (Revels), and *S.G.*, III.ii.149.

15. *Veneris*] Venus, but Almachildes puns on the English word 'venery'.

dead flesh] sexually unresponsive female body: see Partridge, flesh, and cf. *M.D.B.W.*, III.ii.41-2.

16. *construe*] translate orally.

18. *construction*] (1) translation; (2) interpreting.

21-4. 'Necte ... *boy*] Cf. Shakespeare, *Shr*, III.i.31-6 and 40-3 for similar mock construing. Parker notes that 'Comic misconstruing was popular, especially in "school" plays': *C.M. in C.*, I.i.69n (Revels).

21. *noddies*] fools, simpletons: cf. *M.D.B.W.*, III.i.69-70: 'the hour will come, sweetheart, / That I shall make two noddies of my keepers'.

22. *turned colours*] 'perhaps a play on the figurative sense "surrender" as well as a literal reference to the twisted colours of the charm': Corbin & Sedge.

24. *with ... boy*] implies homosexuality.

26. *overcome*] render helpless (to his advances).

27. *whoreson*] literally, son of a whore, but commonly used as a coarsely abusive epithet applied to a person or thing; however, *O.E.D.2* lists no instance of application to a female.

hell-cat] (1) evil woman; (2) witch; (3) close to homonym of Hecate. *O.E.D.2* cites this as the earliest usage.

brain of a cat] Ben Jonson glosses this in *The Masque of Queens* as something which will 'doe a domestick hurt' (*Ben Jonson*, eds. C.H. Herford and Percy and Evelyn Simpson, VII (London, 1941), p. 293), but in this context it is a love charm: see quotation from Scot at I.ii.206-16n.

28-9. *with a vengeance*] possibly proverbial (cf. Tilley, M1003, 'With a mischief') and common throughout Middleton: cf., for instance, *M.W.M.M.*, III.iii.15, *Wid.*, I.i.56, and *G. at C.*, II.ii.82.

29-30. *little ... tail*] another love charm: see quotation from Scot at I.ii.206-16n.

30-1. *with a pestilence*] See II.ii.28-9n, and cf. *H.K.K.*, II.iii.55-6.

32. *cleanly ... handsome*] These two words have the same meaning: elegant or correct, stylistically graceful. Both are specific usages applied to language: see *O.E.D.2*, clean, a., 7, cleanly, a., 6, handsome, a. (adv.), 2a.

38. *take it*] accept or agree to amorous advances: Partridge.

40. *gallery*] usually a place in houses of the period for recreation with open access, and therefore risky as setting for sexual assault: cf. *W.B.W.*, II.ii.270ff (Revels) and, particularly, Jonson, *Volpone*, III.vii.13-14 and n. (Revels).

42. *rudest*] most offensive (with reference to unmannerly behaviour and language).

came at] was present at: see *O.E.D.2*, come, vb., B.38.

45. *I'll ... word*] proverbial: cf. Tilley, W825, 'To eat one's words'.

I'll ... else] or else I'll make everything go to pieces: cf. *R.G.*, IV.ii.79-81 (Revels) and Shakespeare, *MND*, I.ii.24-6, 'I could play 'erc'les rarely, or a part to tear a cat in, to make all split'; proverbial: Dent, A205.1, 'To make all split'.

49. *take*] copulate with: Partridge.

52. *art*] (1) skill; (2) cunning: *O.E.D.2*, art, sb., 13; (3) erotic expertise: cf. Shakespeare, *MM*, II.ii.188-90.

53. *stuff*] 'applied to a lustful person': *O.E.D.2*, sb.^{1}, 7c (a) cites IV.ii.81 and *M.T.*, III.i.205 as examples. See also Partridge, stuff, n., and cf. *M.D.B.W.*, V.ii.249-51.

57. *this means*] i.e. her plans for revenge: see II.ii.69-72 and III.i.

hardness] difficulty.

64. *confusion*] destruction: *O.E.D.2*, 1; cf. Shakespeare, *Mac*, III.v.29.

68-71.] The Duchess refers to preparations for the ensuing bed-trick, a common dramatic device: cf., for example, *G. at C.*, V.ii.75ff, Shakespeare, *MM*, III.i.241ff and *AWW*, III.vii.14ff.

69-70. *dissemble ... entertainment*] pretend to promise him caressing and sexual intercourse with you: see Partridge, mutual entertainment, and cf. Shakespeare, *MM*, I.ii.141-3 and *Per*, xvi.51-3.

72. *Good*] regularly used as a convenient epithet prefixed to titles of high rank: *O.E.D.2*, a., adv. and sb., A.2b.

75-6. *As ... stirring*] an example of nostalgia for a supposedly innocent past: cf. *M.D.B.W.*, IV.ii.186-8: 'Sir, in as plain truth / As the old time walked in, when love was simple / And knew no art nor guile, I affect you'.

76. *tricks*] (1) deceits; (2) sexual stratagems: see Partridge, trick.

stirring] 'active', but with sexual undertone: see II.i.227, n.² and IV.iii.28.

77. *serve your turn*] answer your purpose, suit your need: see *O.E.D.2*, turn, sb., 30b(a); proverbial: Dent, TT25, 'To serve one's turn'.

85. *desertless*] without merit, undeserving.

93. *'Bove*] aphetic form of 'above'.

106. *'T has*] it has.

111. *perform*] carry out what I have undertaken: *O.E.D.2*, 6c.

113. *revenge and love*] Cf. *S.G.*, II.ii.116-18, where Louis says that these two emotions held together would cause 'Distraction in a saint'.

116. *competent*] (1) proper; possibly (2) sufficient.

honesty] sexual virtue: Partridge.

120. *the ... in't*] proverbial: Dent, 250.11, 'The Devil (Fiend) is in it'.

122. *to ... stomach*] proverbial: cf. Tilley, S874, 'To go against one's stomach': cf. *1H.W.*, II.i.57.

stomach] inclination.

125. *Is ... altered*] proverbial: cf. Tilley, C111, 'The case is altered, quoth Plowden'.

ruled] 'Ruled' is justified as an emendation here not only for sense but also for its similar usage throughout the Middleton canon.

127. '*Las*] aphetic form of 'alas'.

venturous] amorous: see II.i.43 and n.

128. *we're ... man*] proverbial: cf. Tilley, F367, 'To be flesh and blood as others are'.

132-4. *Your ... list*] Cf. *W.B.W.*, II.i.113-23 (Revels) for a similar consul of opportunism.

132. *merry*] See II.i.36 and n.

133. *look ... chance*] proverbial: Tilley, E235, 'Have an eye (look) to the main chance'.

134. *list*] wish, desire.

135-7. *By ... others*] 'Bullen notes, "cleped, called." But surely the metaphor is from the clipped wing of a bird in a snare, her "clipped name" being her injured reputation': K. Deighton, *The Old Dramatists* (Westminster, 1896), pp. 175-6. Seduction and birding are often equated in Middleton: cf. *1H.W.*, II.i.277-82 and *H.K.K.*, III.i.138-45.

136. *prate*] boast, blab: *O.E.D.2*, vb., 1.

137. *clipped*] shortened: see *O.E.D.2*, clip, vb.², 5b. If Amoretta's name is shortened to 'Amo', it forms the Latin for 'I love'.

bird] a maiden, girl.

II.iii.

0.1. with a baby] an important stage property: see I.ii.0.1n and Introduction, pp. 58-9. The same property is used for various effects in Middleton: cf. *Y.T.*, v.0.1ff (Revels), for a struggle over a child demonstrating cruelty; *C.M. in C.*, II.i.61.1ff, II.iv.0.1-3 and, in particular, II.ii.127ff (Revels) for a comic version of abandonment; and *F.Q.*, III.ii.0.1-2ff for a compassionate treatment of the newborn infant.

1-3.] Parker notes the parallel between this and *C.M. in C.*, II.i.96-7 (Revels): 'There's tricks enough to rid thy hand on't [a child], wench: / Some rich man's porch, tomorrow before day'.

1. *get*] beget.

2. *house*] i.e. of his tailor: see ll. 5-10.

3. *No ... porch*] I don't need to know the location of the house; I only need to know the location of its porch (because that is where I am going to abandon the baby).

5. *tailor*] The profession was noted for lechery because of the word 'punning on the "tail" = pudendum—hence a male copulator, one who "tail-ers" a woman': Henke. See also Hilda Hulme, 'Three Notes', *J.E.G.P.*, 57 (1958), 722-4.

6. *Well ... sides*] very heavily weighted all round in body (because in late stage of pregnancy): for 'of' = 'on' see *O.E.D.2*, of, 55b and 57.

7. *drab*] (1) slatternly woman; (2) prostitute: Partridge.

9. *scape*] (1) breach of chastity: *O.E.D.2*, sb.1, 2; (2) more accurately, 'the offspring of an illicit sexual union': cf. Shakespeare, *WT*, III.iii.70-1 (this meaning not in *O.E.D.2*).

12. *to a hair*] exactly; proverbial: Tilley, H26, 'To hit (fit) it to a hair'. Cf. *C.M. in C.*, II.iii.5-6 (Revels).

13. *swell ... up*] i.e. by impregnating her.

14. *purse*] (1) money, i.e. because one saves the subsequent expense of bringing up the child; (2) 'perhaps in the sense "scrotum" and, by extension, maintaining a man's sexual freedom': Corbin & Sedge. See also Partridge and cf. Shakespeare, *WT*, IV.iv.611-12.

21. *'Give*] God give.

22. *quick hand*] (1) i.e. for sewing in the tailor's trade; (2) i.e. for stealing.

convey] (1) transport or carry from one place to another; (2) euphemism for 'steal': cf. Shakespeare, *R2*, IV.i.307-8.

cleanly] adroitly.

23. *'Twill ... day*] possibly proverbial: cf. Tilley, M628, 'Let him mend his manners, it will be his own another day'.

'*Twill*] It (i.e. the trade of tailor and/or thief) will.

well said] (1) fittingly or properly spoken: see *O.E.D.2*, well, adv., 5a; (2) proverbial: Dent, WW10.

24. *furnished*] equipped (or, possibly, dressed), i.e. for the journey: *O.E.D.2*, 2c.

28. *It ... better*] it (the delay) renders (our assumed situation) better (more credible). The phantom journey from Scotland to London (see II.i.169 and n.) is a long one, and an unanticipated delay of a day would be commonplace.

30. *safeguard*] an outer skirt or petticoat worn by women 'to protect the lady's costume from dust and soiling by the horse': Linthicum, p. 188.

31. *probably*] plausibly.

32. *marked*] noticed.

33. *monstrous*] exceedingly: *O.E.D.2*, 8b; for adjective used as adverb see Abbott, 1.

34. *country*] always open to bawdy innuendo because of pronunciation and spelling ('cunt') of first syllable.

woodcock] (1) fool: cf. *B.M.C.*, IV.ii.52 and *H.K.K.*, V.i.117; (2) with innuendo of prostitute: Henke; cf. *1H.W.*, II.i.235-9 and *Wid.* V.i.154.

35. *pale I am*] Cf. Jane's paleness from morning sickness in *F.Q.*, II.ii.140-1, and *S.M.T.*, IV.iii.64-6 (Revels): 'She's only pale, the colour of the court, / And most attractive; mistresses must strive for't / And their lascivious servants best affect it.'

36. *box*] cuff, slap.

41. *At*] after: this specific meaning not in *O.E.D.2*, but see prep., 31.

voyage] A 'voyage' is a common metaphor in Middleton for sexual encounter: cf., for example, *M.T.*, I.ii.10-12, *R.G.*, III.i.127 (Revels), *W.B.W.*, II.ii.471-3, IV.i.163 (Revels), and *S.G.*, I.v.87. Cf. also II.i.43 and n.

43. *sweet charge*] pleasing or agreeable cost.

46. *speak with' least*] say (that was) the least: see *O.E.D.2*, least, 5d(b). 'With" is a common form; the scribal apostrophe indicates the missing definite article 'the': see Kökeritz, pp. 274-5.

47. *run out*] exhausted, used up: see *O.E.D.2*, run, vb., B.77c(b), where earliest citation of this usage is 1700.

caudles] warm drinks consisting of thin gruel, mixed with wine or ale, sweetened and spiced, given chiefly to sick people, especially women in childbed: see *O.E.D.2*, caudel, sb., 1.

49.] Cf. *C.M. in C.*, II.ii.161-5 (Revels) where a similar point is made about the cost of childbirth, although in a comic vein.

50. *up*] (1) i.e. onto our horses; (2) i.e. to London: see II.i.193 and n.

51. *wand*] a stick or switch for urging on a horse.

53. *it*] i.e. the whip. Whipping was a standard punishment for fornication: cf. *C.*, IV.iii.86-7 (Revels) and Tourneur, *A.T.*, V.ii.32-5 (Revels).

III.i.

1-8. *This' ... so*] Almachildes's outrage results from his discovery that the woman he has just had sexual intercourse with is not a virgin: see also V.iii.118-21, and cf. *C.*, IV.i.11-13 (Revels) for the convention that a man infallibly discovered a woman's lack of virginity the first time he had sex with her.

1. *This'*] This is.

1-2. *How ... men*] proverbial: cf. Tilley, W716, 'Women naturally deceive, weep, and sin'.

3. *finely handled*] (1) cunningly treated: see *O.E.D.2*, finely, 5; (2) cleverly carressed sexually: see Henke, handle, and Partridge, handle.

5. *tries*] (1) tests; (2) copulates with: see Partridge, try.

11. *gotten*] won (sexually): see *O.E.D.2*, get, vb., 17d.

13. *bird-lime*] a viscous sticky substance prepared from the bark of the holly and used for catching small birds: see *O.E.D.2*, lime, sb.¹, 1a.

My oath's out] The promise I made (at II.ii.135-7) is no longer current (i.e. binding upon my behaviour): see *O.E.D.2*, out, adv., 23.

31. *force*] rape: cf. *S.G.*, I.iii.74.

proud] lascivious: see *O.E.D.2*, a. (sb., adv.), 8a and II.i.98n.

33. *in question*] in a doubtful or undecided state: see *O.E.D.2*, question, sb., 1c.

33-4. *women, / Which*] Ellis's punctuation is possible because 'which' can mean 'who': see Abbott, 265.

36-7. *'Tis ... too*] The Duchess's type of pleasure is not satisfied simply with male copulation followed by a rest so that the man can regain his breath, but it actually wants to kill him as well, and thus rob him of all of his breath. For 'do' = 'to copulate with' see Partridge.

39-40. *Thou'st ... man*] an indication of unworldliness. Cf. *A.F.Q.L.*, IV.i.175: 'O, sir, you're young-sighted'.

40. *Of*] in respect of.

43. *perpetual bonds*] i.e. of marriage.

49. *rising*] (1) social advancement; (2) erection.

50. *perform*] (1) carry out; (2) i.e. sexually; only the sexually potent male is able to 'perform' intercourse: see Partridge, performance, and cf. *T.C.O.O.*, I.i.54-5: 'What lies within the power of my [a courtesan's] performance / Shall be commanded of thee.'

53. *That time*] i.e. for the Duke's assassination.

55. *have ... him*] regard him according to the desire or estimation that he has earned: see *O.E.D.2*, care, sb.¹, 3b, c.

58. *venture hard*] (1) strenuously risk myself: cf. *W.B.W.*, II.ii.404-5 (Revels); (2) earnestly prostitute myself: see II.i.43n.

speed] success, fortune: *O.E.D.2*, sb., 3b.

III.ii.

2. *quean*] prostitute.

3-4. *I ... handsomely*] Cf. II.i.46-7.

4. *look to*] take care of: see *O.E.D.2*, look, vb., 21c.

7. *prick-song*] 'music sung from notes written or "pricked", as distinguished from that sung from memory or by ear': *O.E.D.2*, 1.

close] shut up from observation, secluded.

8. *There's ... in*] The joke rests on the double meaning of 'prick-' in the previous line: (1) musical notation; (2) penis, and, by extension, copulation: see Partridge, prick, n. and vb. and pricking. Cf. *P*., I.ii.105, *Y.F.G.*, II.i.45, and *W.B.W.*, III.iii.122 and n. (Revels), where Mulryne points out that 'The indecent pun in *prick*song is very common'.

11. *complete*] perfect (possessing all the requisite qualities): *O.E.D.2*, a., 5. But see also Peacham, *The Complete Gentleman* (London, 1622), where the adjective is used ironically, as here.

13. *doubtful*] of a questionable or equivocal character: *O.E.D.2*, 1c cites 1838 as the earliest date of this usage.

14. *anon*] shortly, in a little while.

15. *envious*] (1) malicious; possibly (2) vexed at the good fortune of another.

17. *fail*] miss the mark, err.

condition] (1) social position; (2) character, moral nature: *O.E.D.2*, sb., 11a.

20. *panderous*] of the nature of or characterizing one who supplies another with the means of gratifying lust: *O.E.D.2* cites this as an example of the usage.

21-2. *She ... tuck*] She looked different then, more as if she were inclined to favour the city gallants (and, by extension, trade with them). A 'tuck' is a 'sword' (*O.E.D.2*, sb.^{3}, and cf. Shakespeare, *1H4*, II.v.251), which carries the bawdy meaning of 'penis' (see Partridge; sword, and swords and bucklers). Florida has presumably changed appearance (possibly by dressing less flamboyantly) after Antonio's marriage in order to make it less likely that she will be detected or recognized as she continues to provide him with her sexual services.

23. *piece*] a woman regarded as a sexual object: *O.E.D.2*, sb., 9b and Partridge.

transformation] a person transformed: *O.E.D.2*, 1b cites Shakespeare, *MWW*, IV.v.90 as the unique example of this usage.

24. *frailty*] weakness in sexual matters: Partridge.

26. *They ... how*] because servants are not maintained who are so (1) beautifully dressed (see *O.E.D.2*, lusty, 2b), (2) full of sexual desire, nor is she supported (as a mistress) so humbly.

27. *stand*] state of perplexity (or impasse).

31. *at' back door*] at the back door, i.e. a surreptitious exit. The phrase is common: cf., for example, *Pur.*, III.iv.84 and Tourneur, *A.T.*, II.v.116 and 143-4 (Revels). Cf. especially *T.C.O.O.*, III.iii.83-5: 'one master Hoard, with a guard of gentlemen, carried her [a courtesan] out at back door, a pretty while since, sir'.

36. *one ... family*] i.e. a prostitute; for obscene pun on 'falling' cf. *1H.W.*, II.i.30 and *H.K.K.*, III.i.58-9.

37. *Rutneys*] not in Sugden or on any contemporary map of London; probably obscene because 'rut' = 'heat—period of sexual excitement in male deer, goat, ram and other animals': see Partridge, rut-time and rutting.

43. *Bewitched*] (1) enchanted (i.e. by Florida): *O.E.D.2*, bewitch, 2; (2) affected by witchcraft (of Sebastian)—an unconscious irony on Gaspero's part.

45. *happy*] fortuitous.

47. *And*] even though (there are): *O.E.D.2*, conj.[1], C.2.

lighted] alighted, dismounted (i.e. arrived at the door).

48. *waspish*] irascible.

A ... on't] an imprecation or exclamation of irritation or impatience: see *O.E.D.2*, pox, sb., 3.

50. *her*] i.e. Francesca.

52. *fled to shifts*] resorted to stratagems or subterfuges (see *O.E.D.2*, flee, vb., B.2c.

55. *undone*] (1) lost her virginity (see Partridge, undo; undone); (2) ruined, i.e. her future prospects for, presumably, marriage.

58. *'Twas ... herself*] possibly proverbial: cf. Dent, O64.01, 'To not be (be) oneself'.

65. *confusion*] perdition, destruction: *O.E.D.2*, 1; cf. Shakespeare, *Mac*, III.v.29.

68. *coming up*] i.e. to Ravenna, but the phrase was often specifically applied to London: see *O.E.D.2*, come, vb., 74a. Middleton may again be thinking of the geography of England: cf. II.i.169 and 174 and ns.

69. *her ... lightened*] the human evidence of her disgrace (the baby) was removed (through (1) birth and (2) abandonment).

70. *wished*] recommended (in marriage).

71. *surfeit*] sickness or derangement of the system arising from excessive eating or drinking.

75. *speed*] fortune, her success. Isabella is referring to both Francesca's journey and delivery.

78. *service*] (1) duty (in the role of social inferior); (2) devotion ?; (3) help; (4) sexual attention: Partridge, service and services.

81. *Stump*] (1) a landmark; (2) possibly a public house (but no record of such survives); (3) possibly bawdy innuendo because 'stump' = 'penis': Partridge, and cf. *C.M. in C.*, V.iii.1-2 (Revels): 'Ho, my wife's quicken'd; I am a man for ever! / I think I have bestirr'd my stumps, i' faith.'

83. *rod*] a measure of length equal to 5 1/2 yards or 16 1/2 feet or 5.0292 metres.

85. *bleak*] pallid, of a sickly hue.

86. *sharp*] emaciated, thin: the earliest example cited in *O.E.D.2* of this usage is from 1833 (a. and sb.¹, A.10f, but see also A.10a).

riding] (1) i.e. on a horse; (2) i.e. on a man in sexual intercourse: but neither *O.E.D.2*, ride, vb., B.3 and 16 nor Partridge, ride, cite any examples of a woman superincumbent in the sexual act.

sore] with great exertion or effort: *O.E.D.2*, adv., 7.

88. *travelled*] MS spelling, 'travaild', puns on secondary meaning 'laboured in childbirth'.

91. *hand*] handwriting: cf. *M.D.B.W.*, III.iii.79.

101. *strangeness*] (1) unfamiliarity; (2) 'shyness as a stranger': Ellis.

102. *still*] constant, continual: *O.E.D.2*, a. and sb.², A.7.

kept me off] prevented me, made me refrain: see *O.E.D.2*, keep, 27b.

104. *shake ... with*] proverbial: Dent, SS6.

108. *For my part*] proverbial: Dent, PP3, 'For my (own) part'.

his] i.e. Abberzanes.

113. *churching*] 'the public appearance of a woman at church to return thanks after childbirth': *O.E.D.2*, 1.

114. *Give you joy*] proverbial: Dent, JJ2, '(God) give you joy'. Common in Middleton: cf., for instance, *1H.W.*, V.ii.337, 453, *T.C.O.O.*, II.i.221 and *Wid.*, I.ii.204.

where the devil] proverbial: Dent, DD12, 'What (etc.) the devil'.

115. *you*] i.e. the letter.

117. *stuff*] behaviour: this meaning not in *O.E.D.2*, but see sb.¹, 3c; (2) whores: Partridge, n., 2—see also II.ii.53n and IV.ii.81.

120-1. *She ... too*] proverbial: cf. Tilley, S196, 'Trust no secret with a woman', and W347a, 'Do not tell your wife all you know'.

124. *I ... it*] (1) I (would) have (a) uttered, (b) vomited the secret: see *O.E.D.2*, cast, vb., 26, 25b and Abbott, 371; cf. *B.M.C.*, IV.ii.43-4 and *P.*, III.ii.15-16; (2) I have considered the situation: *O.E.D.2*, cast, vb., 42; (3)

possibly, following Dyce's punctuation, the phrase is an exclamation marking the moment that Francesca realizes her plan of action, outlined in ll. 128-39; thus it may mean 'I've got it!': see *O.E.D.2*, cast, vb., 44b, and cf. *B.M.C.*, IV.iii.6 and *H.K.K.*, III.i.24. 'Cast' also meant 'to give birth or bear prematurely' (*O.E.D.2*, vb., 21) and so would come naturally to Francesca's preoccupied mind.

130. *quit*] even by means of retaliation: *O.E.D.2*, a., 3 and see quits, 2a.

132.] In *M.D.B.W.*, III.ii.67 the Duchess plans to disgrace Andrugio in a similar fashion: 'I'll bring his faith in war now into question'.

135. *conceit*] conception, apprehension.

137. *of ... guard*] for a safe defence?: see *O.E.D.2*, sound, a., 5 and guard, 2.

140. *fit him*] (1) requite him as he deserves (in return for what he has done). This usage of 'fit' is common throughout the Middleton canon: cf., for example, *Y.F.G.*, I.i.178, *N.W.H.H.*, II.iii.73-4, and *O.L.*, III.ii.304. Mulholland (*R.G.*, I.ii.142n[2],2 (Revels)) also gives examples from Kyd, *The Spanish Tragedy*, IV.i.70 (Revels) and Beaumont and Fletcher, *Philaster*, II.ii.143 (Revels). Cf. also I.ii.224n above. (2) punish: *O.E.D.2*, fit, vb.[1], 12 gives 1625 as the earliest date for this usage.

144. *conceit*] thought, notion.

in] in reference to.

149. *low*] softly, quietly.

151. *natural love*] love as between blood family relations, and therefore more powerful than that between non-blood family relations: cf. *F.Q.*, IV.ii.85.

153. *lightness*] female wantonness or unchastity: Partridge.

154. *when ... down*] i.e. supposedly to Scotland to her mother for the proposed marriage: see II.i.174-6 and II.i.182 and n.

156. *apparent*] clear, obvious: *O.E.D.2*, a. and sb., 3.

157. *affliction*] trouble of mind, misery: *O.E.D.2*, 2.

164. *straight*] immediately.

172. *speed*] See III.i.58n².

173. *footboy*] 'a boy (in livery) employed in the place of or to assist a footman': *O.E.D.2*, b.

177. *make shift*] (1) manage; possibly (2) manage with effort.

185. *What's ... do*] What's the matter here: see *O.E.D.2*, do, vb., B.33.

186. *toward*] going on: *O.E.D.2*, a. and adv., 2c gives 1838 as the earliest date of this usage, but see also 2b.

191-2. *a ... 'em*] Cf. *M.W.M.M.*, IV.iii.53-4: 'Who keeps a harlot, tell him this from me, / He needs nor thief, disease, nor enemy'.

192. *journey*] sexual anventure: cf. *R.G.*, III.ii.188 (Revels).

193. *country*] See II.iii.34n¹.

208. *stand*] remain steadfast.

cold] (1) indifferent; (2) void of sensual passion: *O.E.D.2*, a., 7c.

212. *lowness*] low condition with regard to station or rank: *O.E.D.2*, 1b.

218. *prefer*] introduce or recommend.

225. *directions*] instruction how to proceed.

III.iii.

0.1. two] i.e. Stadlin and Hoppo. The number of witches entering here is debatable, and all but one of the previous editions have left the number indeterminate. Corbin & Sedge, however, name the two speaking witches not mentioned in the S.D. and argue that three others are necessary, citing V.ii.37 as proof that Hecate 'is habitually accompanied by "five sisters"' (see The Persons, 20n). But in *this* scene, the evidence points to only two witches.

1.] *gallant*] (1) fashionably attired beauty; (2) paramour; (3) pregnant woman (by virtue of being full)? Cf. *C.M. in C.*, I.ii.121-2 (Revels), where Sir Walter Whorehound notes Mrs. Allwit's pregnancy: 'Methinks she shows gallantly, / Like a moon at full, sir.'

brisk] (1) finely dressed; (2) wantonly: not in *O.E.D.2*, but see a. and sb., B.b.

rides] (1) floats in space; (2) i.e. as on a man in sexual intercourse: see III.ii.86 and n².

2. *rich*] splendid, magnificent.

5. *owl*] nocturnal bird of prey and of ill-omen: see Opie & Tatem, pp. 295-6. Cf. Tourneur, *A.T.*, II.i.110-11 (Revels): 'Thou art a screech-owl and dost come i' night / To be the cursed messenger of death', and Shakespeare, *Mac*, II.ii.3-4, 'It was the owl that shrieked, the fatal bellman / Which gives the stern'st good-night'.

6. *'Tis ... then*] proverbial: cf. Dent, HH19, 'It is high time to x'.

14. *betimes*] in a short time, soon: *O.E.D.2*, 4.

15. *a-birding*] (1) searching (i.e. to do evil or, possibly, more specifically, for sexual gratification); (2) flying. Neither definition is in *O.E.D.2*, birding.

17. *sluts*] (1) women of dirty, slovenly or untidy habits or appearance; (2) wanton women, especially if of low origin or as in 1 above: Partridge, slut.

21. *dunghill*] figurative, as an example of the lowest or most degraded situation: *O.E.D.2*, 2a.

23. *ones*] i.e. eggs.

27. *Marmaritin*] See I.ii.164-8n. *O.E.D.2* cites this as the unique example of the word's usage, and offers only a vague definition—'some drug'.

mandragora] the plant mandrake, but since Shakespeare, taken as a type of narcotic: *O.E.D.2*, 1c. Cf. Shakespeare, *Oth*, III.iii.334-7 and *Ant*, I.v.3-6.

28. *panax*] panace or all-heal, a fabulous herb to which was ascribed the power of healing all diseases: *O.E.D.2* cites this example as the earliest usage of the word.

pan] either (1) a socket, as of the thigh: *O.E.D.2*, sb.¹, 4c; or (2) the skull, especially its upper part: *O.E.D.2*, sb.¹, 6; or (3) the patella or knee-pan: *O.E.D.2*, sb.¹, 6b gives 1657 as the earliest date of usage.

29. *selago*] the club moss *lycopodium selago*.

30. *Hedge-hyssop*] *gratiola officinalis*, a plant of Central Europe, formerly noted for its medicinal properties.

32. *moon-calf*] (1) a congenital idiot, a born fool: *O.E.D.2*, 1c cites 1620 as the earliest usage of this meaning; (2) an absent-minded person: *O.E.D.2*, 2 cites *N.W.N.H.*, I.i.112 as earliest usage of this meaning; (3) an unstable person: *O.E.D.2*, 2b. Cf. Shakespeare, *Tmp*, II.ii.135.

35-7. *Hark ... musicians*] Cf. Scot, p. 186: '... frier *Bartholomaeus* saith, that the witches themselues, before they annoint themselues, do heare in the night time a great noise of minstrels, which flie ouer them, with the ladie of the fairies, and then they addresse themselues to their iournie'.

37. *noise*] collective noun for a company or band of musicians.

38.1 Song] See Appendix B for the music to this song.

39-79. *In ... etcetera*] Cf. quotation from Scot at I.ii.38-45n, particularly for ll. 51, 53 and 69-70.

50. *count*] sum total.

51. *mount*] go upwards, ascend.

52.1. cat] See I.ii.235.1n.

53. *coll*] an embrace around the neck: *O.E.D.2*, sb.¹, cites this as the unique example of the usage; cf. I.ii.29n¹.

66. *Malkin*] (1) the proper name of a female spectre or demon; (2) a quasi-proper name for a cat. Cf. Shakespeare, *Mac*, I.i.8.

67. *dainty*] (1) delightful; (2) rare.

70.] Cf. *M.W.M.M.*, IV.i.65, where Succubus invites Master Penitent Brothel to 'dance and sing, and kiss and play'.

toy] 'to play, or disport oneself; especially, amorously: not merely to copulate but also, and predominately, to kiss and caress playful-

passionately': Partridge, vb.

72. *seas ... fountains*] 'The seas are drawn up by the moon (i.e. our mistress, Hecate)': J.M. Nosworthy, *Shakespeare's Occasional Plays*, p. 229.

73. *steep*] Some editors emend this MS reading to 'steeples' on the basis of scansion, the Robert Johnson setting (see Appendix B), subsequent printings of the song in *Macbeth*, and I.ii.22: 'In moonnlight nights o'er steeple-tops'. But the MS is clear and 'steep' makes sense.

77. *noise ... breach*] the roaring of the waves in a violent sea.

77-8. *noise of ... cannon's throat*] considered to be one of the loudest noises: cf. *H.K.K.*, IV.ii.92-5.

80-2. *you ... mortal*] perhaps a parody of Christian ideas of heaven and earth: cf. *M.D.B.W.*, I.ii.99-100: 'The better half, my lord, my mind's there [in heaven] still; / And when the heart's above, the body walks here / But like an idle serving-man below, / Gaping and waiting for his master's coming.'

IV.i.

3. *can ... supper*] Cf. I.ii.240-1 and n.

rub out] cancel: not in *O.E.D.2*.

4. *formal*] (1) regular; (2) precise: *O.E.D.2*, 8.

6. *lunary ... madness*] the moon was thought to cause madness: see Opie & Tatem, pp. 264-5.

7. *bawds ... shop*] 'The two were regarded as inseparable': Corbin & Sedge, who also note the pairing in Marston, *The Malcontent*, V.i.20 (Revels).

8. *wildfire*] (1) will-o'-the-wisp or *ignis factuus*: cf. Shakespeare, *1H4*, III.iii.38; (2) 'a name for erysipelas, especially those in which the eruption spreads from one part to another': *O.E.D.2*, 4; hence, (3) venereal disease by association with 'strumpets' earlier in the line.

8. *beadle from brimstone*] 'beadles were noted for their severity in punishing offenders': Corbin & Sedge.

9. *try the honesty*] Cf. *Wid.*, V.i.361.

11. *as ... woman*] possibly proverbial: cf. Dent, W637.1, 'To be a woman'.

13. *piteous ... tragedy*] Almachildes casts himself as the tragic victim with a theatrical reference.

13-14. A ... Hair-Bracelets] In *W.B.W.*, II.ii.168n (Revels), Mulryne suggests that this might be a reference to the popular play, *A Warning for Fair Women* (1599). Hair bracelets were commonly used as love tokens: cf: Shakespeare, *MND*, I.i.32-3, Donne, 'The Relique', l. 6, 'The Funeral', l. 3 (Helen Gardner, ed., *The Elegies and the Songs and Sonnets of John Donne* (Oxford, 1965), pp. 89-90), and Tourneur, *A.T.*, I.iii.21 (Revels).

15-21.] Cf. *H.K.K.*, II.ii.4-13 for an exact parallel of this situation, and cf. also *H.K.K.*, I.i.1-18 for a similar view of 'the people' and their unruly 'wills'.

19. *rudeness*] (1) ignorance: *O.E.D.2*, 1; (2) uncouthness: *O.E.D.2*, 2; (3) violence in action: *O.E.D.2*, 3; (4) lack of civility: *O.E.D.2*, 4.

21. *raise*] promote or advance a person to a higher rank, office or position: *O.E.D.2*, vb.^{1}, 18a.

23. *crosses*] misfortunes, adversities: see *O.E.D.2*, cross, sb., B.10b.

27. *Goes ... heaven*] i.e. because his belief will not be false?

33. *close*] as near as can be, very near: *O.E.D.2*, a. and adv., B.1.

38. *take ... upon*] affect, feign: *O.E.D.2*, take, vb., B.18d.

43. *spoon-meat*] (1) literally, soft or liquid food to be taken with a spoon: cf. *C.M. in C.*, II.ii.29 (Revels) and *O.L.*, II.ii.4; but also (2) 'broth, in which poison could be easily administered': Ellis.

44. *deed*] Almachildes's 'assassination' of the Duke. Cf. *C.*, III.iv.137 (Revels) and Shakespeare, *Mac*, IV.i.65.

48. *countenance*] assume a particular demeanour or behaviour (here, of superiority): *O.E.D.2*, vb., 1, gives 1519 as the latest date for this usage.

52. *popular*] (1) of the common people; (2) low, vulgar: *O.E.D.2*, 2c.

60. *Dearer*] heavier, more grievous.

64. *rankness*] corruption, festering.

74. *up*] in a state of insurrection, risen in rebellion: *O.E.D.2*, adv.², 10.

82. *her*] herself: see Abbott, 223.

94. *Mischief ... friend*] proverbial (?): for close but not exact analogy, cf. *M.D.B.W.*, I.ii.232-4: 'there is no mischief / But brings one villain[y] or other still / Even close at heels on't'.

IV.ii.

8-12. *for ... fast*] See I.i.3-4 and n.

23-5. *One ... probably*] possible reference to the doctrine that everything in nature has some use or purpose: cf. *R.G.*, IV.i.148 and n. (Revels), *W.B.W.* , I.ii.179-80 (Revels) and *C.*, II.ii. 44 and n. (Revels), where Bawcutt suggests that the doctrine derives from Montaigne's *Essais*, Bk. III, Ch. I, 'De L'Utile et de L'Honneste (Oeuvres, Paris, 1927, V, 3-4), but Mulryne points out, in his note to *W.B.W.* cited above, that the doctrine was traditional. Middleton's closest expression of its use as here is in *M.W.M.M.*, I.i.109-11: 'And therefore I'm contrain'd to use the means / Of one that knows no mean, a courtesan, / One poison for another'.

25. *she*] i.e. Isabella.

26. *him*] i.e. Antonio.

27. *this*] i.e. Florida.

he] i.e. Fernando. Perhaps 'as ... her', ll. 26-7, is an aside? The pronoun cannot logically refer to Antonio, as Corbin & Sedge assume, because Sebastian has not 'taught' him anything.

compound] (1) agree; (2) to make a pecuniary arrangement: *O.E.D.2*, vb., 12; (3) coit: Partridge.

29. *carriage*] (1) 'manner or way of conducting or managing (an affair)': *O.E.D.*2, 17; (2) the way Florida carries herself; (3) the ability to bear men easily during sexual intercourse: Partridge, carriage. Cf. *S.M.T.*, II.i.81 (Revels) and *M.W.M.M.*, I.ii.33-6: 'a woman of an excellent carriage all her lifetime, in court, city and country. *Cour[tesan]*. Sh'as always carried it well in those places, sir;—witness three bastards a-piece.'

34. *betimes*] early in the morning.

35. *Closely*] secretly, covertly.

take] proceed to occupy: *O.E.D.*2, vb., B.27.

37. *a-work*] (1) at work, in activity; (2) i.e. to copulate: see Partridge, work, vb.

41. *cold comfort*] (1) the reverse of encouraging contentment: see *O.E.D.*2, cold, a., 10; (2) no sexual pleasure: see III.ii.208 and n.[2]; (3) proverbial: Tilley, C542.

42. *market*] (1) the action or business of buying and selling, hence; (2) sale (of her body): see Partridge, market-place.

45. *When ... mainly*] proverbial: cf. Tilley, S714, 'Of a little spark a great fire'.

46. *business*] sexual intercourse or intimacy: Partridge.

48. *art*] sexual artifice: cf. *M.W.M.M.*, I.i.126-8 and Shakespeare, *MM*, II.ii.188-90, 'Never could the strumpet, / With all her double vigour—art and nature— / Once stir my temper'.

50-1.] Cf. II.i.215-20.

53. *allusion*] symbolic likening: *O.E.D.*2, 3.

59. *feel*] The MS reading is just plausible if the entire sentence is a projected fantasy of the approaching evening; thus the 'Best of friends' of l. 57 may be Isabella: cf. *C.*, II.ii.147 (Revels), where DeFlores fantasizes embracing Beatrice: 'Methinks I feel her in mine arms already'.

68. *gentlewoman*] a woman of good birth or breeding, but without a titled rank. Fernando's incorrect address is feigned ignorance.

69. *ladyship*] social rank as a lady (*O.E.D.2*, 1), which is higher than that of a gentlewoman.

75. *one*] i.e. Florida.

80. *Cry ... lady*] proverbial: Dent, MM13, 'To cry one mercy'.

81. *stuff*] See II.ii.53 and n.

89. *curtains*] Curtained beds were commonplace: see *R.T.*, II.iii.0.1-2n (Revels), and cf. *M.W.M.M.*, II.ii.1-8, *T.C.O.O.*, IV.v.5, and Tourneur, *A.T.*, V.i.60 (Revels).

90. *disease*] (1) disturb (from rest or sleep): *O.E.D.2*, vb., 1b; (2) discomfort, trouble, annoy: *O.E.D.2*, vb., 1.

97-8.] Cf. *H.K.K.*, I.i.93-4: 'That riches is not best, though it be mighty, / That's purchas'd by the ruin of another'.

102-3.] Cf. *M.D.B.M.*, II.i.100-2: 'better the man / Had never known creation, than to live / Th' unlucky ruin of so fair temple'.

109. *t'affect*] to have an affection for, love: see *O.E.D.2*, vb.^{1}, 2a.

113. *miss*] fail to meet (a person with whom a meeting was intended): *O.E.D.2*, vb.^{1}, 4.

122. *this*] these: *O.E.D.2*, dem. pron. and adj., B.4f.

123. *strumpet*] i.e. Florida.

go] i.e. to Antonio and Isabella's house.

IV.iii.

0.1 *in her chamber*] signified by the upper acting space: see IV.iii.22. Cf. *S.M.T.*, V.i.17.1-2 (Revels), upon which Lancashire comments: 'There appears to have been considerable use in Jacobean drama of the appearance of evil characters *above*, to watch the outcome of activities plotted by them'. See, for example, Chapman, *Bussy D'Ambois*, V.iii.0.1 (Revels).

8. *betimes*] at an early time.

9. *resolved*] convinced: *O.E.D.2*, 2.

10. *There ... us*] probably proverbial: cf. Tilley, L544, 'There is no love lost between them'.

13-14. *pay ... metal*] probably proverbial: cf. Tilley, C507, 'To pay one in his own coin'.

16. *cries*] publicly announces, proclaims, i.e. by snoring loudly; cf. Shakespeare, *Mac*, II.ii.5-6, 'the surfeited grooms / Do mock their charge with snores'.

disease] (1) see IV.ii.90n.; (2) bring into an unhealthy condition (through Antonio's violence): see ll. 37-41 and V.i.71-2.

18. *I ... posset*] Cf. Shakespeare, *Mac*, II.ii.6, 'I have drugged their possets'.

spiced] 'too affect the character or quality of, by means of some addition or modification': not in *O.E.D.2* as applied to persons, but see 'spice', vb., 1b.

posset] See I.ii.89n.

19. *hear*] *O.E.D.2* lists MS spelling, 'heare', as a variant form of 'here', which makes equally good sense.

19-32.] The staging derives from Shakespeare, *Mac*, II.iii.1-20: see Edward J. Esche, review of *Three Jacobean Witchcraft Plays*, eds. Peter Corbin and Douglas Sedge, *Ideas and Production*, 8 (1988), 109 and Introduction, pp. 60-2.

20. *him*] i.e. Antonio.

21. *him*] i.e. Gaspero.

24. *up*] 'used imperatively (with ellipse of verb), as a command or exhortation to action, activity, rising from bed, movement, etc.': *O.E.D.2*, adv.', 28a. Francesca orders Gaspero not only to awake but also to act.

28. *stir*] See II.i.227 and n.

33. *cannot ... but*] proverbial: Dent, CC11.

36. *lodging*] bedroom: *O.E.D.2*, vbl.sb., 4.

37. *Here's*] i.e. in Gaspero's bedroom.

43. *spoiled*] destroyed.

46. *perjurous*] obsolete form of 'perjurious': *O.E.D.2*: cf. *W.B.W.*,
III.iii.280.

51-3.] Cf. *H.K.K.*, I.i.125-6: 'There's nothing makes man feel his
miseries / But knowledge only'.

61. *Above*] beyond, more than: *O.E.D.2*, B.7. Cf. *1H.W.*, I.iv.22-3: 'a
patience aboue mans iniuries'.

100. *goes up*] i.e. as he sheathes it.

101. *new man*] i.e. Sebastian disguised as Celio.

108. *by the way*] (1) incidentally: see *O.E.D.2*, by, prep., adv., 12b; (2)
on: see *O.E.D.2*, by, prep., adv., 19a.

V.i.

0.1. *ANTONIO*] The emendation is required here (and subsequently in
the first two speech headings) because Antonio, not Sebastian, is challenging
Abberzanes, as the following action in the scene makes clear. The error may
indicate Middleton's change of plan in composition, as Corbin & Sedge
suggest, but since Antonio has requested this interview with Abberzanes
(IV.iii.105-7), and since Sebastian does not meet Abberzanes anywhere else
in the play, the error might be Crane's: he could have simply made a mistake
in his transcription and repeated it twice.

2. *untrussed*] 'i.e. the points or tagged laces by which the hose or
breeches were attached to the doublet, being yet untied': Dyce. Cf. *P.*,
III.i.0.1: '*Enter* Falso *untrussed*'.

3. *The ... pity*] proverbial: Dent, MM16.

4. *scape*] escape.

6. *scabbard*] playing on the sense of vagina: cf. *F. of L.*, V.i.54 and
N.W.N.H., I.i.47-8, where Savourwit requests two combatants to sheath their
swords: 'Come, I must have you friends; a pox of weapons! / There's a

whore gapes for't; put it up i' the scabbard'; hence, Abberzanes satisfaction of l. 7.

9. *I ... weapon*] The emphasis on 'wear' as opposed to 'use' indicates Abberzanes is a coward: cf. *O.L.*, IV.ii.261: 'I love to keep good weapons, though [I] ne'er fought.' 'Weapon' here plays on the sense of penis: Partridge.

13. *To ... truth*] proverbial: Dent, TT6, 'To tell (you) the truth (I tell you true)'.

holiday] not fitted for serious action: *O.E.D.*2, 4a.

15. *rip ... navel*] a classic warrior killing: cf. Shakespeare, *Mac*, I.ii.22.

27. *starting-holes*] means of evasion, loopholes: cf. *P.*, I.ii.152-6.

light] discover: *O.E.D.*2, vb.^{1}, 10d.

28. *Go to*] proverbial: Dent, GG7.

play] (1) action, dealing; (2) amorous sport: Partridge.

29. *seed*] offspring, progeny.

41. *friend*] See II.i.36n^2.

50. *it*] i.e. the wine.

60. *falsely*] deceitfully, treacherously.

falsely] erroneously, wrongly: *O.E.D.*2, 2.

61. *by contract*] See I.i.3-4 and n.

74. *fury*] fierce passion, wild fit.

75. *this seven year*] See I.i.23n.

sound] free from venereal disease: Partridge.

78. *at charge*] coiting: see Patridge, charge, vb.

light horse] courtesan: *O.E.D.*2, 2 cites this as its only example.

80. *struck*] (1) beaten; (2) sexually experienced: see Partridge, strike.

doe] young woman, but usually applied to a virgin, thus ironic here: cf. Shakespeare, *Tit*, II.i.118-19: 'Single you thither then this dainty doe, / And strike her home by force'.

87. *conceit*] (1) 'a (morbid) affection or seizure of the body or mind': *O.E.D.2*, sb., 11; possibly (2) personal opinion or judgement.

abuse] (1) injure, hurt: *O.E.D.2*; vb., 5; (2) deceive.

88. *For*] in spite of, notwithstanding: see *O.E.D.2*, A.23a for use with 'any'.

89. *wipes off*] removes, clears away: see *O.E.D.2*, wipe, vb., 2c.

93. *wears your blood*] bears the (noble) ancestry of your family—i.e. through blood-relationship to you.

95. *loud*] (1) clamorous, noisy; (2) emphatic or vehement in expression.

97ff] Cf. *F.Q.*, V.i.210-21 for the plotting of a similar kind of mock indictment designed for a woman to clear herself.

99. *amaze*] overwhelm with wonder, astound.

103. *And*] possibly emphatic usage, i.e. 'and that': see Abbott, 95 and 96.

104. *tempest*] Middleton often uses the image of a tempest or a storm to indicate irrational or uncontrollable anger: cf., for example, *1H.W.*, I.ii.66, *H.K.K.*, IV.ii.127-37, and *S.G.*, V.i.64-5. Cf. also V.iii.25-33 and n.

110. *sureness*] subjective certainty: *O.E.D.2*, 2b.

111. *mistaken*] 'i.e. stabbed in mistake for Isabella': Corbin & Sedge.

112. *privilege*] right of affording security from arrest. *O.E.D.2* notes privileges granted for office, rank, station and place, but not for injury: see sb., B.4, and 7.

114. *she*] i.e. Isabella.

118. *rage*] madness.

122, 123. *stirring*] See II.i.227 and n.

135. *Flatters*] encourages: literally, inspires with hope, usually on insufficient grounds.

V.ii.

2. *fitted*] See I.ii.224n.

4. *His ... molten*] See I.ii.48-9.

5. *blue fire*] See I.ii.10n^2.

8. *Out ... pictures*] proverbial: Dent, OO3, 'Out upon (on) it (etc.)'.

14. *closely*] secretly, covertly.

16. *Worse and worse*] proverbial: Dent, WW34.

17. *scrupulous*] prone to hesitate or doubt, distrustful.

18-29. Cum ... *designs*] Cf. Scot, pp. 225-6:

Moreouer out of Ouid they alledge as followeth.

   Cùm volui ripis ipsis mirantibus amnes

   Infontes rediere suos, concússáq; sisto,

   Stantia concutio, cantu freta nubila pello,

   Nubiláq; ûnduco, ventos abigóq; vocóq,

   Vipereas rumpo verbis & carmine fauces,

   Viuáque saxa, sua conuulsáque robora terra,

   Et syluas moueo, iubeóque tremescere montes,

   Et mugire solum, manesque exire sepulchris,

   Téque luna traho, &c:

   The riuers I can make retire,

   Into the fountaines whence they flo,

   (Whereat the banks themselues admire)

   I can make standing waters go,

   With charmes I driue both sea and clowd,

   I make it calme and blowe alowd.

   The vipers iawes, the rockie stone,

   With words and charmes I breake in twaine

   The force of earth congeald in one,

   I mooue and shake both woods and plaine;

I make the soules of men arise,

I pull the moone out of the skies.

Cf. also *The .xv. Bookes of P. Ouidius Naso, entytuled Metamorphosis, translated oute of Latin into English meeter, by Arthur Golding Gentleman...* (London, 1567), The Seventh Booke, p. 83v:

I haue compelled streames to run cleane backward to their spring.

By charmes I make the calme Seas rough, & make ye rough Seas

plaine,

And couer all the Skie with Cloudes and chase them thence againe.

By charmes I raise and lay the windes, and burst the Vipers jaw.

And from the bowels of the Earth both stones and trees doe draw.

Whole woods and Forestes I remoue: I make the Mountaines

shake,

And euen the Earth it selfe to grone and fearfully to quake.

I call up dead men from their graues: and thee O lightsome Moone

I darken oft, though beaten brasse abate thy perill soone.

See Introduction p. 33 for discussion of Middleton's omission of the sixth line of Ovid's Latin quoted in Scot.

26. *woods walk*] Cf. Shakespeare, *Mac*, IV.i.107-9.

28. *marbles*] marble tombs.

29. *involved*] not straightforward and open, underhand.

38. *howlet-time*] presumably, after the first cry of an owl at night, and thus a time appropriate for performing evil: see III.iii.5-6. 'Howlet' is a dialectic form of 'owlet', an owl, young owl or little owl (see *O.E.D.2*, howlet and owlet). The only use of 'owlet' in the Shakespeare canon is in *Macbeth*, at IV.i.17.

43. semina cum sanguine] seed with blood.

48. *conscionable*] reasonable: this meaning not in *O.E.D.2* for this word, but see 'conscience', 3 and 'conscionably', 2.

50.1. four other *Witches*] Hecate refers to 'five sisters' at l. 37.

52. *marmaritin*] See I.ii.164-8n.

bear-breech] popular name of genus *Acanthus*, brank ursine: *O.E.D.2*, sb.¹, 10.

55. *red-haired*] Parker observes in *C.M. in C.*, III.ii.44n (Revels) that 'red hair was associated with lechery' and cites for comparison *F. of L.*, IV.iii.116, V.i.12-15, and 74-80.

57. *acopus*] either (1) a plant useful in childbirth, or (2) a soothing salve: see Lewis and Short, *Latin Dictionary*, acopus, -us, II. and III., and *O.E.D.2*, acopon, which cites 1661 as the earliest date of usage.

75. *younker*] (1) a young nobleman or gentleman; (2) a young man generally, especially a gay or fashionable one.

83. *tune of damnation*] Cf. *R.T.*, IV.iv.34 (Revels): 'O nimble in damnation, quick in tune'.

84. *burden*] either (1) the bass, undersong, or (2) the refrain or chorus of a song.

85. *strike*] sound.

86.1. Here ... *Dance*] Cf. Scot, p. 42: 'And here some of *Monsieur Bodins* lies may be inserted, who saith, that at these magicall assemblies, the witches neuer faile to danse; and in their danse they sing these words; Har har, diuell diuell, danse here, danse here, plaie here, plaie here, *Sabbath, sabbath*. And whiles they sing and danse, euerie one hath a broome in hir hand, and holdeth it vp aloft.' Dancing is one of the essential constituents of witchcraft: see Valiente, pp. 77-9. See John P. Cutts, 'Jacobean Masque and Stage Music', *Music and Letters*, 35 (1954), 185-200 for a discussion of the possible music for this dance as found in British Library, Add. MS. 10444. See also Corbin & Sedge, pp. 258-9.

V.iii.

3. *this woman*] i.e. Florida.

4. *creature*] The same word is used to describe a whore in *M.W.M.M.*, IV.iii.76-80.

17. *her*] i.e. Florida.

her] i.e. Isabella.

25-33. *A ... castle*] Anne Lancashire suggests that this is an allegorical 'descent into hell pit': see *'The Witch*: Stage Flop or Political Mistake?' in Kenneth Friedenreich, ed., *"Accompaninge the Players": Essays in Celebration of Thomas Middleton, 1580-1980* (New York, 1983), p. 172. The moral of Antonio's death is pointed by a comparison to *F.Q.*, III.i.86-9: 'he that makes his last peace with his Maker / In anger, anger is his peace eternally: / He must expect the same return again / Whose venture is deceitful'. Cf. V.i.104 and n.

26. *my lord*] i.e. Antonio, as the MS punctuation makes clear.

31. *temple's*] church's—especially applied to a large or grand edifice: *O.E.D.*, sb.[1], 2.

38. *light*] (1) sexually immoral; (2) engaged in prostitution: Partridge.

40-2.] Cf. *H.K.K.*, II.iii.166-71 for similar condemnation of illicit female sexual passion.

41. *passion*] overpowering grief (probably generated through past sexual love or physical desire: Partridge).

44. S.D.] the late discovery of a disguised character is a common dramatic technique of the period: cf., for instance, *P.*, V.i.162, *N.W.N.H.*, V.i.352.1-2. and Shakespeare, *MM*, V.i.352.1.

47. *Your ... knowledge*] having worked for you as a servant cannot change me from being known (now).

51. *two ... more*] i.e. mouths, figurative for wounds.

52. *understanding*] 'the intellectual faculty as manifested in a particular person or set of persons': *O.E.D.*, vbl. sb., 2.

54. *Urbin*] Urbino; mistake for Ravenna.

64-5. *One ... now*] This crux may not be as difficult as editors have made it appear. The lines are a statement of the *present* situation; ll. 66-74 are a justification of a decision already made for *future* action: the one night bed-trick has bound Almachildes to her for ever, unless he can be killed. Corbin & Sedge's emendation is inspired, but indefensible.

71-2. *'Tis ... time*] This is a reference to the belief that sexual activity shortened one's life span: cf. *S.M.T.*, I.i.43-8 (Revels): 'He gets me all my children; there I save by't. / Beside, I draw my life out by the bargain / Some twelve years longer than the times appointed, / When my young prodigal gallant kicks up's heels / At one and thirty, and lies dead and rotten / Some five and forty years before I'm coffined.' In her note to these lines, Lancashire quotes *Witch*, V.iii.71-3, *O.L.*, V.i.550-2: 'I would speak with the youthful duke himself; he and I may speak of things that shall be thirty or forty years after you are dead and rotten', and *Wid.*, III.ii.62-4: 'These wenching businesses / Are strange unlucky things and fatal fooleries; / No mar'l so many gallants die ere thirty'.

80.1. discovered] Cf. *S.M.T.*, IV.iii.0.3 (Revels), upon which Lancashire comments, '*Discovered* is the Jacobean theatrical term for the deliberate revealing of a scene by means of opening a door, pulling a curtain, etc.' Cf. also *F.Q.*, IV.ii.0.1 and *S.G.*, I.iii.0.1.

89. *piece*] (1) an individual example of any form of action; (2) a person.

91-2.] Cf. *Y.T.*, x.29-30 (Revels): '*Husband.* My dear soul, whom I too much have wronged, / For death I die, and for this have I longed.'

93. *injury*] i.e. the public and private love tests of pledging drinks to the Duke out of her dead father's skull: see I.i.111ff and II.ii.58-64.

96. *an one*] i.e. united.

98. *cursed fury*] Anger as the cause of destruction is common: cf. V.iii.25-33 and n., and *Y.T.*, v.34 (Revels).

99-101. *my ... adult'ress*] an indication of how corrupted the Lord Governor assumes the Duchess to be: cf. *C.*, V.ii.15-17 (Revels): 'yet he's so foul, / One would scarce touch him with a sword he loved / And make account of'.

109. *known*] (1) been acquainted with; (2) been sexually intimate with: see Partridge, know.

111.] Cf. *1H.W.*, II.i.304: 'This is the common fashion of you all'.

118. *blinded*] (1) blindfolded: see III.i.1-15; (2) deluded: *O.E.D.*, 2; (3) undiscriminating; (4) reckless.

121. *approve*] corroborate, conform: *O.E.D.2*, vb.[1], 2.

123. *haberdasher's shop*] 'In the course of the 16th c. the trade [of haberdasher] seems to have been split into two, those of: a. A dealer in, or maker of, hats and caps, a hatter *obs.*); b. A dealer in small articles appertaining to dress, as thread, tape, ribbons, etc.': *O.E.D.2*.

128. *rise*] The stage action of rising from a kneeling posture often indicates forgiveness: cf. *F.Q.*, IV.iii.106-21.

129. *practice*] (1) treachery; (2) conspiracy, intrigue.

APPENDIX A

Lineation

All departures from MS are recorded in the following list. All arrangements by other editors are cited, whether adopted by the present text or not.

[I.i.]

52-3.] *So MS;* Why ... not; / For ... reputation *Corbin & Sedge.*

81-2. 'Tis ... little] *So Scott; one line in MS.*

84-6. Amsterdam ... Queenhithe] *So MS; as prose Scott.*

88-93.] *So MS; as prose Scott.*

94-6.] *So MS; as prose Scott;* Like ... girls / And ... conclusions *Dyce.*

[I.ii.]

1-7.] *So Corbin & Sedge; Titty ... Suckin / and ... Robin / white ... redd Speritts: / Deuill-Toad ... Dam MS; as prose Dyce.*

8.] *So MS; as prose Dyce.*

49-51. Laid down ... subtly] *So this ed.;* layd-downe ... yet? / they're ... too / good, / then ... subtelly *MS;* Laid down ... too / Good ... subtly *Dyce pres.;* Laid down ... yet? / They're ... Good. / Then ... subtly *Corbin & Sedge.*

58-60.] *So Dyce;* of ... Hog: / fell ... too *MS;* Of ... goslings, / And ... too *Corbin & Sedge.*

62-5.] *So this ed.;* each ... Snakes / shall ... *Dayrie-wenches* / shall ... Curssing *MS;* Each ... snakes / Shall ... all / Beforehand ... dairy-wenches / Shall ... cursing *Dyce;* Each ... send / Those ... beforehand. / The ... stroke / Dry ... cursing *Corbin & Sedge.*

72-82.] *So (as prose) Dyce;* and ... (Mother?) / Noh. / Your ... Bakers; /
you'll ... hundred: / and ... give / yo" ... the / begining ... through / his ... the /
auncientest-Trade ... *Tailor* / prickd-downe ... him *MS.*

88-90. Dear ... shorter] *So MS; as prose Scott.*

90-1. Thou'rt ... villainy] *So Dyce; one line in MS.*

91-2. Not ... think] *So Dyce; one line in MS; as prose Scott; as verse* Not ...
forsooth. / Truly ... think *Corbin & Sedge.*

92-7. How ... daughter] *So Scott;* how ... straight: / ther's ... and / can ... pray
/ give ... the / Night-Mare ... over-lay / a ... Daughter *MS.*

98-100. The ... once] *So Dyce;* the ... Night / make ... once *MS; as prose
Scott.*

107-10.] *So (as prose) Scott;* Vrchins ... ffawnes, / Silence ... Centaures, /
Dwarffes ... Man / i'th ... the / *Puckle ... Hus MS.*

155-6.] *So MS; as one line Corbin & Sedge.*

188-92.] *So Scott;* there's ... the / fineliest ... falne / into ... Childes / Greaze
... in / the ... heeles / with ... eares *MS.*

194-7.] *So (as prose) Scott;* I ... her / honestie ... be / Coverd ... (Mother.)
MS.

198-9.] *So MS; one verse line in Scott;* Call ... methinks, / Very ... tumblers
Dyce.

207-9.] *So MS;* Why ... choice / Of ... ones *Corbin & Sedge.*

213-4.] *So MS; as one line Corbin & Sedge.*

216-17.] *So MS; as one line Corbin & Sedge.*

218-19.] *So Scott;* you ... vnmannerly, / hee'll ... anon *MS.*

226-7.] *So MS; as prose Scott.*

236-7.] *So MS; as prose Scott.*

239-41.] *So (as prose) Scott;* how ... the / Devill ... and / I'll ... twaine / with
... him *MS.*

[II.i.]

34-6.] *So Scott;* I haue ... a-hundred / Gentlewomen ... yeere *MS*.

43-4. These ... children] *So (as prose) Dyce;* Theis ... Gentle women / ten ... Children *MS*.

44-51. If ... fast] *So Scott;* Yf ... Child / so ... whipd / ere ... come / by ... stay / perhaps ... of / Reeking-Water-men ... wyne, / Chewitts ... Cursse / those ... fast *MS*.

52-6.] *So MS; as prose Scott*.

139-40.] *So Dyce;* that ... comes / with ... borne *MS;* That ... 'em. / Oh ... comes / With ... born *Scott*.

140-1. born / To ... I] *So MS;* born to lead / Poor ... I *Scott*.

160.] *So MS; as prose Ellis*.

174-8.] *So Steevens; I ... me / I ... waie / of ... (Son) / nor ... haue / sent ... her MS*.

[II.ii.]

25-6. Here ... gentlewoman] *So Dyce;* Here ... on't / and ... Gentlewoman *MS*.

26-31. The ... pestilence] *So Scott;* The ... the / Brayne ... bad / her ... a / Litle ... Taile / I ... pestlence *MS*.

32-5.] *So MS; as prose Dyce*.

110-11.] *So Dyce; one line in MS*.

118.] *So MS;* Whose ... be. / Oh ... already *Scott*.

[III.i.]

57-8.] *So this ed.;* be ... our-self. / and ... for. / good ... thee *MS;* Be ... for. / Good ... thee *Corbin & Sedge*.

[III.ii.]

2-4.] *So Scott;* I ... of / a ... every / mans ... Wife / half ... handsomely *MS*.

5-6.] *So MS; as prose Corbin & Sedge.*

141-2.] *So Dyce pres.;* Your ... me / you ... wellcome. / where ... she? / who? ... wiffe? / I Sir. / within *MS;* Your ... me / You ... she? / Who ... Within *Corbin & Sedge.*

185-6.] *So Dyce; one line in MS.*

[III.iii.]

4-5. O ... yet] *So Dyce; one line in MS.*

15-19.] *So Scott;* they'are ... night: / they ... day, / I ... Slutts / there ... it, / I'll ... Infect / a ... now *MS.*

18-20. a ... son] *So Scott;* a ... now. / what ... Son *MS;* a ... region *(as prose)* She ... son *(as one verse line) Corbin & Sedge.*

21-2.] *So Scott;* a ... were / too ... me *MS.*

23-4. Nineteen ... eggs] *So MS; as prose Scott.*

28-9. Here's ... 'em] *So Dyce;* heer's ... thee / My ... sure / With ... 'em *MS; as prose Scott.*

31-2. Every ... mother] *So MS; one line Scott.*

34-7.] *So Scott;* Aloft ... once, / that ... Mother. / they ... flying / over ... *Musitians MS.*

44-7.] *So MS; Where's ... Here. / Where's ... Here Corbin & Sedge.*

54-5.] *So MS; one line Scott.*

63-4.] *So Scott;* hark ... in / her ... language *MS.*

80-2.] *So Scott;* Well ... be / gambolling ... here, / like ... Mortall *MS.*

[IV.i.]

1-14.] *So Scott; Though* ... a / pretty ... at / the ... make / myself ... a / Supper ... yong / formall ... there / is ... Condition, / and ... quight / out ... Aqua- / vite-shop ... a / Beadle ... the / honestie ... reckning / the ... be / not ... a / Woman ... about / my ... a / piteous ... be / entituled ... haire-Braceletts *MS.*

[IV.iii.]

56-7. Come ... too] *So Dyce; one line in MS.*

[V.i.]

5-7.] *So Scott;* Nay ... acquainted / greatly ... good / Scabbard ... me *MS.*

9-10.] *So Dyce;* I ... thing / coñendable *MS; one verse line in Steevens.*

12-13. I ... sir] *So this ed.; one line in MS; as prose Scott.*

13-14. 'tis ... side] *So Scott; one line in MS.*

16-17.] *So Bullen pres.;* though ... in't. / are ... Sir? / I'll ... anon. / why ... Sir? *MS;* Though ... in't. / Are ... anon. / Why ... sir? *Corbin & Sedge.*

125-9.] *So this ed.;* pray ... ready. / how ... Surgeon? / hath ... howres. / how ... talkes. / did ... *Master.* / how ... night? / then ... Madam *MS;* Pray ... surgeon! / Hath ... talks! / Did ... master? / Why ... madam *Dyce pres.*

[V.ii.]

13-15.] *So Bullen;* and ... hence. / Canst ... this / Can I? / I ... closely. / so ... too? / so ... cuñingly *MS;* And ... hence. / Canst ... closely? / So ... cunningly? *Corbin & Sedge.*

25.] *So MS;* Te quoque... traho. / Can ... daughter *Steevens.*

30-2.] *So Scott;* I ... mad / and ... then, / and ... Latten *MS.*

46-8.] *So Scott;* they ... eate / vp ... good / conscionable Pudding *MS.*

62-7.] *So Dyce; Titty* ... in / *Fire-Drake* ... *Luckey.* / *Liand* ... in *MS.*

70-3.] *So MS;* Here's ... that! / Here'S ... a grain *Corbin & Sedge.*

83-4.] *So Scott;* A ... warrant / yo^u ... Burthen *MS.*

[V.iii.]

65-6.] *So Scott; one line in MS.*

82-3.] *So Dyce; one line in MS.*

110-11.] *So MS; as one line in Corbin & Sedge.*

APPENDIX B

The songs

This edition has not attempted a full collation of the songs in the text. They have however, been admirably collated by Nicholas Brooke in his edition of *The Tragedy of Macbeth*. The following are the earliest settings available for 'In a maiden time professed' and 'Come away, come away, Hecate'.

1. By John Wilson, Bodleian Library MS. Mus. b.I.f.21 (also extant in Drexel MS. 4357, No. 32). Note that the MS printed overleaf contains an additional two verses which do not appear in the Crane MS of *Witch*, but which do make the bawdy nature of the song absolutely clear.

APPENDIX B

2. By Robert Johnson and found in the Fitzwilliam Museum MU. MS 782, known as the Bull Manuscript, here reproduced. See Nicholas Brooke, ed., Shakespeare, *The Tragedy of Macbeth* (Oxford, 1990), pp. 225-32 for fuller discussion of this song.

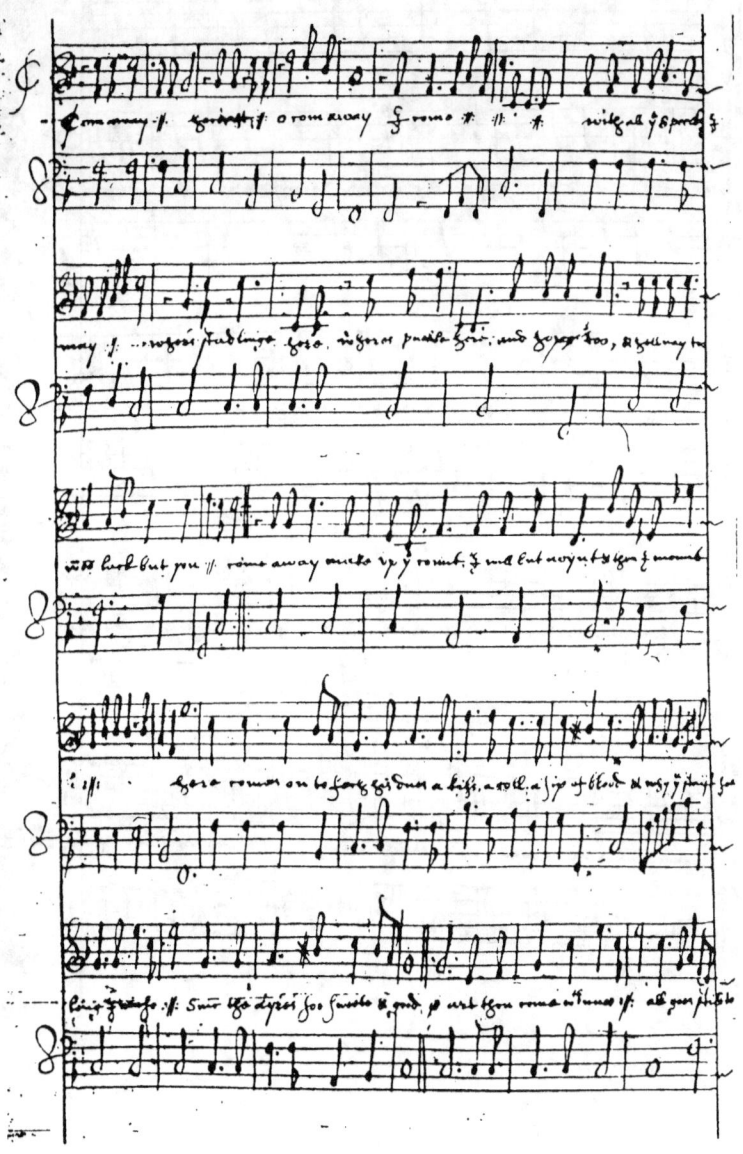

APPENDIX C

Source materials

The following extract is taken from Niccolo Machiavelli, *The Florentine History*, trans. T[homas]. B[edingfield]. (London, 1595), pp. 6-7.

The *Longobardi* beeing (as is aforesaid) entered into those countries neare *Danubio*, who had lately bene abandoned by *Heruli* and *Turingi*, when by their King *Odoacre* they were led into Italy: for a time they there remained. But the kingdome being come to *Alboino* a man couragious & cruel, they passed the riuer *Danubio*, and fought with *Comundo* King of the *Zepedi*, and ouerthrew him in *Pannonio*, which hee then possessed. *Alboino* in this victorie amongst others, happened to take prisoner the duaghter of *Comundo*, called *Rosmunda*, married her, and thereby became Lord of *Pannonia*. Then mooued by the crueltie of his nature, hee made a cup of her fathers hed, whereof in memorie of the victorie) he vsed to drinke. But then called into *Italy* by *Narsete* (with whome in the warres of the *Gotti* hee had acquaintance and friendship) left *Pannonia* to the *Vnni*, who after the death of *Attila* (as is aforesaid) were returned into their countery. Then he came againe into *Italy*, where finding the same into many partes diuided, sodenly wan *Pauia, Millan, Verona, Vicenza*, all *Toscana*, and the more part of *Flamminia*, now called *Romagna*. So that perswading himselfe through so many and so speedie successes, to haue already (as it were) gotten the victorie of all *Italy*, hee celebrated a solemne feast in *Verona*, whereat, beeing by drinking much, become very merry, and seeing the skull of *Comundo* full of wine, hee caused the same to be presented to the Queene

277

Rosmunda, who sat ouer against him at the table (saying vnto her, with so loude a voice that euerie one might heare him) that she should now at this feast drinke with her fater: which speech pearced the Lady to the Heart, and she forthwith determined to reuenge the same. Then knowing that *Almachilde* (a valiant young gentleman of *Lombardi*) loued a maiden of hers, of whome hee obtained to lie with her, and the Queene beeing priuy to that consent, did her selfe tarry in the place of their meeting, which beeing without light, *Almachilde* came thither, and supposing to haue lien with the mayden, enioyed the Queene her mistresse, which done, the Queene discouered her selfe and said vnto him, that it was in his power to kill *Alboino*, and possesse her with her kingdome foreuer: but if hee refused so to do, shee would procure that *Alboino* should kill him, as one that had abused his wife. To this motion and murther of *Alboino*, *Almachilde* consented. After the murther performed, finding that he could not according to his expectation enioy the kingdome, and fearing to be slaine of the *Lonbardes* for the loue they bare to *Alboino*, the Queene and hee taking their princely treasure and iewels, fled to *Longino* at *Rauenna*, who honorably there receiued them. During these troubles, *Iustiniano* the Emperour died, and in his place was elected *Tiberio*, who beeing occupied in the warres against the *Parthi*, could not go to the reliefe of *Italy*. Whereby *Longino* hoped that time would well serue him, with the countenance of *Rosmunda* and helpe of her treasure, to become King of *Lombardy* and all *Italy*. And conferring his intent with the Queene, perswaded her to kill *Almachilde*, and take him for her husband: shee accepted and agreed vnto that which hee perswaded, preparing a cup of wine poisoned, and with her owne hand shee offered the same to *Almachilde*, comming from a bath hote and thirstie: he hauing drunke halfe the wine, and finding his bodie thereby greatly mooued, mistrusting the poison, enforced *Rosmunda* to drinke the rest, whereof both the one and the other within fewe houres died, and *Longino* bereft of his expectation to become King.

APPENDIX D

A note on stage history

I had intended to include a section on the stage history of *Witch* in the Introduction, but all of my numerous letters of inquiry to various institutions remain unanswered. Thus the information that I have is unconfirmed and rather vague, but it is a great deal sharper than it would have been thanks to a recent generous correspondence from Dr. Elizabeth Schafer.

I have heard of three productions. The first two are roughly simultaneous. One was in March of 1984 or so, and done by the Department of Drama at Queens University in Kingston, Ontario, Canada. The Director was Gary Wagner and the Assistant Director was Sara Diederichs. Another production was mounted by students at Warwick University, England, around 1984 and directed by Robert Jones. The third was done in August of perhaps 1988 by Ormond College, Melbourne University, Australia. The venue was the student union theatre.

GLOSSARIAL INDEX TO THE COMMENTARY

280

BIBLIOGRAPHY

Abbott, E.A. *A Shakespearian Grammar: An Attempt to Illustrate some of the Differences between Elizabethan and Modern English.* 2nd ed. London, 1870.

Anglo, Sydney, ed. *The Damned Art: Essays in the Literature of Witchcraft.* London, Henley and Boston, 1977.

Arnold, E.C. *Ink on Paper.* New York, 1963.

Asp, Carolyn. *A Study of Thomas Middleton's Tragicomedies.* Salzburg Studies in English Literature, Jacobean Drama Studies, 28. Salzburg, 1974.

Bald, R.C. 'The Chronology of Thomas Middleton's Plays'. *The Modern Language Review,* 32 (1937), 33-43.

——————. 'Middleton's Civic Employments'. *Modern Philology,* 31 (1933), 65-78.

Baldwin, T.W. *William Shakspere's Small Latine & Lesse Greeke.* 2 vols. Urbana, Illinois, 1944.

Barker, Richard Hindry. *Thomas Middleton.* New York and London, 1958.

Barroll, J. Leeds, *et al. The Revels History of Drama in English, Volume III, 1576-1613.* London, 1975.

Beaumont, Francis and John Fletcher. *The Dramatic Works in the Beaumont and Fletcher Canon.* Gen. ed. Fredson Bowers. 8 vols. [to date]. Cambridge, 1966-.

Benguerel, G. *Thomas Middleton: Part 1.* Nordhausen, Kircher, 1870.

Bentley, Gerald Eades. *The Jacobean and Caroline Stage.* 7 vols. Oxford, 1941-68.

——————. *The Profession of Dramatist in Shakespeare's Time,*

1560-1642. London, 1971.

Berger, Thomas L. and William C. Bradford, Jr. *An Index of Characters in English Printed Drama*. Englewood, Colorado, 1975.

Bibliotheca Steevensiana. A Catalogue of the Curious and Valuable Library of George Steevens, Esq. London, 1800.

Bodin, Jean. *La Demonomanie des Sociers*. Ed. denieres. Paris, 1598.

──────. *De Magorvm Daemonomanie*. Trans. Lotarivm Philoponvm. Basileae, 1581.

──────. *De Magorvm Daemonomanie*. Franncofvrti, 1590.

Bowers, Fredson. *Elizabethan Revenge Tragedy 1587-1642*. Princeton, 1940.

Briggs, Katharine. *A Dictionary of Fairies: Hobgoblins, Brownies, Bogies and other Supernatural Creatures*. London, 1976.

──────. *Pale Hecate's Team: An Examination of the Beliefs on Witchcraft and Magic among Shakespeare's Contemporaries and His Immediate Successors*. London, 1962.

Briquet, J.M. *Les filigranes: dictionnaire historique des marques du papier dès leur apparition vers 1282 jusqu'en 1600. A Facsimile of the 1907 Edition with Supplementary Material Contributed by a Number of Scholars*. Ed. Allan Stevenson. 4 vols. Amsterdam, 1968.

British Museum General Catalogue of Printed Books. London, 1962.

Brittin, Norman A. *Thomas Middleton*. New York, 1972.

Bromham, A.A. 'The Date of *The Witch* and the Essex Divorce Case'. *Notes and Queries*, 225 (1980), 149-52.

──────. and Zara Bruzzi. *'The Changeling' and the Years of Crisis, 1619-1624: A Heiroglyph of Britain*. London and New York, 1990.

Brooks, John B. 'Thomas Middleton'. In *The Popular School: A Survey and Bibliography of Recent Studies in English Renaissance Drama*. Eds. Terence P. Logan and Denzell S. Smith. Lincoln, Nebraska, 1975, pp. 51-84.

Byrne, Muriel St. Clare. 'Elizabethan Handwriting for Beginners'. *The Review of English Studies*, 1 (1925), 198-209.

Catalogue of Early English Poetry and Other Miscellaneous Works Illustrating the British Drama, Collected by Edmond Malone, Esq. and now Preserved in the Bodleian Library. Oxford, 1836.

A Catalogue of the Greater Portion of the Library of the Late Edmond Malone, Esq. Editor of Shakespeare &c. (Including a Few Duplicates of His Early English Poetry.). London, 1818.

Chambers, E.K. *The Elizabethan Stage.* 4 vols. Oxford, 1923.

Christ, Karl. *Quellenstudien zu den Dramen Thomas Middleton.* Borna-Leipzig, 1905.

Christian, Mildred G. 'An Autobiographical Note by Thomas Middleton'. *Notes and Queries*, 175 (1938), 259-60.

——————. 'Middleton's Residence at Oxford'. *Modern Language Notes*, 61 (1946), 90-1.

——————. 'A Sidelight on the Family History of Thomas Middleton'. *Studies in Philology*, 44 (1947), 490-6.

Clark, Stuart. 'King James's *Daemonologie*: Witchcraft and Kingship'. In *The Damned Art: Essays in the Literature of Witchcraft.* Ed. Sydney Anglo. London, Henley and Boston, 1977, pp. 156-81.

Clowes, William. *A Short and Profitable Treatise Touching the Cure of the Disease Called (Morbus Gallicus).* London, 1579.

——————. *A Profitable and Necessarie Booke of Obseruations.* London, 1596.

Crane, Ralph. *Certaine selected Psalms of David, (in Verse) different from those usually soong in the Church.* Bodleian MS Rawl. poet. 61.

——————. *Diuers Zealous Meditations; aswell Vpon the Sufferings and Passion of Christ: as also Vpon the 17th. Chaper. of Iob: y^e. I. & 13. Verses.* Bodleian MS Rawl. D.301.

——————. *The Pilgrimes New-yeares-Gift; or, Fourteen Steps to the*

Throne of Glory. London, 1621. Bodleian Vet. A2 f. 257.

Cutts, John P. 'The Original Music to Middleton's *The Witch*'. *Shakespeare Quarterly*, 7 (1956), 203-9.

Dawson, Giles E., and Laetitia Kennedy-Skipton. *Elizabethan Handwriting, 1500-1650: A Guide to the Reading of Documents and Manuscripts*. 1966; rpt. London, 1968.

Day, John. *Law Tricks*. Ed. John Crow (with assistance from W.W. Greg and F.P. Wilson). Malone Society Reprints, Oxford, 1950 for 1949.

——————. *The Works of John Day*. 2 vols. Ed. A.H. Bullen. London, 1881.

Deighton, K. *The Old Dramatists: Conjectural Readings on the Texts of Marston: Beaumont and Fletcher: Peele: Marlowe: Chapman: Heywood: Greene: Middleton: Dekker: Webster*. Westminster, 1896.

Dekker, Thomas. *The Dramatic Works of Thomas Dekker*. 4 vols. Ed. Fredson Bowers. Cambridge, 1953-61.

Dent, R.W. *Proverbial Language in English Drama Exclusive of Shakespeare, 1495-1616*. Berkeley, Los Angeles, London, 1984.

Dobell, Bertram. *Catalogue of Books Printed for Private Circulation*. London, 1906.

Donovan, Dennis. *Elizabethan Bibliographies Supplements I: Thomas Middleton 1939-1965, John Webster 1940-1965*. London, 1967.

Eccles, Mark. 'Middleton's Birth and Education'. *The Review of English Studies*, 7 (1931), 431-41.

——————. '"Thomas Middleton a Poett"'. *Studies in Philology*, 54 (1957), 516-36.

Esche, Edward J. 'Comments on the Visual Semoitics of Middleton's *The Witch*. In *Ideas and Production: A Journal in the History of Ideas*, IV (1985), 101-7.

——————. Review of Peter Corbin and Douglas Sedge, eds. *Three Jacobean Witchcraft Plays: John Marston, 'The Tragedy of*

Sophonisba'; Thomas Middleton, 'The Witch'; William Rowley, Thomas Dekker, John Ford, 'The Witch of Edmonton'. Manchester, 1986. In *Ideas and Production: A Journal in the History of Ideas*, VIII (1988), 108-10.

Ewbank, Inga-Stina. 'The Middle of Middleton'. In *Arts of Performance in Elizabethan and Early Stuart Drama; Essays for G.K. Hunter*. Eds. Murray Biggs, *et al*. Edinburgh, 1991, pp. 156-72.

Ewen, C.L. l'Estrange. *Witch-hunting and Witch Trials: The Indictments for Witchcraft from the Records of 1373 Assizes Held for the Home Curcuit A.D. 1559-1736*. London, 1929.

Fleay, Frederick Gard. *A Biographical Chronicle of the English Drama 1559-1642*. 2 vols. London, 1891.

Fletcher, John. *Demetrius and Enanthe*. Eds. Margaret McLaren Cook and F.P. Wilson. Malone Society Reprints. Oxford, 1951 for 1950.

—————. *The Tragedy of Sir John Van Olden Barnavelt*. Ed. Wilhelmina P. Frijlinck. Amsterdam, 1922.

—————, and Philip Massinger. *Sir John van Olden Barnavelt*. Ed. T.H. Howard-Hill. Malone Society Rerints. Oxford, 1980 for 1979.

Friedenreich, Kenneth, ed. *'Accompaninge the players': Essays Celebrating Thomas Middleton, 1580-1980*. New York, 1983.

Frost, David L. *The School of Shakespeare: The Influence of Shakespeare on Elizabethan Drama 1600-42*. Cambridge, 1968.

Fuzier, Jean and Jean-Marie Maguin. 'Archetypal Patterns or Horror and Cruelty in Elizabethan Revenge Tragedy'. *Cahiers Elisabéthains*, 19 (1981), 9-25.

Genest, John. *Some Account of the English Stage, from the Restoration in 1660 to 1830*. 10 vols. Bath, 1832.

The Geneva Bible. Geneva, 1560.

George, David. 'The Problem of Middleton's *The Witch* and Its Sources'. *Notes and Queries*, 212 (1967), 209-11.

—————. 'Thomas Middleton at Oxford'. *The Modern Language Review*, 65 (1970), 734-6.

—————. 'Thomas Middleton's Sources: A Survey'. *Notes and Queries*, 216 (1971). 17-24.

Gerarde, John. *The Herball or Generall Historie of Plantes*. London, 1597.

Gifford, George. *A Discourse of the Subtill Practises of Deuilles by Witches and Sorcerers*. London, 1587.

—————. *A Dialogue Concerning Witches and Witchcraftes*. London, 1593.

Giraldi-Cinthio, Giovanni Battista. *Hecatommithi*. Venezia, 1574.

Gover, J.E.B., Allan Mawer and F.M. Stenton. *The Place-Names of Wiltshire*. English Place-Names Society. Vol. 16. Cambridge, 1939.

Graves, Thornton S. 'Ralph Crane and the King's Players'. *Studies in Philology*, 21 (1924), 362-6.

Greg, W.W. *Dramatic Documents from the Elizabethan Playhouses: Stage Plots: Actors' Parts: Prompt Books*. Oxford, 1931.

—————. *Dramatic Documents from the Elizabethan Playhouses: Stage Plots: Actors' Parts: Prompt Books* (Commentary). Oxford, 1931.

—————. *English Literary Autographs, 1550-1650*. 3 vols. London, 1932.

—————. 'Prompt Copies, Private Transcripts, and the "Playhouse Scrivener"'. *The Library*, 4th series, 6 (1925-6). 148-56.

Harbage, Alfred. *Annals of English Drama 975-1700: An Analytical Record of All Plays, Extant or Lost, Chronologically Arranged and Indexed by Authors, Titles, Dramatic Companies, etc*. London, 1940.

Harris, Anthony. *Night's Black Agents: Witchcraft and Magic in Seventeenth-Century English Drama*. Manchester, 1980.

Hartnoll, Phyllis, ed. *Shakespeare in Music*. London, 1964.

Hazlitt, Carew W., ed. *A Select Collection of Old English Plays*. Ed. Robert Dodsley. 15 vols. London, 1875.

Heawood, Edward. 'Papers Used in England after 1600: I. The Seventeenth
  Century to c. 1680'. *The Library*, 4th series, 11 (1930-1), pp. 263-99.
——————. *Watermarks: Mainly of the 17th and 18th Centuries.*
  Hilversum, Holland, 1950.
Heinemann, Margot. *Puritanism and Theatre: Thomas Middleton and
  Opposition Drama under the Early Stuarts.* Cambridge, 1980.
Henke, James T. *Reniassance Dramatic Bawdy (Exclusive of Shakespeare):
  An Annotated Glossary and Critical Essays.* Salzburg Studies in
  English Literature, Jacobean Drama Studies, 40. Salzburg, 1974.
Henslowe, Philip. *Henslowe's Diary.* R.A. Foakes and R.T. Rickert.
  Cambridge, 1961.
Herford, C.H. 'Middleton (Thomas)'. In *The Dictionary of National
  Biography.* Vol. XIII. Eds. Leslie Stephen and Sidney Lee. 1885-90;
  rpt. Oxford, 1921-2, pp. 357-8.
Herrick, Marvin T. *Tragicomedy: Its Origins and Development in Italy,
  France, and England.* Illinois Studies in Language and Literature,
  39. Urbanna, 1955.
Holmes, David M. *The Art of Thomas Middleton: A Critical Study.* Oxford,
  1970.
The Holy Bible: The Authorized King James Version. London, 1611.
Howard-Hill, T.H. '"Lizards Braine" in Middleton's *The Witch'. Notes and
  Queries*, 218 (1973), 458-9.
——————. 'Ralph Crane's Parentheses'. *Notes and Queries*, 210 (1965),
  334-40.
——————. *Ralph Crane and Some Shakespeare First Folio Comedies.*
  Charlottesville, 1972.
——————. 'Shakespeare's Earliest Editor, Ralph Crane', *Shakespeare
  Survey 45* (1992), 113-129.
Howard, T.B. *A Complete Collection of State Trials. Vol. 2: 1603-1627.*
  London, 1816.

Hoy, Cyrus. *Introductions, Notes, and Commentaries to the Texts in 'The Dramatic Works of Thomas Dekker' Edited by Fredson Bowers*. 4 vols. Cambridge, 1980.

Hulme, Hilda. 'Three Notes: *Troilus and Cressida*, V.vii.11; *Midsummer Night's Dream*, II.i.54; *Measure for Measure*, II.i.39'. *Journal of English and Germanic Philology*, 57 (1958), 721-5.

James I. *Daemonologie*. Edinburgh, 1597.

—————. *Newes from Scotland*. Edinburgh, 1591.

Jonson, Ben. *The Masque of Queens*. In *Ben Jonson*. Vol. VII. Eds. C.H. Herford and Percy and Evelyn Simpson. Oxford, 1941, pp. 265-319.

Jones, Marion. 'Early Moral Plays and the Earliest Secular Drama'. In *The Revels History of Drama in English, Volume I, Medieval Drama*. London and New York, 1983, pp. 211-91.

Jung, Hugo. *Das Verghältnis Thomas Middleton's zu Shakspere*. Müchener Beiträge zur Romanischen und Englishchen Philologie, 29. Leipzig, 1904.

Kittredge, George Lyman. 'English Witchcraft and James the First'. In *Studies in the History of Religions Presented to Crawford Howell Toy by Pupils Colleagues and Friends*. New York, 1912, pp. 1-65.

—————. *Witchcraft in Old and New England*. Cambridge, Massachusetts, 1929.

Kökeritz, Helge. *Shakespeare's Pronunciation*. New Haven and London, 1953.

Krzyzanowski, Juliusz. 'Conjectural Remarks on Elizabethan Dramatists (Pt. III)'. *Notes and Queries*, 195 (1950), 400-2.

Lake, David J. *The Canon of Thomas Middleton's Plays*. Cambridge, 1975.

Lamb, Charles. *Specimens of English Dramatic Poets Who Lived about the Time of Shakespeare*. London, 1808.

Lancashire, Anne. '*The Witch*: Stage Flop or Political Mistake?'. In *'Accompaninge the players': Essays Celebrating Thomas Middleton*.

Ed. Kenneth Friedenreich. New York, 1983, pp. 161-81.

Larner, Christina. 'James VI and I and Witchcraft'. In Alan G.R. Smith, ed., *The Reign of James VI and I*. London, 1973, pp. 74-90.

——————. *Witchcraft and Religion: The Politics of Popular Belief*. Ed. Alan Macfarlane. Oxford, 1984.

Lawrence, W.J. 'The Mystery of *Macbeth*: A Solution'. In *Shakespeare's Workshop*. Oxford, 1928, pp. 24-38.

Le Loyer, Pierre. *A Treatise of Specters*. Trans. Zachery Jones. London, 1605.

Lee, Sidney and C.T. Onions, eds. *Shakespeare's England: An Account of the Life and Manners of His Age*. 2 vols. Oxford, 1916.

Leech, Clifford. 'On Editing One's First Play'. *Studies in Bibliography*, 23 (1970), 61-70.

Levack, Brian P. *The Witch-Hunt in Early Modern Europe*. London and New York, 1987.

Levin, Richard. *The Multiple Plot in English Renaissance Drama*. Chicago and London, 1971.

Lewis, Charlton T. *A Latin Dictionary Founded on Andrews' Edition of Freund's Latin Dictionary*. Oxford, 1879.

Linthicum, M. Channing. *Costume in the Drama of Shakespeare and His Contemporaries*. Oxford, 1936.

Logan, Terence P., and Denzell S. Smith, eds. *The Popular School: A Survey and Bibliography of Recent Studies in English Renaissance Drama*. Lincoln, Nebraska, 1975.

Lyly, John. *The Complete Works*. Ed. R. Warwick Bond. Oxford, 1902.

Macfarlane, Alan. *Witchcraft in Tudor and Stuart England*. London, 1970.

Machiavelli, Niccolo. *The Chief Works*. 3 vols. Trans. Allan Gilbert. Durham, North Carolina, 1965.

——————. *The Florentine History*. Trans. T[homas]. B[edingfield]. London, 1595.

——————. *Tutti le Opera.* Vol. 1. Firenze, 1929.

McElroy, John F. *Parody and Burlesque in the Tragicomedies of Thomas Middleton.* Salzburg Studies in English Literature, Jacobean Drama Studies, 19. Salzburg, 1972.

Madan, Falconer. *A Summary Catalogue of Western Manuscripts in the Bodleian Library at Oxford which have not hitherto been Catalogued in the Quarto Series with Reference to the Oriental and other Manuscripts.* 7 vol. Oxford, 1897.

Middleton, Thomas. *The Changeling.* Ed. N.W. Bawcutt. London, 1958.

——————. *A Chaste Maid in Cheapside.* Ed. R.B. Parker. London, 1969.

——————. *A Game at Chess.* Bodleian MS Malone 25.

——————. *The Ghost of Lucrece.* Ed. Joseph Quincy Adams. New York, 1937.

——————. *Honourable Entertainments.* Ed. R.C. Bald. Malone Society Reprints, Oxford, 1953.

——————. *The Puritan; or the Widow of Watling Street.* Ed. C.F.Tucker Brooke. In *Shakespeare Apocrypha: Being a Collection of Fourteen Plays which have been Ascribed to Shakespeare.* Oxford, 1908.

——————. *A Tragi-Coomodie, Called the Witch: Long since Acted by His Maties. Seruants at the Black-Friers.* Bodleian MS Malone 12.

——————. *A Tragi-Coomodie, Called The Witch; Long Since Acted by His Maties Servants at the Black-Friers.* Ed. George Steevens. London, 1778.

——————. *The Witch.* In *Ancient British Drama.* Vol. 3. Supposed ed. Walter Scott. London, 1810.

——————. 'Thomas Middleton's *The Witch*'. Ed. Frank Sullivan. Ph.D. dissertation, Yale University, 1939.

——————. *The Witch.* Eds. L. Drees and Henry de Vocht. In *Materials for the Study of Old English Drama.* Vol. 18. Louvain, 1945.

——————. *The Witch.* Eds. W.W. Greg and F.P. Wilson. Malone Society

Reprints, Oxford, 1950 for 1948.

—————. *The Works of Thomas Middleton*. 8 vols. Ed. A.H. Bullen. London, 1885.

—————. *The Works of Thomas Middleton*. 5 vols. Ed. Alexander Dyce. London, 1840.

—————. *Thomas Middleton*. 2 vols. Ed. Havelock Ellis. Introduction by Algernon Charles Swinburne. London, 1887 and 1890.

—————. *The Witch*. Eds. Peter Corbin and Douglas Sedge. In *Three Jacobean Witchcraft Plays*. Manchester, 1986.

—————. *Women Beware Women*. Ed. J.R. Mulryne. London, 1975.

—————, and Thomas Dekker. *The Roaring Girl*. Ed. Paul A. Mulholland. Manchester, 1987.

Mulholland, Paul. 'Notes on Several Derivatives of Crane's Manuscript of Middleton's *The Witch*'. *The Papers of the Bibliographical Society of America*, 78 (1984), 75-81.

The National Union of Catalogue Pre-1956 Imprints. Vol. 382. London, 1975 or Chicago, 1975.

Nosworthy, J.M. *Shakespeare's Occasional Plays: Their Origin and Transmission*. London, 1965.

Notestein, Wallace. *A History of Witchcraft in England from 1558 to 1718*. New York, 1911.

Onions, C. T. *A Shakespeare Glossary*. 3rd ed. Revised and enlarged by Robert D. Eagleson. Oxford, 1986.

Opie, Iona and Moira Tatem. *A Dictionary of Superstitions*. Oxford, 1989.

The Oxford English Dictionary. Oxford, 1973.

The Oxford English Dictionary. 2nd ed. Oxford, 1989.

Painter, William. *The Firste Tome of the Palace of Pleasure*. London, 1575.

Partridge, A.C. *Orthography in Shakespeare and Elizabethan Drama: A Study of Colloquial Contractions, Elisions, Prosody and Punctuation*. London, 1964.

Partridge, Eric. *Shakespeare's Bawdy: A Literary & Psychological Essay and a Comprehensive Glossary*. 3rd ed. London, 1969 for 1968.

Paul, Henry N. *The Royal Play of 'Macbeth': When, Why, and How It Was Written by Shakespeare*. 1948, 1950; rpt. 1971, New York.

Perkins, William. *A Discovrse of the Damned Art of Witchcraft*. Cambridge, 1608.

Phialas, P.G. 'Middleton's Early Contact with the Law'. *Studies in Philology*, 52 (1955), 186-94.

Potts, Thomas. *The Wonderfvll Discoverie of Witches in the Covntie of Lancaster*. London, 1613.

Power, W. 'Thomas Middleton vs. King James I. *Notes and Queries*, 202 (1957), pp. 526-34.

Proudfoot, G.R. 'Dramatic Manuscripts and the Editor'. In *Editing Renaissance Dramatic Texts English, Italian, and Spanish: Papers Given at the Eleventh Annual Conference on Editorial Problems, University of Toronto, 31 October - 1 November 1975*. Ed. Anne Lancashire. New York and London, 1976, pp. 9-39.

Pruvost, René. *Matteo Bandello and Elizabethan Fiction*. Paris, 1937.

Reed, Robert Rentoul, Jr. *The Occult on the Tudor and Stuart Stage*. Rpt. Boston, 1965.

Ristine, Frank Humphrey. *English Tragicomedy: Its Origins and History*. 1910; rpt. New York, 1963.

Robbins, Rossell Hope. *The Encyclopedia of Witchcraft and Demonology*. 1959; rpt. Feltham, Middlesex, 1984.

Roberts, Gareth. 'A Re-examination of the Sources of the Magical Material in Middleton's *The Witch*', *Notes and Queries*, 221 (1976), 216-19.

Rogers, Kenneth. *The Mermaid and Mitre Taverns in Old London*. London, 1928.

Rowe, George, E., Jr. *Thomas Middleton and the New Comedy Tradition*. Lincoln and London, 1979.

Rubinstein, Frankie. *A Dictionary of Shakespeare's Sexual Puns and their Significance*. 2nd ed. London, 1989.

Schanzer, Ernest. 'The Marriage-Contracts in *Measure for Measure*'. *Shakespeare Survey 13* (1960), 81-9.

Schelling, Felix E. *Elizabethan Drama 1558-1642: A History of the Drama in England from the Accession of Queen Elizabeth to the Closing of the Theaters, to which is Prefixed a Résumé of the Earlier Drama from Its Beginnings*. 2 vols. London, 1908.

——————. 'Some Features of the Supernatural as Represented in the Plays of the Reigns of Elizabeth and James'. *Modern Philology*, 1 (1903-4), 31-47.

Schoeck, R.J., ed. *Editing Sixteenth Century Texts: Papers Given at the Editorial Conference University of Toronto October 1965*. Toronto: For the Editorial Conference Committee, 1966.

Schoenbaum, Samuel. Revisor of Alfred Harbage. *Annals of English Drama 975-1700*. London, 1964.

——————, *Annals of English Drama 975-1700 ... A Second Supplement to the Revised Edition*. Evanston, Illinois, 1970.

——————. 'Editing English Dramatic Texts'. In *Editing Sixteenth Century Texts: Papers Given at the Editorial Conference University of Toronto October 1965*. Ed. R.J. Schoeck. Toronto: For the Editorial Conference Committee, 1966, pp. 12-24.

——————. *Internal Evidence and Elizabethan Dramatic Authorship: An Essay in Literary History and Method*. London, 1966.

——————. 'Marston, Middleton, and Massinger'. In *English Drama (excluding Shakespeare): Selected Bibliographical Guides*. Ed. Stanley Wells. London, 1975, pp. 69-99.

——————. 'Middleton's Tragicomedies'. *Modern Philology*, 54 (1956), pp. 7-19.

——————. '*The Revenger's Tragedy* and Middleton's Moral Outlook'.

Notes and Queries, 196 (1951), 8-10.

Scot, Reginald. *The Discouerie of Witchcraft*. London, 1584.

——————. *The Discoverie of Witchcraft*. Ed. Brinsley Nicholson. London, 1886.

Scott, A.F. *Witch, Spirit, Devil*. London, 1974.

Scott, Mary Augusta. *Elizabethan Translations from the Italian*. Boston and New York, 1916.

The Second Maiden's Tragedy. Ed. Anne Lancashire. Manchester, 1978.

A Shakespeare Bibliography: The Catalogue of the Birmingham Shakespeare Library. By Birmingham Public Libraries. 7 vols. London, 1971.

Shakespeare, William. *The Complete Works*. Gen. eds. Stanley Wells and Gary Taylor. Oxford, 1986.

——————. *Macbeth*. Ed. Horace Howard Furness. Revised by Horace Howard Furness Jr. 1873; rev. London, 1903.

——————. *Macbeth*. Ed. John Dover Wilson. Cambridge, 1947.

——————. *Measure for Measure*. Ed. N.W. Bawcutt. Oxford, 1991.

——————. *The Plays of William Shakspeare*. 8 vols. Notes by Sam. Johnson. London, 1768.

——————. *The Plays of William Shakespeare*. 10 vols. Notes by Samuel Johnson and George Steevens. London, 1773.

——————. *The Plays of William Shakspeare*. 10 vols. Notes by Samuel Johnson and George Steevens. 2nd ed. London, 1778.

——————. *The Plays of William Shakspeare*. Notes by Samuel Johnson and George Steevens. 3rd ed. Revised by Isaac Reed. 10 vols. London, 1785.

——————. *The Plays and Poems of William Shakspeare in Ten Volumes*. Nots by Edmond Malone. 10 in 11 vols. London, 1790.

——————. *The Plays and Poems of William Shakspeare*. Eds. Edmond Malone and James Boswell. 21 vols. London, 1821.

—————. *Macbeth, a Tragedy: With all the Alterations, Amendments, Additions, and New Songs*. London, 1674.

—————. *The Tragedy of Macbeth*. Ed. Nicholas Brooke. Oxford, 1990.

Sharpe, Kevin. *Criticism and Compliment: The Politics of Literature in the England of Charles I*. Cambridge, 1987.

Simpson, R.R. *Shakespeare and Medicine*. Edinburgh and London, 1959.

Smith, Alan G.R. *The Reign of James VI and I*. London, 1973.

Smuts, R. Malcolm. *Court Culture and the Origins of a Royalist Tradition in Early Stuart England*. Philadelphia, 1987.

Sprenger, Jakob and Heinrich Krämer. *Mallevs Malificarvm*. ? 1486.

Stevens, John. 'Shakespeare and the Music of the Elizabethan Stage: An Introductory Essay'. In *Shakespeare in Music*. Ed. Phyllis Hartnoll. London, 1964

Stow, John. *A Survey of London*. London, 1603. Ed. Charles Lethbridge Kingsford. 2 vols. Oxford, 1971.

Sugden, Edward H. *A Topographical Dictionary to the Works of Shakespeare and His Fellow Dramatists*. Manchester, 1925.

Sullivan, Frank. '"Swathie"'. *The Times Literary Supplement*, 24 June 1939, p. 373.

Summers, Montague. *The History of Witchcraft and Demonology*. London, 1926.

Supplement to the Edition of Shakespeare Plays Published in 1778 by Samuel Johnson and George Steevens. Ed. Edmond Malone. 2 vols. London, 1780.

Tannenbaum, S.A. *Handwriting of the Renaissance*. London, 1930.

Thomas, Keith. *Religion and the Decline of Magic: Studies in Popular Beliefs in Sixteenth- and Seventeenth-Century England*. London, 1971.

Tilley, Morris Palmer. *A Dictionary of the Proverbs in England in the Sixteenth and Seventeenth Centuries*. Ann Arbor, Michigan, 1950.

Tourneur, Cyril. *The Atheist's Tragedy, or, The Honest Man's Revenge.* Ed. Irving Ribner. London, 1964.

──────. *The Revenger's Tragedy.* Ed. R.A. Foakes. London, 1966.

Trevor-Roper, H.R. *The European Witch-Craze of the 16th and 17th Centuries.* 1967; rev. Harmondsworth, 1969.

Turner, Robert K., Jr. 'Act-End Notations in Some Elizabethan Plays'. *Modern Philology*, 72 (1975), 238-47.

Valiente, Doreen. *An ABC of Witchcraft Past & Present.* 1973; rpt. London, 1984.

Villare Angicum: or, A View of the Townes or England. Collected by the Appointment of Sir Henry Spelman Knight. London, 1656.

Vinson, James, ed. *Renaissance Drama.* London, 1980.

Virgilius, Publius Maro. *The Bvcoliks.* Trans., A[braham]. F[leming]. London, 1589.

W.W. *A True and Iust Recorde, of the Information, Examination and Confession of All the Witches, Taken at S.Oses in the Countie of Essex.* London, 1582.

Wagonheim, Silvia Stoler. Revisor of Samuel Schoebaum's revision of Afred Harbage. *Annals of English Drama 975-1700.* 3rd ed. London, 1989.

Walker, David M. *The Oxford Companion to Law.* Oxford, 1980.

Ward, Adolphus William. *A History of English Dramatic Literature to the Death of Queen Anne.* 3 vols. London, 1875.

Wells, Stanley, ed. *English Drama (excluding Shakespeare): Selected Bibliographical Guides.* London, 1975.

──────, and Gary Taylor. *Modernizing Shakespeare's Spelling, with Three Studies in the Text of 'Henry V'.* Oxford, 1979.

Westersdorf, Karl P. 'The Marriage Contracts in *Measure for Measure*'. *Shakespeare Survey 32* (1979), 129-44.

West, Robert Hunter. *The Invisible World: A Study of Pneumatology in*

Elizabethan Drama. 1939; rpt. New York, 1969.

Wickham, Glynne. 'To Fly or Not to Fly? The Problem of Hecate in Shakespeare's *Macbeth*'. In *Essays on Drama and Theatre: Liber Amicorum Benjamin Hunnigher.* Amsterdam, 1973, pp. 171-82.

—————. 'Hell-Castle and Its Door-Keeper'. *Shakespeare Survey 19* (1966), 68-74.

Wilson, F.P. 'Ralph Crane, Scrivener to the King's Players'. *The Library,* 4th series, 7 (1926-7), 194-215.

Wolff, Dorothy. *Thomas Middleton: An Annotated Bibliography.* New York and London, 1985.

Yachnin, Paul. '"This Great Game": The Opportunism of Thomas Middleton'. Ph.D. thesis, University of Toronto, 1983.

For Product Safety Concerns and Information please contact our EU
representative GPSR@taylorandfrancis.com
Taylor & Francis Verlag GmbH, Kaufingerstraße 24, 80331 München, Germany